Debt Relief and Sustainable Development in Sub-Saharan Africa

Debt Relief and Sustainable Development in Sub-Saharan Africa

George C. Abbott
University of Glasgow, Scotland

Edward Elgar

Published by
Edward Elgar Publishing Limited
Gower House
Croft Road
Aldershot
Hants GU11 3HR
England

Edward Elgar Publishing Company
Old Post Road
Brookfield
Vermont 05036
USA

A CIP catalogue record for this book is available from the British Library

Library of Congress Cataloging-in-Publication Data
Abbott, George C.
Debt relief and sustainable development in sub-Saharan Africa/by George C. Abbott.
p. cm.
Includes bibliographical references and index.
1. Debt relief–Africa, Sub-Saharan. 2. Debts, Public–Africa, Sub-Saharan. 3. Structural adjustment (Economic policy)–Africa, Sub-Saharan. I. Title.
HJ8826.A22 1993
336.3'6'0967–dc20 92–34369
CIP

ISBN 1 85278 513 6

Printed in Great Britain at the University Press, Cambridge

Contents

Tables

Figures

Abbreviations

AAF-SAP	African Alternative Framework to Structural Adjustment Programmes for Socio-economic Recovery and Transformation
APPER	African Priority Programme for Economic Recovery
BSFF	Buffer Stock Financing Facility
CCFF	Compensatory and Contingency Financing Facility
CMEA	Council for Mutual Economic Assistance
DAC	Development Assistance Committee of the Organization of Economic Co-operation and Development
ECA	Economic Commission for Africa
EFF	Extended Financing Facility
ESAF	Enhanced Structural Adjustment Facility
FAO	Food and Agriculture Organization of the United Nations
GDP	Gross Domestic Product
HICs	Highly Indebted Countries
IDA	International Development Association of the World Bank Group
IMF	The International Monetary Fund
kgs	kilogrammes
m.	million
NICs	Newly Industrializing Countries
OAU	Organization of African Unity
ODA	Official Development Assistance
OECD	Organization of Economic Co-operation and Development
OPEC	Organization of Petroleum Exporting Countries
PFP	Policy Framework Paper
RTA	Retroactive Terms Adjustment
SAF	Structural Adjustment Facility
SAL	Structural Adjustment Loan
SBAs	Stand-by Arrangements
SECAL	Sectoral Adjustment Loan
SPA	Special Programme of Assistance for SSA Countries
SSA	Sub-Saharan Africa
STABEX	Stabilization of Export Earnings Scheme of the Lomé Convention

SYSMIN	Mineral Products Support Scheme of the Lomé Convention
UNCTAD	United Nations Trade and Development Conference
UNDP	United Nations Development Programme
UNIDO	United Nations Industrial Development Organization
UNPAAERD	United Nations Programme of Action for African Economic Recovery and Development, 1986–90
WB	World Bank

Introduction

Sub-Saharan Africa (SSA) is facing a debt crisis of no less international significance than that experienced by the so-called highly indebted countries (HICs). However, it is the latter which have consistently monopolized the international headlines. This has now begun to change. While still greatly exercised with the crisis facing the HICs, the international community has increasingly turned its attention to the crisis in SSA countries, where debt levels have risen sharply, output and exports stagnated and standards of living fallen drastically. Many of them are, in fact, back to where they were in the early 1960s.

The plight of these countries has been widely discussed and analysed. During the 1980s the World Bank produced several reports which diagnosed the region's problems in great detail and outlined various policy measures for restoring growth and long-term development. SSA countries also mounted a series of studies, and their governments adopted numerous comprehensive programmes for achieving specific regional goals and objectives. There is therefore no shortage of information on the region's problems. Opinions do, however, differ sharply as to the cause and what should be done to restore growth and promote sustainable development. The World Bank, for example, blames domestic mismanagement and other internal factors for the region's poor economic performance. Many SSA countries, on the other hand, regard external factors as largely responsible for their problems.

Whatever the cause, it is generally agreed that (a) SSA countries are experiencing a serious debt crisis which they cannot resolve on their own; (b) the conventional methods of debt consolidation are inappropriate and of limited use in their case; and (c) SSA countries need to undertake major policy and structural reforms if they are to get out of debt and achieve long-term sustainable development.

This study accepts these premisses, and argues, first, that the debt crisis is neither a recent nor a temporary phenomenon. It can, in fact, be traced back at least to the 1960s, when SSA countries were accumulating foreign debts faster than they were growing or their exports increasing. Secondly, the crisis is not self-correcting. Contrary to conventional wisdom, therefore, SSA countries cannot grow out of debt. They need help. Thirdly, the debt crisis is a serious drain on their resources, as it pre-empts an increasing share of available foreign exchange and limits the scope for effective management of the domestic economy. Fourthly, the interdependence of debts and development establishes a series of interlocking and mutually reinforcing vicious circles which militate against faster growth and the achievement of sustainable development. SSA countries cannot reduce existing debt levels unless they achieve faster growth, which itself depends on a substantial reduction in existing debt levels, and this is not possible without faster growth and development. The circle is thus complete.

The study argues that debt relief holds the key to this particular circle. Not only does it provide relief to reduce the debt crisis, this relief can also be used to finance and promote sustainable development. In essence, therefore, debt relief performs two functions: (a) it is an *end* in itself (debt reduction); and (b) it is a *means* to an end (sustainable development). However, in order to perform both roles properly, appropriate measures must be taken to ensure that it is efficiently administered and productively utilized, and that it is combined, co-ordinated and effectively integrated with structural adjustment programmes, the *sine qua non* of sustainable development in SSA countries.

The relationship of debt relief to structural adjustment is thus of crucial importance. However, its significance is not fully understood nor its developmental potential explored. Structural adjustment, for example, tends to neglect or underplay the dead weight of outstanding debts in adjusting countries, with the result that improvements in economic performance have been compromised by the steady deterioration in their external debt position. Also, many SSA countries 'in adjustment' have had their debts rescheduled several times without any appreciable improvement in their overall performance. This has called into question the concept and practice of structural adjustment, as advocated by the World Bank and the IMF. It has also led SSA governments to develop their own model of structural adjustment, the so-called African Alternative to Structural Adjustment.

Although there are fundamental conceptual and policy differences between the two models, both recognize the need for debt relief and reforms in SSA countries. However, these are treated as separate policy objectives to be achieved independently of each other. Consequently, there has developed a two-track approach to debt reduction and sustainable development. Within this scenario, debt reduction plays a minor and subsidiary role. This study contends that such a strategy is misconceived and counterproductive. If debt reduction is to be effective, it must be integrated with reforms and recovery. Similarly, if structural adjustment is to work, it must be accompanied by a substantial reduction in existing debt obligations. Debt relief and structural adjustment are, in fact, complementary elements of any strategy to achieve long-term sustainable development in these countries. The general principles and operational guidelines of an integrated debt-development strategy are set out in the final chapter.

Chapter 1 outlines the principal characteristics of SSA countries and shows that, notwithstanding the range and diversity of their conditions, they exhibit a remarkable degree of similarity in respect of their basic economic and social features. A review of long-term trends shows that the macroeconomy of SSA countries is in bad shape (and has been for a long time). The reasons for this long-term deterioration are examined and the performance of key sectors, specifically agriculture, foreign trade and the public sector are analysed in depth. SSA countries urgently need to introduce major policy and institutional changes to put their economies on a sounder footing.

At the same time, they have to deal with a debt crisis which shows no signs of abating. Chapter 2 analyses the nature, causes and present dimensions of this crisis in aggregate terms as well as in respect of particular debtor groups and types of debts. The structure and composition of external debts and their servicing costs are also analysed and supported by detailed statistics both for the region and for major debtor countries to show that the crisis is neither temporary nor self-correcting. All the indicators show that it is, in fact, getting worse. The costs and consequences of this worsening situation could well spell disaster for SSA countries. Among other things, mounting service costs militate against the achievement of long-term sustainable development. The outlook is not optimistic.

Chapter 3 argues that conventional debt relief measures are largely ineffectual and inappropriate for dealing with this crisis. Those debtor countries which have had multiple reschedulings are now deeper in debt. They have also consistently under-performed over the last decade. More comprehensive and systematic measures are clearly needed. This is accepted by the creditor countries and multilateral financial institutions who have launched a number of initiatives, debt relief measures and programmes for reducing the debt burden of poor countries. Sub-Saharan Africa, being one of the poorest regions in the world, has benefited from these schemes. Other relief programmes have been devised specifically for them. Several of these relief measures are examined in detail and their contribution to the crisis analysed. While collectively, as well as individually, they are a major improvement on past practices, by themselves they are unlikely to resolve the crisis. They need to be combined with other policy reform measures in order to ensure that SSA debtor countries make full and effective use of the total resource package available to them.

There is a clear need for structural adjustment in SSA countries. Both the international community and SSA governments accept it as a *sine qua non* for long-term growth and sustainable development. Opinions differ, though, as to the nature and purpose of adjustment, its priorities and policy reform requirements and how it should be implemented in the context of SSA countries. The general principles, procedures and reform measures of the conventional (IMF/World Bank style) model of adjustment are discussed in Chapter 4. The various facilities of the IMF for financing adjustment, including its highly concessional facilities – the Structural Adjustment Facility (SAF) and the Enhanced Structural Adjustment Facility (ESAF) – are analysed and their contribution to the recovery and promotion of sustainable development in SSA countries evaluated. So too are the policy-based lending programmes of the Bank, in particular, its Special Programme of Assistance for SSA countries (SPA). Finally, the essential features and policy requirements of the African Alternative to Structural Adjustment (AAF–SAP) are outlined.

The present strategy for achieving long-term sustainable growth and development adopts a two-track approach. The concept and operation of this strategy are critically examined and the need for a new integrated strategy based on the interdependence of debt relief, structural adjustment and new funding is established. The general principles, policy guidelines and requirements are developed, and its operation and administrative procedures set out. So too are the roles and responsibilities of the respective parties to the crisis (creditors, debtors and multilateral financial institutions). This is followed by a diagrammatic presentation of the way the integrated debt-development strategy would work in practice in order to demonstrate its feasibility and improvement on present practices.

G. C. A.

1. The Macroeconomy of SSA Countries

A. GENERAL CHARACTERISTICS

Geographically, Sub-Saharan Africa (SSA) covers the whole of Africa south of the Sahara, excluding South Africa. It is comprised of 45 countries with a total area exceeding 22 million square kilometres. The countries which make up this compact and extensive landmass differ in size, population, geographical and climatic conditions, natural resources and other economic, political, social and cultural characteristics. A few basic statistics are enough to put the vast disparity of conditions into perspective.

In size, the countries range from Sudan, with a total of more than 2.5 million square kilometres, to the Seychelles and São Tomé and Príncipe which are small island states of less than 100,000 square kilometres. In 1987 their population ranged from Nigeria, with over 107 million, to the Seychelles and São Tomé and Príncipe, each with a population of less than 100,000. Similar disparities are reflected in population densities, with the smaller states in general having a higher density than the larger ones. Mauritius, for example, has a population density of 574 persons per square kilometre, as compared with Botswana, Mauritania and Namibia, each of which has a population density of two.

The region experiences almost every type of geographical and climatic condition from tropical rain forests to semi-arid and desert conditions. It also has enormous natural resources. Five countries – Angola, Cameroon, Congo, Gabon and Nigeria – are major oil exporters. Others have extensive deposits of minerals and precious metals. Botswana's diamond deposits are among the richest in the world. Guinea has substantial deposits of high-grade bauxite, and Ghana has considerable potential in gold. There is uranium in Niger, iron ore in Liberia, and copper in Zambia and Zaire, to give a few examples. The region's fishing, forestry and energy resources are largely untapped, and agriculture, which is the mainstay of its economic life, is conducted under a variety of production systems and practices.

There are major differences in respect of economic, financial and political systems and forms of government. Membership of the Franc Zone, for example, extends only to the former French colonies, and the common currency (the cfa) is tied in a fixed relationship to the French franc. The Sterling Area, a similar arrangement which included the former British colonies in Africa, was disbanded a long time ago, and the members pursue independent economic and financial policies. History has also played a major role in shaping the social, cultural and linguistic traditions and customs which differ markedly between francophone Africa on the one hand and anglophone Africa on the other.

These disparities enable the region to be subdivided into different groupings and categories to suit particular forms and emphasis of analysis. The World Bank, for example, uses a cut-off point of $480 per capita (1987) to differentiate between low-income and middle-income countries. It further differentiates between lower- and upper-middle-income countries. Other studies distinguish between oil-importing and oil-exporting SSA countries. There are any number of further distinctions and divisions, such as between land-locked and island economies; producers of primary commodities and countries with large mineral resources; severely indebted, middle-income countries and debt-distressed, low-income countries, and so on.

Notwithstanding the heterogeneity of existing conditions and characteristics, SSA countries exhibit an overwhelming degree of similarity in terms of the basic structure, problems and performance of their economies. The majority of them have low per capita incomes, high population growth rates and experience appalling poverty. Drought and famine are endemic to the region, and the lack of basic health, education and social infrastructure makes these countries some of the poorest in the world. Of the world's 42 poorest countries, 28 are, in fact, located in Sub-Saharan Africa.

Their economies are open, with foreign trade accounting for about 20 per cent of the region's GDP. Most of them are heavily dependent on one or two export crops, which makes them particularly vulnerable to the vagaries of world commodity markets. Export incomes have fallen, and there is a growing dependence on imports of food and food aid. Additionally, the region faces a serious debt crisis which is greatly aggravated by reduced capital inflows and the steady deterioration of its existing capital stock.

Administrations are weak and inefficient and their domestic economies badly mismanaged. There is an acute shortage of human and institutional capacities, and major social problems are building up as increasing numbers of people migrate to the cities and towns. And, to top it all, the continent is experiencing major environmental degradation through a reinforcing process of desertification, deforestation and land degradation. Basic economic and social indicators for individual SSA countries are given in Appendix A.1.

B. TWO CRISES

Quite simply, what this adds up to is that there is an enormous and pervasive crisis facing SSA countries. Indeed, it can be argued that the region has been in a state of crisis for a very long time, and that at any one time there are several overlapping and interconnecting crises in this part of the world. In other words, a state of crisis is not only endemic to the region, it is systemic as well. However, there are several characteristics about the present crisis which set it apart from previous crises.

First, it is deep-seated and long-standing. Secondly, it is not self-correcting. Major structural changes and policy reforms are required in order to reverse the decline and to ensure a sustained improvement in living standards. Thirdly, SSA countries have committed themselves to implement the necessary reforms; and finally, various initiatives and programmes have been launched by the rich countries, multilateral financial institutions and other organizations to help SSA countries get out of this crisis. There is, therefore, a firm consensus internationally on the nature and extent of the crisis and, more importantly, the need for a major collective and cooperative international effort to resolve it. This is the starting point of this study.

It starts from the premiss that the present crisis is essentially the combined and visible manifestation of several crises but, in particular, the crisis in agriculture and the debt crisis. Although these two crises manifest themselves differently, together they create enormous economic, social and political problems for SSA countries. Being of a long-term nature, the crisis in agriculture has acquired a sort of permanent status. People have got used to living with it. Its slow and inexorable deterioration gives it an elemental force to which they adjust within the limits of their individual capacity. Producers switch crops or go out of production if prices and incomes fall. Workers leave the land and head for the city where life seems less precarious. Governments, too, have tended 'to walk away' from it, regarding it as a long-term crisis, which has been caused by factors beyond their control. The solution is also perceived to be beyond their ability and/or resources. Consequently, they have either kept agriculture short of funds or neglected it, thereby contributing to the intensification of the crisis.

On the other hand, faced with a debt crisis, governments have to act. They cannot walk away from it. Foreign debts are a priority claim on their foreign exchange earnings and international reserves. They reduce the scope for manoeuvrability for financing development and meeting balance of payments needs. Also, being part of the complex web of international economic relations and foreign policy, foreign debts have wide-reaching international ramifications and repercussions which put the debt crisis at the top of the government's agenda. In short, the debt crisis determines the policy parameters within which they operate. Everything is subordinated to it and economic policy management is formulated and implemented in a crisis environment.

Both crises operate in different time-frames. The agricultural crisis is not only long-standing, it requires a long-term sustainable effort for the sector to recover. There are no 'quick fixes'. The debt crisis, on the other hand, requires the opposite strategy. If corrective measures are not taken quickly, the economy is likely to collapse. These operational requirements have led to the compartmentalization of policy, with the result that policy measures for dealing with the debt crisis concentrate on its financial and monetary aspects without regard to their effects on the agricultural sector or elsewhere in the real economy. This shows a serious misunderstanding of the nature and cause of the debt crisis in SSA countries. More importantly, it is more difficult to deal with both crises at the same time as vital linkages are ignored and internal economies not exploited. Various anomalies and dichotomies then develop, which ultimately lead to wrong or unrealistic strategies.

While there are undoubtedly major differences between them, the two crises are, in fact, closely interrelated. Progress on one front depends crucially on improvements on the other, and vice versa. The debt crisis cannot be resolved without a significant improvement in the performance of the agricultural sector. Similarly, the recovery of agriculture in SSA countries depends to a large extent on how the debt crisis is handled. Not only are the two interrelated, they reinforce each other, giving rise to a series of interlocking vicious circles which consolidate the interdependent nature of the relationship.

For example, SSA countries urgently need accelerated growth and long-term sustainable development in order to provide higher standards of living, better social facilities, and so on, for their peoples as well as to service their foreign debts. However, the short-term effect of accelerated growth would be to increase total foreign debts and debt service payments and pre-empt a greater share of their foreign exchange earnings, thus jeopardizing the whole process of development. On the other hand, if there is no development, SSA countries will not be able to service their foreign debts which, in turn, intensifies the debt crisis. The circle is thus closed but at a higher level, from which another spiral begins.

A similar circularity can be identified in respect of the agricultural crisis. The long-term decline in agricultural production reduced the amount of food for domestic consumption and increased the demand for food imports. Increased expenditure on food imports, in turn, reduced the amount of foreign exchange available for development financing and service payments, which then fed directly into the vicious spiral of debts and development. Exports have also fallen, adding another twist to the spiral.

The effects of these developments have been particularly severe on the agricultural sector. Imports of food, fertilizers, fuels and other inputs, which are essential to the sector's recovery, were curtailed to such an extent that SSA countries were described as suffering from acute import strangulation. It requires a substantial and sustained effort, therefore, to break the agricultural crisis. Without growth and additional investment in this sector, SSA countries will not be able to feed their growing populations and earn enough foreign exchange to pay their foreign debts. This will reduce their capacity to borrow more funds to sustain development, which starts the process all over again.

The way out of this double-bind depends ultimately on the achievement of long-term sustainable growth and development but also, more immediately, on a substantial reduction of present debt levels in the near and medium term. The essential dichotomy, therefore, is to resolve the debt crisis without jeopardizing the performance of the agricultural sector: or, to put it more positively, to use debt relief measures to promote the rehabilitation of the agricultural sector and to strengthen its role and performance as the leading sector. It is ultimately the key to the region's recovery and long-term development.

C. A REVIEW OF MACROECONOMIC TRENDS

All the principal economic and social indicators show that the macroeconomy of Sub-Saharan Africa is in bad shape. They also show that this is neither a recent nor a temporary phenomenon. The deterioration can, in fact, be traced back to the 1960s when things started going wrong. During that decade, real per capita GDP grew on average by 1.2 per cent per annum, less than half the rate for the developing countries as a whole. Between 1970 and 1980, it fell to 0.9 per cent per annum. The downward trend continued into the 1980s, with real per capita GDP falling on average by –1.9 per cent per annum between 1980 and 1987. In summary, a period of slow growth (1960–69) was followed by one of stagnation (1970–79) which, in turn, gave way to rapid decline (1980–87). Although there has been some improvement recently, this has not been enough to reverse the steady deterioration. Since 1960, real per capita GDP has fallen, on average, by –1.7 per cent per annum. Effectively, therefore, all the gains registered during the 1960s have been whittled away, and SSA countries are now worse off than at the start of that decade.

Within this overall picture, real per capita GDP growth rates were spread very unevenly across countries and over time. Table 1.1 gives annual per capita growth rates for the best and worst performers between 1961 and 1987. These ranged from Botswana with an average of 8.4 per cent per annum at one end, to Uganda with –2.2 per cent per annum at the other. In countries like Liberia, Niger and Nigeria, real per capita incomes have fallen by more than a quarter since 1980. In terms of income groups, the economic performance of SSA countries has been equally disappointing. Six countries – Equatorial Guinea, Ghana, Liberia, Nigeria, São Tomé and Príncipe and Zambia – previously classified as middle-income, are now classified as low-income countries as a result of their poor economic performance over the last decade.

Table 1.1 *Per capita GDP growth rates for selected SSA countries, 1961–87 (% per annum)*

Best performers	(+)	Worst performers	(–)
Botswana	8.4	Chad	–2.0
Cameroon	3.0	Ghana	–1.8
Congo	3.8	Madagascar	–1.6
Lesotho	3.1	Niger	–1.8
Mauritius	2.6	Uganda	–2.2
Seychelles	3.0	Zaire	–1.5
		Zambia	–1.7

Source: World Bank data.

One of the main reasons for the steady deterioration in real per capita incomes is the massive increase in population, which has been growing at the rate of 3 per cent per annum since the 1970s. This makes SSA the fastest growing region in the world in terms of population, and contrasts sharply with the declining trend of population growth rates elsewhere in the developing countries. The present population of 451 million is expected to reach 1 billion by 2010.

Over the last two decades, the rate of growth of population has exceeded the rate of growth of food production, with the result that SSA countries have to rely to an increasing extent on imports of food and food aid to feed their rapidly expanding populations. This has led to a serious food crisis which has been exacerbated by droughts, famine and other natural disasters. Additionally, the need to provide housing, education, health, medical and other social services for their rapidly rising population puts a severe strain on the domestic economy and contributes to its under-performance.

SSA countries have not, in fact, exploited their enormous agricultural potential or mineral resources. They have allowed agriculture to decline, notwithstanding its importance to their economic life. In 1987 it accounted for 34 per cent of total GDP, as against 43 per cent in 1965. This contraction has had knock-on effects throughout the region. The number of people working in agriculture has fallen. So, too, has the sector's share of total foreign exchange earnings. This, in turn, has led to a fall in the level of both domestic savings and government revenue, given the heavy burden of taxation which the sector bears.

Following independence, most SSA countries engaged in a massive programme of state-sponsored industrialization. As a result, the industrial sector grew on average by 8 per cent per annum during the 1960s, and accounted for 15 per cent of the region's GDP. For a variety of reasons, however, such a rapid expansion could not be sustained, and by the end of the 1970s the sector had entered a period of stagnation and de-industrialization from which it has not recovered. During the 1980s, growth, as measured by manufacturing value added (MVA), averaged 0.5 per cent per annum. In 1987 manufactures accounted for 10 per cent of total GDP, roughly the same figure as in 1965. Many of the industries which had been financed by buoyant commodity export earnings and cheap international credits during the 1970s were in deep trouble, once international interest rates turned positive and the world recession deepened. Those that experienced the most serious decline in annual MVA growth rates during the 1980s include transport equipment (–6.9 per cent), wood and cork (–5.8 per cent), furniture (–3.8 per cent), glass (–3.5 per cent) and plastic products (–2.3 per cent).

A recent World Bank study reports that over the last two decades a total of 21 SSA countries have suffered extensive de-industrialization, the most serious cases being Benin, Ghana, Liberia, Madagascar, Mozambique, Togo and Zaire.[1] Depletion of the region's capital stock was further aggravated by the so-called 'import strangulation' of the 1980s – the shortage of foreign exchange to pay for essential imports of capital goods for restructuring, rehabilitation and maintenance purposes. As a result, capital utilization rates fell sharply. Recently, the situation has improved somewhat, but the industrial sector generally is characterized by heavy over-capitalization and considerable capacity under-utilization. In Zambia, for example, capacity utilization in 1988 was put at 30 per cent.

Two related points flow from this analysis. First, the industrial sector in SSA countries is under-performing. In 1987 per capita MVA (expressed in terms of 1980 dollars) ranged from $5 in Zaire to $282 for Mauritius. The latter is, however, widely regarded as the success story, and not typical of performance throughout the region, the average for which was $32 MVA per capita. Secondly, stagnation and de-industrialization mean that the sector cannot provide enough jobs for those people who leave agriculture as well as for new entrants to the labour force. In most SSA countries, the rate of growth of employment in manufacturing has fallen sharply since the drive to rapid industrialization of the mid-1960s. During the 1970s, for example, negative growth rates were recorded in several countries, the worst cases being –10.4 per cent in Congo, –8.4 per cent in Cape Verde, –7.1 per cent in Gambia and –6.4 per cent in Zaire, all on an average annual basis. There was a further deterioration in the overall picture during the 1980s, when employment in manufacturing grew on average by 1.2 per cent per annum for the region, with the worst performance being recorded in Cape Verde (–5.1 per cent p.a.) and Zaire (–3.5 per cent p.a.).

In summary, the performance of the manufacturing sector has been disappointing. It has not been able to sustain itself or to provide the growth and employment which SSA countries need. There are also many large and unproductive projects, the so-called 'white elephants', and inefficient public sector enterprises which do not pay their way but, rather, are a sizeable drain on the countries' limited foreign exchange and international reserves. Finally, de-industrialization has exacerbated the problem of unemployment. Macroeconomic data on SSA countries, excluding Nigeria, are given in Table 1.2.

Although the data are self-explanatory, a few remarks are in order. First, gross capital formation is now running below 20 per cent per annum, which is generally regarded as the minimum rate necessary to sustain growth in these countries. This is due, in no small measure, to the extensive disinvestment and depletion of capital stock which have taken place. Other contributory factors include poor overall performance and domestic economic mismanagement, both of which have served to reduce the average rate of return on investment from 30.7 per cent per annum over the period 1961 to 1973 to 2.5 per cent per annum between 1980 and 1987. What this means, in effect, is that apart from petroleum and a few extractive industries, SSA countries have ceased to be an attractive proposition for foreign investors. The inflow of private foreign capital has virtually dried up since the onset of the debt crisis. This was accompanied by a sharp fall in gross domestic investment, averaging –8.2 per cent per annum between 1980 and 1987. The most severe cases of gross annual disinvestment occurred in Mozambique (–23.1 per cent), Liberia (–16.7 per cent), Uganda (–15 per cent), Nigeria (–14.8 per cent) and Benin (–12.7 per cent).

Secondly, there has been a considerable increase in the annual rate of inflation over the average recorded during the 1970s. The picture is, however, a lot more disparate than the figures suggest. Between 1980 and 1987, for example, the average annual rate of inflation ranged from 95.2 per cent for Uganda to 1.5 per cent in Liberia (that was, of course, before the civil war destroyed most of the latter's economy).[2] Thirdly, rising levels of public expenditure on the one hand, and falling or stagnant revenues on the other,

Table 1.2 Macroeconomic data on SSA countries[a]*, 1971–90*[b]

	Average[c] 1971–80	1981	1982	1983	1984	1985	1986	1987	1988	1989	1990
Real GDP (% p.a.)	2.9	2.9	2.2	–0.2	0.9	3.3	3.6	1.8	1.5	2.0	1.7
Real GDP per capita (% p.a.)	–	–	–0.4	–3.1	–1.6	0.5	0.6	–1.0	–1.6	–0.8	–1.2
Gross capital formation (% of GDP)		20.9	19.7	16.8	17.0	17.9	19.0	18.4	18.1	18.6	18.8
Consumer prices (% p.a.)[d]	18.5	29.3	19.2	25.6	21.4	20.1	21.1	23.9	19.5	15.4	19.7
Central gov't fiscal bal. (% of GDP)		–6.9	–7.2	–5.9	–5.1	–5.6	–6.0	–7.1	–6.8	–6.0	–7.2
Export volumes (% p.a.)	1.1	–2.1	1.4	1.4	5.1	–0.2	8.7	2.4	–0.5	4.4	4.8
Import volumes (% p.a.)	2.6	0.1	–4.8	–7.9	–0.7	–0.5	–1.9	–1.2	3.1	–0.2	–2.7
Export unit values (% p.a. US$)	13.0	–8.5	–8.0	–2.2	3.8	–3.5	–7.0	2.0	2.6	2.7	–0.2
Import unit values (% p.a. US$)	14.0	–3.7	–5.1	–3.4	–2.8	–2.3	12.2	11.3	4.9	4.4	7.9
Terms of trade (% p.a.)	–0.9	–5.0	–3.0	1.3	6.8	–1.2	–17.2	–8.3	–2.2	–1.6	–7.6
Non-oil commodity t. of t. (% p.a.)[e]	10.2	–17.8	–8.2	7.5	4.9	–8.8	4.0	–2.4	13.9	–0.8	–5.2
Official reserve holdings ($ bill.)		3.4	2.8	3.0	3.1	4.1	5.1	5.9	6.3	7.4	7.1
Reserves as ratio of imports (%)		8.6	7.6	8.8	9.3	12.4	13.7	14.6	14.5	16.2	14.8
Net credit from IMF ($ bill)[f]		1.6	0.7	1.3	0.5	–	–0.4	–0.5	–0.2	–	–0.2

Notes

[a] Excluding Nigeria and South Africa.

[b] Except where otherwise indicated, arithmetic averages of country growth rates weighted by the average US dollar value of GDP over the preceding three years.

[c] Compounded annual rates of change.

[d] Geometric averages of country indices weighted by the average US dollar value of GDP over the preceding three years.

[e] In US dollar terms.

[f] Includes net disbursements from programmes under the General Resources Account, Trust Fund, Structural Adjustment Facility (SAF) and Enhanced Structural Adjustment Facility (ESAF). Projected net disbursements incorporate the impact of projected programmes. The data are on a transaction basis, with conversions to US dollar values at annual average exchange rates.

Source: Data abstracted from *World Economic Outlook*, Statistical Appendix (various issues), Washington, D.C., IMF, 1989.

Table 1.3 The agricultural sector in SSA countries[a]

	% share of GDP			Rate of growth (ave annual) %			Index of per cap food prod. (1979–81=100)	Food imports as % of total imports			Labour force in agriculture (%)	
	1965	1980	1987	1965–73	1973–80	1980–87	1985–7	1965	1980	1987	1965	1980
Angola	50	43	46	0.2	–9.7	—	88	18	—	—	79	74
Benin	59	48	46	4.5	3.4	2.5	114	18	19	11	83	70
Botswana[b]	34	12	3	12.4	0.6	–7.8	75	9	8	9	89	70
Burkina Faso	53	45	38	0.9	1.3	6.1	118	23	19	16	89	87
Burundi	—	62	59	4.7	1.6	1.7	100	16	14	12	94	93
Cameroon[b]	33	28	24	4.6	4.5	2.4	94	11	8	13	86	70
Cape Verde[b]	—	25	19	—	—	—	99	—	—	—	67	52
Cen. African Rep.	46	40	41	2.1	1.8	2.4	94	13	20	13	88	72
Chad[b]	42	53	43	0.2	0.5	2.6	104	13	—	—	92	83
Comoros	—	—	36	0.3	3.4	0.8	95	—	—	—	88	83
Congo[b]	19	12	12	4.1	2.1	1.5	92	15	18	16	66	62
Côte d'Ivoire	47	33	36	4.9	3.3	1.6	105	18	17	19	81	65
Ethiopia	58	51	42	2.1	0.6	–2.1	89	6	7	4	86	80
Gabon[b]	26	7	11	2.1	—	—	97	16	19	18	83	75
Gambia	35	31	35	4.5	0.9	7.1	126	19	11	43	88	44
Ghana[b]	44	58	51	4.5	0.0	0.0	106	12	9	6	61	56
Guinea[b]	75	42	30	2.1	2.5	—	93	12	—	—	87	81
Guinea-Bissau[b]	52	52	61	0.9	–3.4	5.7	129	25	—	—	86	82
Kenya	35	32	31	6.2	3.7	3.4	93	10	8	9	86	81
Lesotho	65	26	21	6.5	1.1	0.4	83	49	17	–7	92	86
Liberia	26	36	37	6.5	4.0	1.2	96	16	18	19	79	74
Madagascar[b]	31	39	43	2.1	–0.4	2.2	97	19	8	9	89	87
Malawi	50	40	37	–2.9	4.8	2.5	87	15	7	5	92	83

Mali[b]	65	58	54	0.9	7.1	0.3	101	20	16	12	90	86
Mauritania	32	31	37	–2.1	–0.3	1.5	90	9	29	26	89	69
Mauritius	16	12	15	6.4	–6.0	5.2	103	34	26	19	37	28
Mozambique	47	—	50	0.2	—	–11.1	84	17	—	—	87	85
Niger[b]	68	43	34	–2.9	1.4	2.8	87	12	13	18	95	91
Nigeria	54	26	30	2.8	–1.4	0.6	105	9	17	8	72	68
Rwanda[b]	75	46	37	2.1	8.7	1.1	86	12	9	12	94	93
São Tomé & Príncipe	—	45	30	—	7.2	–7.3	68	—	—	—	—	—
Senegal[b]	25	19	22	0.2	0.4	4.2	105	36	24	32	83	81
Seychelles	—	7	6	—	—	–2.9	—	36	20	14	—	—
Sierra Leone	34	33	45	1.5	3.9	1.6	98	17	19	17	78	70
Somalia	71	68	65	4.5	10.9	2.8	102	31	13	13	81	76
Sudan	54	34	37	0.3	3.4	0.8	100	23	26	17	82	71
Swaziland	35	30	24	8.0	3.5	3.9	104	7	—	—	85	74
Tanzania	46	44	61	3.1	0.2	3.8	90	10	13	6	—	—
Togo[b]	45	27	29	2.6	1.9	0.8	89	15	19	20	78	73
Uganda	52	72	76	3.6	–2.3	–0.5	123	7	5	5	91	86
Zaire[b]	21	29	32	0.9	0.9	3.2	99	18	19	13	82	72
Zambia[b]	14	14	12	2.0	1.6	3.2	97	9	8	7	79	73
Zimbabwe	18	14	11	3.7	–0.3	2.3	91	13	15	10	79	73
Sub-Saharan Africa[c]	43	30	34	2.2	–0.3	1.3	100	14	16	12	77	71

Notes

[a] Excluding Djibouti and Equatorial Guinea for which data are not available.

[b] GDP and its components are at purchaser values.

[c] Weighted average.

— Not available.

Source: World Bank, *Sub-Saharan Africa: From Crisis to Sustainable Growth.* Washington, D.C.: World Bank, November 1989, Statistical Appendix (various tables).

have resulted in substantial fiscal deficits. Although foreign grants have increased, these have not been enough to cover the growing deficits which are higher than elsewhere in the developing countries. In 1987, for example, the fiscal deficit of SSA countries averaged 7.1 per cent of GDP, as compared with 5.3 per cent for the developing countries as a whole.

The consequences of such large deficits are obvious. Among other things, they put the government under severe pressure to borrow from domestic banks and the monetary authorities in order to maintain existing levels of public expenditure and services, which is precisely what most SSA governments have done. This contributes to the rate of domestic inflation, which then spills over into and intensifies their balance of payments problems. The picture on the financial side is equally depressing. Their official reserves are low by international standards, and spread unevenly among the members. Notwithstanding some improvement in recent years, their financial position is likely to remain precarious for the foreseeable future. In effect, therefore, SSA countries face severe problems in the monetary and financial sector which are not only interlocking, but have now reached crisis proportions in the shape of the debt crisis.

D. THE AGRICULTURAL SECTOR

Agriculture is the mainstay of the economic life of SSA countries. Its contribution to the macroeconomy is shown in Table 1.3. In 1987 it accounted for 34 per cent of the region's GDP. For Guinea-Bissau, Somalia, Tanzania and Uganda the proportion exceeded 60 per cent. But these were exceptional. The general pattern is one of contraction and decline which goes back to 1965. The worst period was between 1973 and 1980, when the rate of growth of agricultural production declined on average by –0.3 per cent per annum. There has been some improvement since then, but there is still a long way to go before the sector can regain its position and role as the leading sector.

The per capita index of food production shows that there was no deterioration during the period 1985–7, as compared with 1979–81. This was due largely to the recent improvement in food production in most countries, particularly in Gambia, Guinea-Bissau and Uganda. However, this does not adequately reflect the true nature and extent of the food crisis facing SSA countries. The base year (1979–81) was, in fact, a period of low per capita food production as compared with the 1970s.[3] Effectively, therefore, the improvement in per capita production since 1985 has arrested rather than reversed the decline of earlier years. During the 1960s, for example, the region was able to feed itself as well as export significant quantities of food and raw materials. Over the intervening years, however, the balance has been reversed. It no longer produces enough food to feed itself and has to rely on imports of food and food aid to make up the deficit.

Although Table 1.3 shows that by 1987 food imports as a percentage of total imports was down to 12 per cent, the food situation is still critical throughout Sub-Saharan Africa. The figures for Gambia (43 per cent), Mauritania (26 per cent) and Senegal (32 per cent) speak for themselves.

Secondly, food aid is now a major item of domestic food consumption, accounting for about 30 per cent of total food imports. In 1986 SSA countries imported over 3 million tons of food aid in cereals (mainly wheat and rice). This was more than three times the amount imported ten years earlier. In terms of per capita consumption, this was equivalent to 7 kg of imported food aid for the region. In Botswana and the Sudan, per capita consumption of food aid averaged 44 kg in 1986. Other major importers, on a per capita basis, were Somalia (31 kg), Mozambique (24 kg), Lesotho (20 kg) and Ethiopia (15 kg).

Thirdly, agriculture provides employment for the vast majority of the population. In 1965 more than three-quarters of the labour force were employed in agriculture. In Burundi, Chad, Lesotho, Mali and several other SSA countries, the proportion exceeded 90 per cent. By 1980 the overall average had fallen to 71 per cent. As the table shows there was not a single SSA country in which the proportion of the labour force in agriculture increased between the two dates.

Finally, exports of agricultural commodities account for over 30 per cent of total foreign exchange earnings. This was estimated to be worth over $18 billion in 1988. The proportion was much higher for those countries whose exports are concentrated in one or two primary commodities. Between 1982 and 1986, for example, 91 per cent of Burundi's export earnings came from coffee (87 per cent) and tea (4 per cent). In the case of Uganda, coffee accounted for 95 per cent of total export earnings, while virtually all of Equatorial Guinea's export earnings came from three exports: cocoa (54 per cent), timber (41 per cent) and coffee (5 per cent).

The deterioration in the performance of the agricultural sector is due to a combination of internal and external factors. Among the former are:

(a) the long-term bias in the internal terms of trade against agriculture. The sector has not, for example, been allowed to protect itself against inflation by raising prices in line with other prices. Also, producer prices have been kept artificially low either because marketing boards pass on excessive costs to producers, or the share which producers receive fails to cover the cost of production, even for those commodities in which the country has a comparative advantage. In 1987 producer prices for cocoa in Ghana averaged 41 per cent of the export price. For tobacco in Malawi the proportion was 21 per cent, and for cotton in Mozambique it was 31 per cent;

(b) production structures and crop patterns that are rigid and inflexible. This, along with low supply elasticity, limits the scope for diversification and the development of alternative crops. Land which is given over to cocoa or sugar cannot be converted immediately to other uses when the prices of these crops fall. This, combined with falling levels of productivity and poor agronomic practices, has reduced the output of both domestic food production and export crops, leading to acute food shortages, loss of international markets and reduced export earnings;

(c) the over-burdening of the agricultural sector by export taxes, marketing board levies and the like. Although these provide much needed revenue for the government, they reduce the amount of resources available to the sector. They are a serious disincentive to increased production and greater efficiency. Also, the various tax benefits and incentives enjoyed by the industrial sector discriminate against agriculture, for which there are no comparable incentives and benefits. Effectively, therefore, the agricultural sector carries the economy and its surplus is used to subsidize and underwrite industrial development. The sector is further penalized by being kept short of funds, with the result that essential research, extension work and other ancillary services are not adequately funded;

(d) the long-term bias against agriculture that is further systematized by government trade and exchange rate policies. Restrictive trade and payments regimes not only over-protect industry and penalize agriculture, but also create serious distortions within the domestic economy. High tariffs, for example, favour production for the domestic market and discourage exports. Additionally, over-valued rates of exchange have encouraged the importation of food and contributed to the decline of food production in SSA countries;[4]

(e) high population growth rates which create severe pressure on limited physical resources. The long-term relationship between population growth rates and the performance of the agricultural sector is forcefully illustrated in Table 1.4. During the first phase (1965–73), 19 countries registered positive rates of growth of per capita agricultural production, with the best performances recorded in Botswana (9.1 per cent p.a.) and Swaziland (8.4 per cent p.a.). Twenty countries recorded negative per capita rates of growth, the worst cases being Malawi (–5.7 per cent pa) and Niger (–5.2 per cent p.a.). The position worsened considerably during the second period (1973–80), when the number recording positive rates of per capita growth fell to 14 and those with negative rates rose

Table 1.4 Annual average per capita rate of growth of agricultural production, 1965–87[a]

	Negative rates of growth in % p.a.					Positive rates of growth in % p.a.				
	4.00 and over	3.9–3.0	2.9–2.0	1.9–1.0	<1	<1	1.0–1.9	2.0–2.9	3.0–3.9	4 and over
1965–73	Malawi(–5.7) Mauritania Niger (–5.2)		Comoros Sudan	Angola Burkina Faso Chad Mali Mozambique Rwanda Senegal Togo Zaire Zambia	Ethiopia Guinea-Bissau Madagascar Sierra Leone Tanzania	CAR Côte d'Ivoire Gabon Guinea Uganda	Benin Congo Gambia Somalia Zimbabwe	Cameroon Ghana Kenya	Burundi Liberia	Botswana(9.1) Lesotho Mauritius Swaziland (5.4)
1973–80	Angola(–13.2) Guinea-Bissau (–8.6) Mauritius (–7.8) Uganda	Botswana Madagascar Tanzania Zimbabwe	Gambia Mauritania Nigeria Senegal Zaire	Burkina Faso Chad Côte d'Ivoire Ethiopia Ghana Lesotho Niger Zambia	Burundi CAR Congo Kenya Togo	Benin Guinea Liberia Sudan Swaziland	Cameroon Comoros Malawi Sierra Leone			Mali Rwanda(5.3) São Tomé and Príncipe(5.4) Somalia(8.3)
1980–87	Botswana (–11.2) Mozambique (–13.2) São Tomé and Príncipe (–10.3)	Ghana Seychelles Uganda	Comoros Côte d'Ivoire Mauritania Nigeria Senegal Sudan Togo	Burundi Congo Liberia Malawi Mali Rwanda Zimbabwe	Benin Cameroon CAR Kenya Madagascar Niger Sierra Leone Somalia Zambia	Chad Mauritius Swaziland Tanzania Zaire		Burkina Faso Lesotho	Gambia	Guinea-Bissau

Note
[a] As measured by the difference between the growth rate of aggregate production and aggregate population for each country where data are available.
Source: World Bank data.

to 27. The deterioration accelerated during the third phase (1980–87), with the number on the positive side of the scale falling to 9, and those on the negative rising to 30.

The deterioration is most marked in respect of per capita food production, which declined on average by –2.3 per cent per annum between 1969 and 1973. In Mauritania and Niger, two of the worst affected countries, it fell by –10.1 and –11.6 per cent per annum, respectively. There was a slight recovery between 1973 and 1984 but not enough to compensate for the years of neglect or the ravages of drought, famine and other disasters. In 1970 per capita grain production for 24 SSA countries most seriously affected by drought averaged 150 kg. By 1975 it had fallen below 140 kg, which is regarded by the Food and Agriculture Organization (FAO) as the minimum for a healthy diet. It continued to decline and, notwithstanding one or two good years, by 1984 had fallen below 100 kg per capita. The deterioration is shown in Figure 1.1.

Figure 1.2 compares per capita food production in Sub-Saharan Africa with that of Latin America and Asia between 1961 and 1984. The comparison is at once informative and depressing. Whereas per capita food production rose appreciably for both Latin America and Asia, it fell almost 25 per cent

Figure 1.1 Per capita grain production in 24 African countries affected by drought, 1970–84

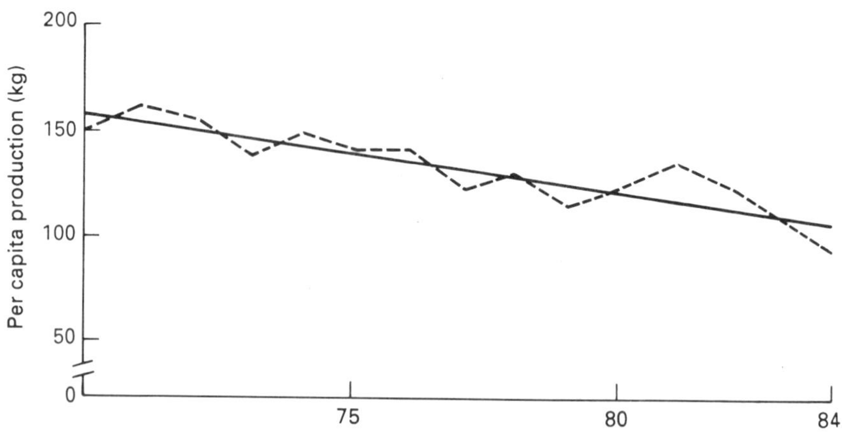

Source: Based on Food and Agriculture Organization (FAO) data, except that the 1984 figure is a projection using data from FAO, the US Agency for International Development and the US Department of Agriculture.

Figure 1.2 Index of per capita food production, from 1961–5 to 1983 (1961–5 average = 100)

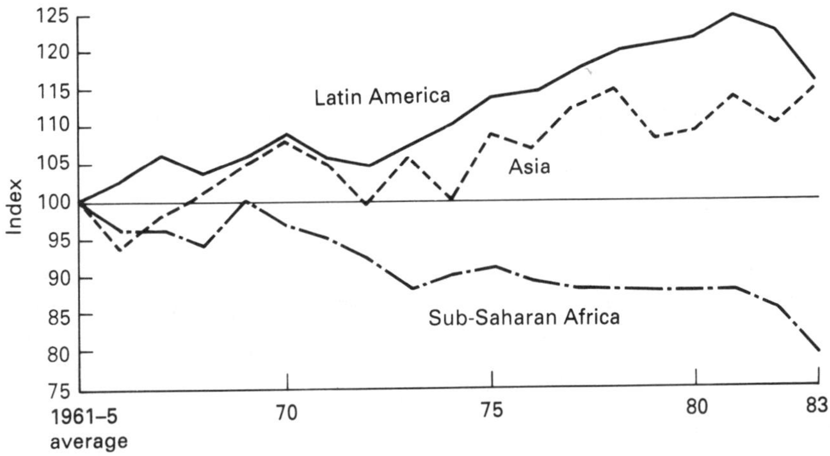

Source: Based on data provided by the US Department of Agriculture, and published in World Bank, *Towards Sustained Development in Sub-Saharan Africa: A Joint Program of Action*, Washington, D.C.: World Bank, 1984.

for Sub-Saharan Africa. This clearly has serious long-term implications for the region, only three of which need be mentioned. First, it will exacerbate the problem of shortages and food insecurity. Secondly, it will reduce exports even further and increase the region's dependence on food imports and food aid to relieve annual production shortfalls. Thirdly, it will reduce considerably government revenues, given the heavy burden of taxation which the sector bears. This will have a knock-on effect on the level of government expenditure on a vast range of services including agriculture, which, in turn, will set off another vicious circle of contraction within the sector.

A recent United Nations study on Africa's commodity problems sums up the situation as follows:

> The main reasons for the failure in Africa's commodity sector, reflected in low productivity and uncompetitive production, also include ill-advised government policies, unenlightened administration and organisation, a serious lack of agricultural scientists and extension officers, a poor knowledge of international markets, a lack of investment in transport and other infrastructure essential to effective competitive production and an economic policy framework which offers an inadequate environment in which productivity growth and competitiveness could be maintained, let alone increased, and in which commodity production could be increased to meet Africa's needs.[5]

E. TRADE AND PAYMENTS

SSA countries have also done badly on the trade and payments front. During the 1960s export volumes increased on average by 5.9 per cent per annum. These were the good years. Since then there has been a steady deterioration in their export performance. Between 1971 and 1980 export volumes either stagnated or declined markedly. The most notable exceptions were Botswana, Lesotho, Mali and Niger, for which the growth of exports of merchandise trade exceeded 15 per cent per annum between 1973 and 1980. Nevertheless, for the region as a whole, the volume of exports only expanded on average by 1 per cent per annum throughout the decade.

By 1980 export volumes had fallen to their lowest level since 1961.[6] They subsequently recovered, though their performances throughout the 1980s can, at best, be described as variable and well below the average trend of the previous two decades. For low-income SSA countries, exports declined on average by –3.6 per cent per annum between 1980 and 1987, while for middle-income SSA countries, they rose on average by 4.5 per cent per annum over the same period. However, this was not enough to compensate for the steady and protracted deterioration of previous years, and the region's share of world exports of non-fuel primary commodities fell from 7 per cent in 1970 to less than 4 per cent in 1987. This is estimated to have cost them between $9 and $10 billion in lost foreign exchange earnings in 1987 alone.

Part of the reason for this loss is the decline in the terms of trade which SSA countries have experienced, irrespective of whether they are exporters of primary commodities, petroleum or minerals. Starting back in the 1960s, their terms of trade steadily deteriorated up to 1973, with the heaviest falls being experienced by the oil-importing low-income countries. This was followed by a rapid though uneven improvement, which culminated in 1980 when the terms of trade for the region as a whole reached an all-time peak. Since then, they have again deteriorated, though not to the levels recorded during the worst years of the 1970s.

Movements in the terms of trade of SSA countries are heavily influenced by the performance of the five oil-exporting members. Buoyant oil prices brought on by the two oil crises were clearly the driving force behind the upsurge in the index during the 1970s. By the same token, its subsequent decline can be attributed to the fall in oil prices and the collapse of the international oil market in 1986. If one excludes the oil exporters, the picture which emerges is one of steady long-term deterioration in both the net barter terms of trade and the income terms of trade for the vast majority of the other members, particularly the poorer ones. Table 1.5 shows the terms of trade and the purchasing power of exports for Africa, excluding South Africa, for selected years between 1960 and 1988.

Table 1.5 Africa's terms of trade and purchasing power of exports, 1960–88 (1980=100)

Year	Terms of trade	Purchasing power of exports
1960	49	23
1965	37	31
1970	36	47
1975	67	64
1980	100	100
1985	95	74
1988	59	52

Source: UNCTAD, *Handbook of International Trade and Development Statistics, 1988*, New York, 1989, Tables 2.5 and 2.6, reproduced as Table 7 in *Africa's Commodity Problems: Towards a Solution*, New York: United Nations, 1990, p. 123.

The two most obvious points which the table makes are: (a) the terms of trade fell by almost 40 per cent between 1980 and 1988; and (b) the purchasing power of exports virtually halved over the same period. Terms of trade estimates for SSA countries for which data are available are given in Appendix A.2.

The deterioration in both indices reflects the perennial weakness of commodity export prices and the over-dependence of SSA countries on a limited range of primary commodity exports and minerals. In addition, SSA governments allowed the rate of domestic inflation to get out of line with that of their main trading partners. They also refused to devalue their currencies. Consequently, rates of exchange became seriously over-valued, leading to a loss of markets and valuable foreign exchange earnings. In 1973, for example, the real effective rate of exchange index (REER) for Malawi, Sudan, Tanzania, Uganda and Zambia ranged between 121 and 166, taking 1965 as the base year. By 1982 it exceeded 200 for more than a dozen countries and, in the case of Ghana, Uganda and Sierra Leone, the nominal rate of exchange ceased to have any meaning.

More recently, there has been a considerable improvement in the index, particularly in those countries which have devalued domestic currencies as part of their structural adjustment programmes with the IMF and the World Bank. According to the latter institution,

> Since the mid-1980s, the divergence between real effective exchange rates in Africa and those of its competitors in other developing regions has ceased to widen and may be beginning to narrow.[7]

Whether or not this is so, there is little doubt that over-valued rates of exchange contributed greatly to SSA countries' balance of payments problems, by over-pricing exports and under-pricing imports. Instead of devaluing their currencies to correct the distortion, they resorted to tariffs, import controls and other quantitative restrictions to protect domestic markets. These were reinforced by import-substituting industrialization policies aimed at promoting local industries and saving foreign exchange. But these policies served only to aggravate the problem. As Table 1.2 shows, export volumes grew on average by 1.1 per cent per annum between 1971 and 1980, whereas import volume increased by 2.6 per cent per annum.

They managed to sustain this policy mainly with the help of increased capital inflows; but with the onset of the debt crisis, these virtually dried up and the policy became unsustainable. Imports had to be cut back drastically, the worst year being 1983, when they fell by –7.9 per cent. Between 1980 and 1987 import volumes fell on average by –5.8 per cent per annum; the worst-affected cases were Liberia (–10.2 per cent), Nigeria (–14.0 per cent) and Sierra Leone (–15.1 per cent).

The massive cut-back in imports helped to reduce the current account deficit to $3.3 billion by 1984. However, as Table 1.6 shows, this improvement was short-lived, and by 1988 the overall deficit had again risen to $8.2 billion, the same level as in 1982. The factors which were largely responsible for this were (a) the sharp swing in the movement of oil prices between 1986 and 1987; and (b) the rapid increase in interest payments, which actually doubled over the decade.

The table also shows that since 1984 international reserves have more than trebled. This can be attributed in part, to the sharp rise in oil prices following the 1986 slump, and partly to the fact that many SSA countries borrowed heavily to build-up their reserves. The position is thus not as healthy as the figures suggest. Also, these reserves are very unevenly spread among the members. In 1987, for example, about 40 per cent of the region's reserves were held by Botswana. The overall improvements in the figures for import cover should therefore be read with caution. In many SSA countries the import cover can, in fact, be counted in days rather than months.

SSA countries have drawn on a variety of sources to finance their deficits. In 1987, for example, they managed to raise a total of $4.6 billion in medium- and long-term loans, including net purchases from the IMF. They were also able to attract a significant amount of non-debt-creating flows, principally foreign private investment and grants. Additionally, many of them drew

Table 1.6 Current account deficit for SSA countries, 1981–90 ($ billion)

Year	Deficit		Reserves	Import cover (months)
	Total	of which interest payments		
1981	–9.6	–3.0	3.4	1.0
1982	–8.2	–3.1	2.8	0.9
1983	–5.6	–3.1	3.0	1.1
1984	–3.3	–3.7	3.1	1.1
1985	–3.3	–3.9	4.1	1.5
1986	–5.9	–4.3	5.1	1.6
1987	–6.7	–4.9	5.9	1.8
1988	–8.2	–5.6	6.3	1.7
1989	–7.4	–5.6	7.4	1.9
1990	–7.8	–6.0	9.8	2.4

Source: *World Economic Outlook*, Washington D.C. IMF (various issues).

down their reserves to dangerously low levels. Clearly, each source creates its own problems. Additional loans increase existing debt burdens, while private investment flows are attracted mainly to those countries with good investment prospects. Consequently, the improvement registered in a few individual countries has been largely lost in the overall pattern of deterioration on the balance of payments front.

F. THE PUBLIC SECTOR

A common feature of all SSA countries is the rapid growth and expansion of the public sector. Part of this has been due to the requirements of independence and statehood, but there have been strong political and ideological reasons as well, such as a deep distrust of the market system and private enterprise and a commitment to socialism, state ownership and central planning. Whatever the reason, the results have been the same throughout. The public sector took on new duties and responsibilities and expanded into several commercial and productive activities previously undertaken by the private sector, for example, mining, manufacturing, transport, marketing and distribution.

Accordingly, it developed a variety of structures and institutions which give it a decisive say in the way the economy is run. These operate at all levels of government (central, local, district, village) and include such organizations as parastatals, state-owned enterprises, marketing boards, cooperatives and the like. Collectively, these provide an extensive network of administrative and organizational forms and bureaucratic arrangements for managing the economy. The concept and scope of the public sector in SSA countries thus extend beyond the range of activities conventionally associated with the term in the developed countries, and account for a major share of domestic resources. In 1987 central government expenditure exceeded 40 per cent of GNP for Gabon, Togo and Zimbabwe.

Partly as a result of, as well as contributing to, the rapid expansion of the public sector, there has been a massive increase in employment in that sector. It is now the largest single employer in most SSA countries. A World Bank study of public sector employment in seven SSA countries for which data were available showed that the proportion ranged between 40 per cent and 74 per cent of 'formal' or recorded employment. In Ghana, for example, the figure rose from 51.4 per cent in 1957 to 71.5 per cent in 1970. In Tanzania the increase was even more spectacular: it rose from 27 per cent in 1960 to 66 per cent in 1974. And in Zambia, public sector employment was 72 per cent of total recorded employment in 1976. These increases have been largely at the expense of private sector employment which, in the case of Ghana declined by –2.2 per cent from 1957 to 1972. For Tanzania the decline averaged –4.8 per cent per annum between 1962 and 1974.[8]

However, the growth in public sector expenditure has not helped to improve the efficiency and management of the economy. Rather, there has been a steady deterioration in the performance of the sector, which is seriously over-extended and badly managed. Further, the rapid growth in public sector employment has led to considerable over-staffing, top-heavy administration, inefficient management and over-ambitious investment programmes. In addition, the scope of public sector activities and the open-ended subsidies which underpin the operations of parastatals and state-owned enterprises have stifled private entrepreneurial activity in agriculture, industry and commerce. They are also a serious drain on government resources as their operating losses have to be covered from public funds.

Among the reasons for the poor performance of the public sector, the World Bank lists the following:

(a) the uncontrolled expansion of staff in the civil service and public enterprises, which have often functioned as welfare agencies for unemployed school leavers;
(b) the rapid promotion and turnover of poorly qualified staff who have little in-depth understanding of either the institutions they manage or of the broader context in which they are expected to function;

(c) difficulties faced by managers in motivating and disciplining their staff owing to the social and political context in which they operate;
(d) in an increasing number of countries, the compression of civil service pay scales at the expense of higher-level staff.[9]

It should be said, though, that several SSA governments have introduced a series of measures to reduce the size of the private sector, cut its workforce and improve its management and efficiency. For example, Mali, Rwanda, Somalia and Togo have abandoned their policy of providing automatic employment for school-leavers and university graduates. Others – the Central African Republic, Gambia, Ghana, Guinea, Mauritania and Senegal – have introduced comprehensive programmes of administrative reforms for revamping the civil service and improving its efficiency. Salaries, the largest single item of central government expenditure, have been cut or frozen and staff made redundant.

In Gambia, 20 per cent of civil service staff was identified as superfluous and made redundant. A similar exercise in Ghana and Guinea resulted in the retrenchment of some 24,000 and 14,000 staff, respectively. The introduction of competitive entrance examinations for the civil service and more effective recruitment and management procedures resulted in a saving of 8 per cent in the salary bill in the Central African Republic. Elsewhere, in-service training schemes have been instituted and measures taken to improve institutional and human capacities. Several non-viable public enterprises have been closed and non-strategic ones sold. For those that remain, better management has cut operating losses through higher prices, better cost accounting and shedding staff.[10]

The various measures which have been put in place throughout the region have had a major impact on rationalizing the public sector. As a proportion of GDP, central government consumption expenditure fell on average by –0.7 per cent per annum between 1980 and 1987 for the region as a whole (in Zaire and Mozambique the figure exceeded –10 per cent).[11] There is a danger, though, that rapid retrenchment of personnel and cuts in public expenditure will leave many public enterprises short of funds for vital maintenance, equipment and supplies. There are, in fact, reports of factories and equipment lying idle for lack of funds for maintenance, schools without books, chalk and other materials, and clinics having to close because they have run out of funds to pay staff or buy medicines. A balance must therefore be struck between improved efficiency and better management, on the one hand, and the requirements of proper maintenance and utilization of existing capacity and enterprises, on the other.

Within the existing pattern of public expenditure, heavy emphasis is placed on administration and defence. During the 1970s the average annual rate of growth of expenditure on these two items averaged 10 per cent of GDP per annum, ranging from countries like Burundi and Mauritius, with an average of less than 5 per cent, to Mauritania (18 per cent), Kenya (17 per cent) and Sudan (16 per cent). Things really got out of hand during the 1980s, when there was a massive expansion in public sector expenditure, ultimately precipitating the demand for massive retrenchment and reforms. Table 1.7 shows government expenditure as a share of GDP and defence expenditures as a share of government expenditure in 1987, the year in which for the first time, there was a significant contraction in the level of public expenditure.

Although the average level of public expenditure as a proportion of GDP is not excessive when compared with other developing countries, there are several members in which it clearly needs to be reduced, Gambia, Guinea-

Table 1.7 Government expenditure as a share of GDP, and defence expenditure as a share of government expenditure for selected SSA countries in 1987 (%)

Countries	Government expenditure/ GDP	Defence/government expenditure
Burkina Faso	19.4	17.3
Ethiopia	35.7	30.6
Gambia	52.0	—
Guinea-Bissau	57.7	5.1[a]
Kenya	31.4	10.1
Lesotho	57.2	9.6[a]
Malawi	30.2	5.2
Nigeria	19.1	4.5
Seychelles	64.6	—
Sudan	26.2	10.7
Swaziland	29.1	5.4
Tanzania	25.1	14.1[b]
Uganda	6.4	13.9
Zambia	36.7	—
Zimbabwe	39.7	17.2
All Africa	31.2	10.6[b]

Notes
[a] 1984
[b] 1985
— Not available.
Source: *Africa's Commodity Problems: Towards a Solution*, United Nations, 1990, Annex, Table 9, pp. 127–8 (as amended).

Bissau, Lesotho and Seychelles being obvious examples. Perhaps, though, the most significant point which the table makes is that, contrary to popular belief, expenditure on defence does not account for a major share of public expenditure except in a few countries (Burkina Faso, Ethiopia and Zimbabwe). A reduction in existing levels of defence expenditure would obviously release resources for other purposes such as increased investment in agriculture, one of the main priorities of the United Nations Programme of Action for African Economic Recovery and Development (UNPAAERD).[12]

About half the number of SSA countries have already taken steps to implement the necessary reforms for raising investment expenditure in agriculture to 20–25 per cent of total public expenditure, the target set in UNPAAERD. However, as Table 1.8 shows, the level of expenditure on agriculture is well below that target. Also, it has remained remarkably stable since 1975. It will require, therefore, a massive transfer of resources to the agricultural sector, which cannot be achieved in the given time period without

Table 1.8 Central government expenditure on agriculture as % of total expenditure for selected SSA countries, 1975–87

Country	1975–9	1980–87
Botswana	9.2	9.1
Burkino Faso	4.2	4.5
Cameroon	5.5[a]	4.6[b]
Ghana	9.1	8.7
Kenya	9.0	9.9
Liberia	7.2	5.5
Malawi	13.1	12.5[b]
Mauritius	8.2	6.4
Niger	7.6[a]	4.5[b]
Nigeria	2.0	0.3[b]
Swaziland	10.9	9.1
Tanzania	11.6	9.8
Uganda	10.3	5.6
Zimbabwe	8.8[a]	9.0

Notes
[a] 1976–9
[b] 1980–86
Source: Simon Commander, 'Prices, Markets and Rigidities: African Agriculture, 1980–1988', paper presented at Overseas Development Institute Conference on *The Design and Impact of Adjustment Programmes on Agriculture and Agricultural Institutions*, ODI, London, 10–11 September 1987 (mimeo).

a major upheaval and reordering of public expenditure. In the case of Malawi, the country with the best ratio, expenditure will have to double.

The low proportion of central government funding of agriculture has at least two serious long-term implications for SSA countries. First, not only does agriculture make the greatest contribution to the economy, it is the sector in which they have the greatest comparative advantage in terms of domestic production and export crops. However, having been neglected for so long, there are no 'quick-fix' solutions to the sector's problems. It will require a major and sustained long-term effort to enable it to realize its full potential. Secondly, given that the agricultural sector provides a major share of government tax revenues, its long-term neglect has caused the tax base to shrink, which, in the context of rapidly expanding public sector expenditure, has resulted in massive budgetary deficits in most countries. In 1987 the overall fiscal deficit as a proportion of GDP was –28.2 per cent for Botswana, –26.2 per cent for Guinea-Bissau and –15.8 per cent for Zimbabwe.

G. SOCIAL CONDITIONS AND TRENDS

In the early days of independence, SSA countries placed a high priority on the improvement of social conditions and living standards. Many of them launched major projects for eliminating poverty and malnutrition as well as providing universal education and other essential social services. However, after a series of early successes, many of these programmes had to be cut back and most of the improvements have since been lost. Conditions have, in fact, steadily deteriorated. By 1995 the number of people living in absolute poverty in SSA countries is expected to exceed 405 million, almost double the number in 1980. The food situation has also worsened. Whereas in 1970 about two-thirds of the population lived in countries where the per capita consumption of food was increasing, by 1980 the proportion had fallen to one-quarter. Between 1984 and 1986 the daily calorie supply for SSA countries averaged 91 per cent of the region's requirements.[13]

Life expectancy at birth averages 51 years as against 62 years for all developing countries. Forty-five per cent of its population have access to health services compared with 61 per cent for all developing countries. In SSA countries, 37 per cent of the population have access to safe water. In all developing countries the proportion is 55 per cent, and adult literacy rates average 48 per cent against 60 per cent in all developing countries.

The education sector provides the best indication of the extent to which the early gains in social development have been eroded. Between 1980 and 1988 total public spending on education fell from $11 billion to $7 billion in real terms. For a sample of 26 countries, spending per pupil declined from

$113 to $89 with the result that primary school enrolment rates fell from 77 per cent in 1980 to 67 per cent in 1990. At present, just under half the number of children in the 6 to 11 age group attends school. Teachers' income fell by at least a third in real terms. Finally, although the average

Table 1.9 Social indicators for least developed SSA countries (%)

	Infant mortality rate[a] (1988)	Rural population with access to safe water (1988)	Primary school enrolment rates in 1987[b] % Male	Female	Total	Daily calorie supply as % of needs (1984–6)
Benin	109	35	84	43	63	95
Botswana	66	33	107	114	111	96
Burkina Faso	137	69	41	24	32	86
Burundi	111	34	77	57	67	97
Cape Verde	65	49	112	105	108	125
Cent Afr Rep	131	11	82	51	66	86
Chad	131	na	73	29	51	69
Comoros	79	na	90	70	80	82
Djibouti	121	21	53	37	45	na
Eq Guinea	126	na	120	107	114	na
Ethiopia	153	11	46	28	37	71
Gambia	142	50	76	47	61	103
Guinea	146	24	41	18	30	77
Guinea-Bissau	131	27	73	39	56	105
Lesotho	99	45	101	125	113	101
Malawi	149	50	73	59	66	102
Mali	168	36	29	17	23	86
Mauritania	126	na	61	42	52	92
Mozambique	172	17	76	59	68	69
Niger	134	49	37	20	29	100
Rwanda	121	64	69	66	67	81
São Tomé & Príncipe	66	45	na	na	na	103
Sierra Leone	153	22	68	49	58	81
Somalia	131	22	20	10	15	90
Sudan	107	20	57	40	49	88
Tanzania	105	46	67	66	66	96
Togo	93	41	124	78	101	97
Uganda	102	18	76	63	70	95

Notes
[a] Per 1000 live births
[b] Because of enrolment by older students, ratios may exceed 100%.
na = Not available
Source: *Africa Recovery Briefing Paper*, No 2, August 1990 'Africa LDCs: Among the Most Vulnerable and Least Developed', p. 8, New York: United Nations Dept of Public Information.

number of pupils per teacher has fallen, the expansion of educational opportunities has not kept pace with the rapidly growing population. In 1990 the number of adult illiterates was estimated at 139 million. This is expected to increase to 147 million by the year 2000.[14]

There are, of course, vast disparities within this broad scenario of averages. Some of these are shown in Table 1.9 for least developed SSA countries, the most socially deprived group within the region. Infant mortality rates for the group averaged 121 per 1000 live births in 1988, the highest in the world. In countries like Ethiopia, Mali, Mozambique and Sierra Leone, where the rate exceeded 150, only 75 per cent of the children survive to age 5. In addition, fertility rates in most countries exceed the average (6.2 children per mother) for SSA countries as a whole, which itself is considerably higher than elsewhere in the developing world. If population growth rates are to fall to the projected rate of 2.75 per cent per annum by the year 2020, fertility rates in SSA countries will have to be cut by half.

In 1950 about 85 per cent of the population of SSA countries lived in rural areas. Over the years, this figure has gradually fallen due to high population pressure and accelerated migration to urban centres. In 1990 the population living in rural areas was put at 70 per cent, of which only about one-third had access to safe water. In Ethiopia and the Central African Republic, the proportion was as low as 11 per cent. Additionally, in most cases, people have to travel long distances to fetch and carry water.

Among other things, migration has aggravated the problem of urban unemployment and led to large slum areas and squatter settlements with overcrowding and poor sanitation. It has also created additional demand on very limited and inadequate public health resources. Further, migration has had deleterious effects on the rural areas, since it is usually the most active in the rural labour force which leave the land and head for the cities. This, in turn, contributes to low agricultural output and food production. By the end of this century there will be about 350 million urban dwellers in SSA countries.

It is not necessary to go into the reasons why social conditions have deteriorated, but clearly poor economic performance, rising population pressure and cuts in social expenditure have all contributed greatly to the decline. Urgent measures need to be taken to reverse the trend and restore growth in SSA countries. If they are to achieve the rate of growth of 4.6 per cent per annum which the World Bank considers necessary for long-term sustainable growth, SSA countries will have to increase gross domestic investment to 25 per cent of GDP from its current level of 15 per cent. Food production will also have to double in order to cope with rising population pressure and to achieve self-sufficiency in the medium-term. Most importantly, they will have to increase social expenditure to between 8 and 10 per cent of GDP per annum by 2000 in order to provide universal access to minimum food requirements, basic education, primary health care, family planning services, safe drinking water and sanitation, and to enhance the status and role of women so that they can participate fully in the process of economic and social development. Social expenditure for SSA countries currently averages about 4.5 per cent of GDP per annum.[15]

NOTES

1. World Bank, *Sub-Saharan Africa – From Crisis to Sustainable Growth: A Long-Term Perspective Study*. Washington, D.C.: World Bank, November 1989, p. 110.
2. For the average annual rate of inflation in individual SSA countries since 1965, see Appendix A.1.
3. An index based on the period 1974–6 showed that by 1981–3, per capita food production for SSA countries had fallen to 94. See World Bank, *Financing Adjustment with Growth in Sub-Saharan Africa, 1986–90*. Washington D.C.: World Bank, April 1986, Statistical Annex.
4. For a fuller discussion of the domestic constraints and the bias against agriculture, see World Bank, *Accelerated Development in Sub-Saharan Africa: An Agenda for Action*. Washington D.C.: World Bank, October 1981, Chs 4 and 5; and Tore Rose (ed.) *Crisis and Recovery in Sub-Saharan Africa: Realities and Complexities*. Paris: OECD, Development Centre, Paris, June 1985, Working Document CD/R (85); Jean-Jacques Faucher and Hartmut Schneider, 'Agricultural Crises: Structural Constraints, Prices and other Policy Issues', in Rose (1985), pp. 50–65.
5. United Nations, *Africa's Commodity Problems: Towards a Solution*, a Report by the United Nations Secretary General's Expert Group on Africa's Commodity Problems. Geneva: UNCTAD Secretariat, 1990, pp. 29–30.
6. In the case of primary commodities, the volume of exports in 1980 was down to 80 per cent of their 1961 level; see World Bank, *Sub-Saharan Africa: From Crisis to Sustainable Growth*, p. 20.
7. World Bank and United Nations Development Programme, *Africa's Adjustment and Growth in the 1980s*. Washington, D.C.: World Bank, March 1989, p. 21.
8. World Bank, *Accelerated Development in Sub-Saharan Africa: An Agenda for Action*. Washington, D.C.: World Bank, 1981, p. 41.
9. World Bank, *Sub-Saharan Africa: From Crisis to Sustainable Development*, p. 55.
10. For a fuller account of measures aimed at rationalizing the public sector, see *Financing Adjustment with Growth in Sub-Saharan Africa, 1986–90*, pp. 21–4.
11. Compare this with the period of most rapid expansion (1965–73) when public consumption as a proportion of GDP rose on average by 9 per cent per annum. In the case of Nigeria and Somalia the annual rate of growth exceeded 16 per cent.
12. See United Nations Department of Public Information, Division for Economic and Social Information, *Africa: United Nations Programme of Action for African Recovery and Development, 1986–1990*, New York: United Nations, 1986.
13. The corresponding figure for the developing countries as a whole was 107 per cent, and 132 per cent for the industrialized countries.
14. For details, see *Africa Recovery*, Vol. 6, No. 1, April 1992, New York. United Nations Dept of Public Information, pp. 12–13.
15. The essential requirements of an effective long-term programme of social development are outlined in World Bank, *Sub-Saharan Africa: From Crises to Sustainable Development*, Ch. 3, pp. 63–88.

2. The Debt Crisis

A. ITS NATURE AND CAUSES

There are three features of the debt crisis affecting SSA countries that need to be stressed at the outset. First, it is not confined to a few of them. They are all, to a lesser or greater extent, affected by it. Secondly, it has deepened dramatically over the last decade. Thirdly, and related to the latter point, SSA countries have been accumulating external debts at a much faster rate than other developing countries. In several respects, therefore, this crisis is no less serious than that affecting the highly indebted countries (the so-called HICs), the group which has dominated the international headlines.[1]

There are, of course, major differences between the two, particularly in the perception and international response which they have elicited. The Mexican debt crisis, for example, was first regarded as an acute liquidity problem for which adequate and appropriate measures existed within the framework of conventional debt consolidation exercises. However, the speed with which it spread to other Latin American countries (the so-called contagion effect) and the amounts involved quickly changed this perception. The possibility of widespread defaults was seen as a serious and immediate threat to the stability and efficient functioning of the international monetary and financial system. Consequently, a major international effort was required to save the system from collapse. This largely explains the heavy emphasis and attention paid to the debt crisis in the HICs.

On the other hand, the debt problems of SSA countries were not considered a threat to the stability and prosperity of the world economic and financial system. The amounts involved were small in relation to the global total of Third World debts. Also, their debts were considered to be due, in part, to the process of long-term growth and development and the need for external resources to finance that process. Once the rate of growth picked up and the development process took off, they would be able to service these debts. Conceptually as well as operationally, therefore, a distinction was drawn between the short-term liquidity crisis facing the HICs and the long-term development debts of the SSA countries. The former (a liquidity crisis) was a threat to the world monetary and financial system and had to be dealt with immediately. The latter (an insolvency crisis) was not. It could wait until the world economy recovered. Effectively therefore, SSA countries were expected to grow out of their debt problems with time.

This basic distinction provided the parameters for policy formulation in the period immediately following the outbreak of the 1982 Mexican debt crisis. However, it proved largely artificial. After numerous proposals, plans and initiatives, and a decade of rescheduling and refinancing packages, the so-called liquidity crisis of the HICs has not eased.[2] Of more direct interest to this study, SSA countries have not grown out of their debts. They are, in fact, more heavily indebted now than at the start of the crisis. Further, as already indicated, their economic performance deteriorated dramatically during the 1980s. Many of the assumptions regarding the nature and course of the crisis were thus largely unfounded.

First, although a substantial proportion of SSA countries' debts are development-related, ability to service them depends not only on growth and development in the debtor countries but also on a healthy and expanding world economy; neither of these were obtained during the 1980s. The expected growth and development did not materialize and, instead of contributing to the process of development, these development loans retarded it by pre-empting an increasing share of their limited foreign exchange resources for debt service payments. The problem was further aggravated by the inordinate number of prestige projects (the so-called 'white elephants') and ill-conceived and over-ambitious development plans which effectively railroaded the development effort.

Secondly, the notion that SSA countries brought the crisis on themselves has largely been dispelled by the course of subsequent events. The vast majority of them have, in fact, gone to great lengths to meet debt service payments (often sacrificing urgent domestic development needs in the process). However, despite their best efforts, the crisis has not abated. The level of total external debts outstanding has continued to rise. So, too, have debt service ratios. In many ways they are considerably worse off than when the crisis broke.

Part of the reason for this can be attributed to external factors. The recent rise in protectionism in the developed countries, particularly the so-called new protectionism, and the proliferation of non-tariff measures have hurt SSA countries in terms of market access, the development of new products and the processing of raw materials domestically. Further, increases in international interest rates are estimated to have added between \$8 and \$10 billion to their external debts. Also, having the majority of their debts denominated in dollars added a further \$1 to 2 billion to debt service payments, due to the weakness of the dollar during most of the 1980s. Rescheduling and refinancing cost them an extra \$1 billion.

Other external factors included the weak and sluggish performance of the world economy during the 1980s. The international recession combined with the massive fall in commodity prices hit SSA countries particularly hard. Export markets were lost and foreign exchange earnings fell disastrously, thereby constraining their ability to service outstanding debts as well as finance urgent development work. This contrasts sharply with the commodity boom of the 1970s when exports expanded and easy access to international capital markets enabled them to run up substantial foreign debts.

In addition, net resource flows to SSA countries declined sharply between 1982 and 1984, that is, at the time when additional resource flows were most needed. Although they have recovered, net resource flows in 1987, in real terms, were some \$3 billion below their 1982 level. The severe financial squeeze which they experienced between 1982 and 1984 was clearly due to the virtual disappearance of private capital flows and commercial bank lending which dominated the 1970s. Although there has been some recovery particularly since 1985, private flows are nowhere near the levels reached during the 1970s. Consequently, the increase in net resource flows has come mainly from official development finance (ODF) sources, principally official development assistance (ODA). In 1987 this amounted to \$15 billion, an increase of 50 per cent on the 1984 level. Data on net resource flows to SSA countries for the period 1980–87 are given in Appendix A.3.

SSA countries have also contributed in large measure to their own debt problems in a variety of ways. The most obvious of which include:

(a) unrealistic development plans with outsize and unproductive projects;
(b) a top-heavy and poorly trained bureaucracy;
(c) bloated public expenditure, including funding of parastatals and other state-owned enterprises;
(d) weak or non-existent organizational and institutional infrastructure;
(e) acute shortage of managerial, administrative personnel and skills;
(f) inefficient monetary, fiscal and exchange rate policies;
(g) insufficient domestic savings and low investment;
(h) lack of political will to take politically unpalatable decisions;
(i) no effective debt management strategy.

It is this combination of internal and external factors which has given the debt crisis in SSA countries its peculiar characteristics. Basically, their debts are regarded as long-term and developmental in nature. As part of the process of development, they are not amenable to a 'quick fix' solution, but need to be related to the debtor's long-term development profile and ability to pay.

Secondly, the amounts involved are small by world standards. Also, the debts themselves are mainly long-term public debts contracted on concessional terms. Quantitatively as well as qualitatively, therefore, there are major substantive differences between them and the debts of the HICs.

Thirdly, most SSA countries exist on the periphery of the world's economic and financial system. They account for a small proportion of world trade and offer limited investment opportunities for foreign private capital. Their ability to raise loans in international capital markets is severely constrained by their low credit-rating. They were, in fact, largely bypassed in the recycling process. Consequently, although they were accumulating debts at an alarming rate, these were not considered a threat to the stability and well-being of the international monetary and financial system.

Basically, this is still the case. However, the distinction between a liquidity and a solvency crisis is rather arbitrary and artificial in the context of SSA countries, given (a) the interdependence of the debt crisis and the crisis in agriculture; (b) their extreme vulnerability to fluctuations in international commodity markets; and (c) the impact of major external shocks such as the oil crisis on their domestic economy. Nigeria is a case in point. During the 1970s it was one of the richest countries in Sub-Saharan Africa. The international oil market was booming, foreign exchange earnings were at record levels and the country enjoyed a high international credit-rating. Ten years later the position was completely changed. The bottom fell out of the oil market, its agriculture had virtually collapsed and the country was deep in debt. It is, in fact, now ranked as an IDA-eligible country.

While it is true that SSA countries' debts do not feature prominently in the overall picture, they impose major economic, financial and social costs on the debtor countries. They also have serious implications for international economic and political relations between the rich creditor countries (the North) and the poor debtor nations (the South). They cannot, therefore, be ignored or subsumed in the wider context of the need for a healthy and expanding world economy. This much is agreed among the parties to the crisis. They also agree that urgent and effective international action is needed to deal with the crisis. This is the new and positive dimension which has characterized the approach to the debt crisis in this part of the world since the mid-1980s.

B. THE TAXONOMY OF DEBTORS

The World Bank estimates that the total external debts of SSA countries, defined as all medium- and long-term debts, public as well as private (whether publicly-guaranteed or not), IMF credits and short-term debts were less than $10 billion in 1972. Over the next decade they shot up to $70 billion. A further $60 billion were added over the next five years to bring the total to

$130 billion in 1987, including arrears of almost $11 billion. Of these debts, 22 per cent were owed by Nigeria and 9 per cent by Côte d'Ivoire, making them the two largest debtors. They are also the only SSA countries to be classified as members of the HICs.

These two countries, along with Congo and Gabon, obtained about two-thirds of their external borrowing between 1978 and 1982 from commercial creditors. The IMF categorized this group as market borrowers, a term which reflected their high credit-rating and greater access to international capital markets. It also distinguished them from the vast majority of other SSA countries, whose external debts are owed to official creditors. The main group (official borrowers) obtained two-thirds of their external loans between 1978 and 1982 from official sources. In all, there are 30 of them, mainly low-income SSA countries with a few middle-income countries.[3] A third group of some ten countries are classified as other or diversified borrowers.[4]

The World Bank adopts a different taxomony of debtors, or to be more precise, uses a variety of categories and sub-sets to reflect specific conditions. Its most usual classification, based on per capita income levels, divides SSA countries into low-income and middle-income debtors. The former category, by definition, includes the vast majority of SSA countries. Since the division was first made, two countries, Liberia and Nigeria, have been reclassified as low-income countries and added to this group of debtors. There is, however, a problem with Nigeria. In terms of per capita income, it is clearly a low-income debtor country and as such qualifies for assistance from the International Development Association (IDA) and the various international debt relief programmes open to low-income SSA countries. However, the nature and size of its external debts put it firmly in the category of HICs, for which different relief proposals and programmes are available. Does Nigeria, therefore, have a liquidity crisis or a solvency crisis? The World Bank gets round this dilemma by including Nigeria as a low-income country, but shows data for it separately.

Within the category of low-income debtors, the World Bank identifies two main sub-groups. The first of these, the debt-distressed, includes countries which urgently need debt relief and substantial inflows of new concessional funding. The concept of debt-distressedness is not precisely defined. Rather, it incorporates a number of short- and long-term factors which collectively indicate the debtor's inability to service its foreign debts beyond some manageable threshold which can vary from year to year, depending on the country's circumstances.

According to the World Bank, these countries were unique in that their debt service ratios exceeded 30 per cent in 1988, which was substantially above what they had experienced in recent years. Also, they suffered a 17 per cent decline in real per capita income between 1980 and 1986, with exports and investment falling by 30 per cent and 15 per cent, respectively, over the same period. Originally, the group included 22 SSA countries, 21 of which were low-income and one (Liberia) was middle-income.[5] In 1987 the external debts of this group were put at $60 billion. The number of debt-distressed SSA countries is now up to 30.

Apart from being the worst-case debt scenario, so to speak, the debt-distressed countries also provide strong evidence of the crisis in agriculture. In virtually all of them there has been a steady decline in the annual average per capita rate of growth of agricultural production over two decades. In Mali and Senegal this exceeded 5 per cent per annum between 1965 and 1973. In a more recent period (1973–84), annual per capita output declined on average by 4 per cent in Guinea-Bissau, 4.7 per cent in Gambia and 5.1 per cent in Ghana. What is perhaps more indicative of the steady deterioration in these debt-distressed countries is the fact that in none of them did the annual per capita rate of growth of agricultural output average 1 per cent per annum (or more) over the period from 1965 to 1984.

The other category which the World Bank differentiates is the IDA-eligible countries. Eligibility for IDA credits is confined to the poorest members of the World Bank. In 1987 the operational cut-off point for purposes of entitlement was set at $580 per capita GNP. Other criteria, such as the level of poverty, the need for concessional assistance and the ability to use such funding effectively are also taken into account in determining a member's entitlement, subject to what is known as an 'historical ceiling'. In 1987 this ceiling was set at $940 per capita GNP. In all, there are some 35 SSA countries in this group, some of which are middle-income countries. In 1987 their total external debts, excluding Nigeria, exceeded $58 billion.

Middle-income SSA countries are also often divided into two categories for debt purposes, depending on whether they are oil importers or oil exporters. The former group includes Botswana, Cape Verde, Côte d'Ivoire, Djibouti, Mauritius, Seychelles, Swaziland and Zimbabwe. The latter is comprised of Cameroon, Congo and Gabon. Only Cameroon has regularly maintained service payments on its external debts. In 1987 the external debts of all middle-income SSA countries exceeded $15 billion. In 1989 the World Bank adopted a new classification to differentiate debtors in terms of whether they are severely indebted or moderately indebted. The classification is based on ratios of debt to exports, debt to GNP, debt service to exports and interest payments to exports. In all, there are 26 severely indebted low-income countries (SILICs), of which 24 are SSA countries. The next largest group is the severely indebted middle-income countries with 20 members. Only three of these (Congo, Côte d'Ivoire and Senegal) are SSA countries. Central African Republic, Ethiopia, Gambia and Uganda are categorized as moderately

Table 2.1 *SSA countries main debtor classification*

Countries	Low-income	Middle-income	Debt-distressed[a]	IDA-eligible	Severely indebted[b]		Moderately indebted[c]	
					Low-income	Middle-income	Low-income	Middle-income
Angola		*						
Benin	*		*	*	*			
Botswana		*						
Burkina Faso	*			*				
Burundi	*		*	*	*			
Cameroon		*						*
Cape Verde		*		*				*
Central Afr. Rep.	*		*	*			*	
Chad	*		*	*				
Comoros	*		*	*	*			
Congo		*				*		
Côte d'Ivoire		*	*			*		
Djibouti		*		*				
Equatorial Guinea	*		*	*	*			
Ethiopia	*			*			*	
Gabon		*						*
Gambia	*		*	*			*	
Ghana	*		*	*	*			
Guinea	*		*	*	*			
Guinea-Bissau	*		*	*	*			
Kenya	*		*	*	*			
Lesotho	*			*				
Liberia		*	*	*	*			
Madagascar	*		*	*	*			

Malawi	*		*	*	*			
Mali	*		*	*	*			
Mauritania	*		*	*	*			
Mauritius		*						
Mozambique	*		*	*	*			
Niger	*		*	*	*			
Nigeria		*	*	*	*			
Rwanda	*			*				
São Tomé & Príncipe	*		*	*	*			
Senegal	*		*	*		*		
Seychelles		*						
Sierra Leone	*		*	*	*			
Somalia	*		*	*	*			
Sudan	*		*	*	*			
Swaziland		*						
Tanzania	*		*	*	*			
Togo	*		*	*	*			
Uganda	*		*	*			*	
Zaire	*		*	*	*			
Zambia	*		*	*	*			
Zimbabwe		*						*
Total	31	14	30	35	24	3	4	4

Notes
[a] The World Bank applies the debt-distressed categorization only to Sub-Saharan Africa.
[b] Defined as countries in which three of the four key ratios are above critical levels. These ratios and their critical levels are debt to GNP (50%), debt to export of goods and all services (27.5%), accrued debt service to exports (30%), and accrued interest to exports (20%).
[c] Defined as countries in which three of the four key ratios fall in the following ranges: debt to GNP (30–50%), debt to exports of goods and all services (16.5–27.5%), accrued debt service to exports (18–30%), and accrued interest to exports (12–20%).
Source: World Bank and IMF publications for earlier classification, and World Bank, *World Debt, Tables 1990–91, vol. 1: Analysis and Summary Tables* (Washington, D.C.: World Bank, 1991) for later classification.

indebted low-income countries (MILICs), and Cameroon, Cape Verde, Gabon and Zimbabwe as moderately indebted middle-income countries (MIMICs).[6]

Three points need to be made in respect of Table 2.1. First, the groups are not mutually exclusive. Most SSA countries belong to more than one group. All low-income countries are, in fact, additionally classified as either debt-distressed or IDA-eligible, and many of them belong to both groups. Secondly, there is a definite deterioration in respect of the middle-income countries. Liberia and Nigeria have slipped to low-income status, while others (Cape Verde and Djibouti) now rank as IDA-eligible. This reclassification flies in the face of the basic principle of graduation and maturation which underlies the operation of IDA-eligibility. Thirdly, IDA-eligible SSA countries now constitute the largest group. This is the group on which both the IMF and the World Bank have targeted their programmes of long-term concessional assistance.

Regardless of the various classifications, the debt crisis exhibits the same characteristics throughout SSA. First, the rate of accumulation of external debts shot up sharply during the 1980s. It exceeded by a wide margin the rate of growth of output, or to put it another way, SSA countries have been getting into debt faster than they have been growing. Secondly, and as a consequence of the former point, the size of their external debts in relation to other key macroeconomic variables, such as exports and the level of reserves, has increased substantially, which in turn, has exerted severe strain on their balance of payments. Thirdly, there is now a massive overhang of arrears currently estimated at 10 per cent of total debts outstanding. This proportion will obviously increase as the number of countries falling into arrears increases.

C. STRUCTURE AND COMPOSITION OF DEBTS

Although the debt crisis has been building up for a long time, it is not necessary to go back beyond the last decade to identify the main factors behind its growth and development. During the 1980s the external debts of SSA countries rose rapidly not only in aggregate terms but also in relation to other Third World countries. This rise took place in the context of stagnating or declining growth rates and export levels.

Secondly, net inflow of resources fell by more than one-third, in real terms, between 1982 and 1984. This contraction was by no means uniform throughout the region. There were many countries for which the net flow of resources remained negative for the whole of the decade, despite the partial recovery in total resource flows after 1985.

Thirdly, SSA countries, in common with other developing countries, borrowed heavily from the private sector during the 1970s when funds were cheap. Euro-credits and commercial bank lending alone increased by 40 per cent, and suppliers' credits by 20 per cent. These credits virtually disappeared when the Mexican debt crisis broke in 1982. The effects on SSA countries were disastrous. Not only did a major source of external funding dry up overnight, they were left with a serious debt overhang problem, which was greatly exacerbated by the fact that these credits were used mainly to support current levels of consumption (through subsidies, price support schemes and so on) rather than for investment purposes. Consequently, when commodity prices fell and the real cost of borrowing and servicing existing debts rose during the 1980s, SSA countries were in deep trouble. It was clearly a case of injudicious borrowing and inappropriate use of funding.

Finally, although public sector inflows increased during the 1980s, they were not enough to make up for the shortfall in private inflows and in addition meet the mounting costs of debt servicing. Many SSA countries were, in fact, forced to reschedule their debts on more than one occasion. Zaire, for example, undertook 15 debt rescheduling exercises between 1975 and 1988. However, despite repeated reschedulings, SSA countries are still deeply in debt and arrears continue to pile up. Table 2.2 shows the total disbursed debt of Sub-Saharan African countries by source and terms of lending over the period from 1980 to 1988.

Two sets of data are given for 1982, the year in which a new system of compiling and presenting statistics on indebtedness was adopted by the Organization for Economic Cooperation and Development (OECD). This enables a detailed comparison to be made with the old system (1975–82) as well as to maintain continuity. The principal changes concern the inclusion of new items in official credits and a new way of presenting the data on bank lending.

The data cover only public and publicly-guaranteed debts (that is, those debts which the government know of, and have undertaken to provide the necessary foreign exchange to service). They do not include unguaranteed debts contracted in the private sector, mainly because, in the past, these were not considered to be significant, but more importantly, it was very difficult to monitor them. The government often only becomes aware of them when presented with an application for foreign exchange to service them. Better data coverage and more effective debt management have enabled SSA countries to provide estimates of these private long-term unguaranteed debts, but there is still a long way to go before the coverage can be considered adequate. The countries with the largest unguaranteed debts in 1987 were Cameroon ($530 million), Côte d'Ivoire ($3,264 million), Kenya ($496 million), Niger ($254 million), Nigeria ($352 million) and Sudan ($405 million).

That said, the most obvious point the table makes is that the external debts, including use of IMF credits, doubled between 1982 and 1988. Each

Table 2.2 Total disbursed debt of Sub-Saharan African countries by source and terms of lending, 1980–88 ($ billion)

	1980	1981	1982	1982	1983	1984	1985	1986	1987	1988
Long-term debt										
I OECD countries and capital markets	28	30	32	36	41	41	47	58	68	72
A. ODA	6	6	6	6	6	7	9	11	15	16
B. Total export credits	15	15	16	16	17	17	23	30	37	38
Official export credits	..	..	..	5	7	7	10	16	22	..
Guaranteed supplier credits	..	..	..	5	4	3	4	3	3	..
Guaranteed bank credits	..	..	..	6	6	7	9	11	12	..
C. Financial markets	7	8	9	13	16	14	12	13	13	15
Banks	7	8	9	13	16	14	12	13	13	..
Bonds	1	1	–	–	–	–	–	–	–	..
D. Other private	1	1	1	–	2	3	4	4	4	4
II Multilateral	8	10	11	11	13	14	17	22	28	31
of which: Concessional	5	6	7	7	8	9	11	13	17	..
Non-concessional	3	4	4	4	5	5	7	9	12	..
III Non-OECD creditor countries	8	9	10	10	12	12	13	13	14	14
Sub-total: Long-term debt	44	49	54	58	66	67	77	93	110	117
of which: Concessional	16	18	20	20	22	23	27	32	40	..
Non-concessional	28	30	34	37	44	44	50	60	70	..
Short-term debt										
Banks	..	..	..	8	9	7	9	12	15	15
Export credits	..	..	..	3	4	3	4	5	7	9
Sub-total: Short-term debt	..	..	..	11	12	10	14	17	22	24
Total external debt excl. IMF credit	..	..	..	69	78	77	91	110	133	141
Use of IMF credit	..	..	..	4	5	5	6	6	7	7
Total external debt incl. IMF credit	..	..	..	72	83	82	97	116	140	148
Other identified liabilities	..	..	..	1	1	0	1	1	1	..

Notes
.. Not available
– Nil or negligible
Source: *Financing and External Debt of Developing Countries, 1988 Survey*, Paris: OECD 1989, Table V.11, p. 58 (as amended).

of the three main types of debt also doubled, with the result that, proportionally, their respective share of the total remained remarkably stable throughout, long-term debts accounting for about 80 per cent of the total. There were, nevertheless, significant changes within each group. The share of total export credits, for example, rose from 44 per cent of all long-term debts owed to OECD countries and capital markets in 1982 to 53 per cent in 1988. On the other hand, the share of debts owed to financial markets fell from 36 per cent to 22 per cent, reflecting the extent to which commercial banks reduced lending to SSA countries.

Although 80 per cent of SSA countries' external debts are owed by the low-income countries, there is considerable concentration in the overall pattern of disbursement. In 1987 Nigeria alone was responsible for 29 per cent of the group's total. Other major low-income debtors were Kenya, Sudan, Tanzania, Zaire and Zambia. Among the middle-income countries, Côte d'Ivoire was by far the largest debtor, with about 10 per cent of the region's total. Taken together, these seven debtors accounted for 59 per cent of all SSA countries' external debts.

Secondly, most debts are bilateral official, or government-to-government, loans. In 1987 these accounted for almost 70 per cent of all public long-term debts. In the case of IDA-eligible countries, the proportion averaged 87 per cent, though there was considerable variation among the members. In Benin, for example, the proportion was 57.5 per cent, whereas it reached 97.9 per cent for Rwanda. For small debtors like Comoros, Cape Verde and São Tomé and Príncipe, bilateral official loans have been the principal and, indeed, the only form of loans since 1982.

Thirdly, a growing proportion of SSA countries' debt is held by multilateral creditors, such as the World Bank, Regional Development Banks and other multilateral financial institutions. In 1982 these debts accounted for 21 per cent of all public and publicly-guaranteed long-term debts. By 1987 the proportion had risen to 28 per cent. Clearly, this figure will rise as these institutions continue to provide more finance for development. Significantly, the proportion of non-concessional debt has been rising faster than concessional, which increases the overall debt burden.

Fourthly, about 70 per cent of all SSA bilateral official debts are owed to OECD countries. Notwithstanding efforts to standardize lending policies and practices, there is still a wide range and diversity of terms and conditions attaching to loans from these sources. In addition, substantial sums are owed by countries such as Mali, Guinea, Guinea-Bissau, Mauritania, Somalia and Sudan to Eastern European countries (formerly the CMEA countries) and the members of OPEC under an equally bewildering set of terms and conditions. The diversity of creditors, each with its own terms and conditions, creates major problems for the debtors; for example, the degree of

Table 2.3 External debt situation of IDA-eligible SSA countries at year end 1987 (US$ millions unless otherwise shown)

Country	Per capita GNP	Per capita debt[b]	Public long-term debt		Debt service on long-term debt[b]		1988 debt Service[c] 1987 exports (%)	Use of IMF credit	Number of multilateral debt reschedulings 1975–88[d]
			Total	Official creditors (%)	1987 (actual)	1988 (scheduled)			
Benin	310	263	929	57.5	34	110	52.1	0	0
Burkina Faso	200	104	794	95.2	31	57	n.a.	0	0
Burundi[a]	250	151	718	97.4	42	46	41.8	0	0
Cape Verde	500	437	121	97.5	7	10	n.a.	0	0
Central African Republic[a]	330	217	520	95.2	22	41	22.3	37	3
Chad	150	60	270	84.1	6	10	6.1	10	0
Comoros	370	507	188	99.9	1	10	33.3	0	0
Djibouti	n.a.	453	152	98.0	13	13	n.a.	0	0
Equatorial Guinea	n.a.	483	175	94.9	9	18	45.4	8	0
Ethiopia	120	58	2,434	83.3	180	274	n.a.	63	0
Gambia[a]	220	399	273	93.8	15	19	16.7	23	2
Ghana[a]	390	230	2,207	87.7	183	258	n.a.	778	0
Guinea[a]	320	274	1,616	93.9	111	191	n.a.	30	2
Guinea-Bissau[a]	160	471	391	79.0	9	22	91.6	2	1
Kenya[a]	330	269	4,482	82.6	588	640	36.8	381	0
Lesotho	370	151	237	92.8	15	21	6.1	0	0
Liberia	450	703	1,152	82.9	11	135	n.a.	291	5
Madagascar[a]	200	281	3,113	91.2	147	397	95.7	144	7

Malawi[a]	180	179	1,155	95.8	71	102	33.5	110	5
Mali[a]	210	258	1,847	96.7	32	71	21.8	75	0
Mauritania[a]	440	1,071	1,868	93.2	86	193	40.8	47	3
Mozambique[a]	150	85	n.a.	n.a.	n.a.	n.a.	n.a.	0	3
Niger[a]	260	247	1,259	81.7	151	183	57.0	91	7
Rwanda	300	90	544	97.9	20	25	14.1	0	0
São Tomé and Príncipe[a]	290	870	84	99.3	4	9	98.9	0	0
Senegal[a]	510	528	3,068	91.6	285	341	26.4	267	8
Sierra Leone	310	173	513	83.0	5	56	n.a.	83	5
Somalia	290	450	2,321	92.8	9	110	n.a.	154	2
Sudan	330	480	7,876	78.7	48	1,013	142.3	859	9
Tanzania[a]	220	181	4,068	89.4	83	383	85.3	65	1
Togo[a]	290	371	1,042	92.1	63	143	31.6	78	8
Uganda[a]	260	89	1,116	94.9	70	139	37.5	229	3
Zaire[a]	150	264	7,334	84.7	247	798	41.3	833	15
Zambia	250	889	4,354	86.0	129	563	59.0	957	4
Totals			58,233	86.9	2,726	6,399	n.a.	5,615	94

Notes

[a] Countries currently eligible for the World Bank's Special Program of Assistance.

[b] Not including arrears, Fund repurchases and charges, or interest on short-term debt.

[c] Scheduled debt service on long-term debt.

[d] To September 1988.

n.a. = Not available

Source: *World Debt Tables. External Debt of Developing Countries*, vol. I: *Analysis and Summary Tables, 1988–89 edition.* Washington D.C.: World Bank, 1988, p. xxxvi.

concessionality on official loans varies from creditor to creditor, debts build up at different rates and debt burdens differ. This aspect of the crisis needs to be addressed urgently.

Fifthly, there has been a significant increase in short-term debts. Originally, these debts were not considered part of the debt problem, on the grounds that, as trade-related credits, they would liquidate themselves in the normal course of events. However, this is no longer the case. Notwithstanding the drastic reduction in imports, SSA countries have experienced severe problems with financing their trade flows. Consequently, a substantial proportion of these debts has had to be rolled over and/or converted to medium- and long-term debts, thereby increasing the total stock of debt outstanding. Short-term debts also include accumulation of arrears of interest on public long-term debts which have risen sharply since the crisis began. In 1987 the short-term debts amounted to $24 billion, or 16 per cent of total external debt outstanding. The corresponding figure in 1982 was $11 billion. Countries with short-term debts in excess of $1 billion in 1987 were Côte d'Ivoire ($1.3 billion), Nigeria ($1.7 billion), Sudan ($2.1 billion) and Zambia ($1.1 billion).

Finally, the use of IMF credits has increased by more than threefold since 1980. These credits now exceed $6.5 billion per annum. This massive increase in what is essentially short-term debt is regarded by several analysts as one of the main causes of the debt crisis in SSA countries. IMF credits, in common with debts to the World Bank and other multilateral financial institutions, enjoy 'preferred creditor' status. Debts to these institutions cannot be rescheduled. They have to be serviced, irrespective of what is happening elsewhere in the domestic economy. In the context of SSA countries, this means that bilateral creditors as well as the debtors' domestic economy bear the brunt of servicing multilateral debts. Several SSA countries are in fact net creditors to the fund; in other words, their repurchase of past credits exceeds current use of new credits. Others are no longer current on their service payments, which effectively excludes them from further use of the Fund's resources. Table 2.3 shows the external debt situation of IDA-eligible SSA countries at the end of 1987.

D. THE DYNAMICS OF DEBT SERVICING

One of the earliest and most authoritative analyses of the dynamics of debt servicing was given by Keynes in his article on the German transfer problem.[7] He argued that in order to pay its war reparation debts, Germany had first to extract the necessary funds from the pockets of the German people. He called this the budgetary problem. Secondly, having raised the necessary funds domestically, Germany then had to convert them into foreign currency in order to service its debts. This gave rise to the so-called transfer problem which consisted 'in reducing the gold-rate of efficiency-earnings of the German factors of production sufficiently to enable them to increase their export to an adequate aggregate total'. The process was thus essentially a two-stage operation which gave rise to two different sets of problems and measures.

Keynes's article engendered a lot of controversy and there was a spirited debate, principally between himself and Ohlin, as to whether debt servicing involved one or two separate sets of problems; or more specifically, whether the transfer problem did in fact exist.[8] By 1932 the debate had lost most of its urgency and significance for the international economy, and these issues receded into the background. However, with the onset of the debt crisis and the steady deterioration of economic and social conditions in the debtor countries over the last decade, the debate has been reopened.

Although the causes of the German war reparation problem were different to those of the present debt crisis in SSA countries, there are obvious parallels in terms of the dynamics of debt servicing and its impact on their economies. SSA countries have to cut their budgetary deficits and reduce the rate of domestic absorption so as to extract the necessary domestic currency from national income (the budgetary problem). Secondly, they have to earn a surplus on their external account in order to provide the additional foreign exchange to meet their debt service obligations. There is also a remarkable degree of similarity in their respective underlying economic and financial conditions. Germany's economy lay in ruins, its currency was worthless and it faced the urgent task of rebuilding and restructuring its economy. At the same time it faced a crippling debt burden without the prospect of any new capital inflows. To a lesser or greater extent, these conditions pertain in SSA debtor countries.

(a) The Budgetary Problem

This arises from the debtor country's need not only to cut its budgetary deficit by reducing the level of domestic absorption, but more crucially, to extract the additional domestic savings out of current national income in order to secure the necessary domestic resources for servicing its external obligations. Effectively, therefore, a budgetary surplus must first be created either by reducing domestic consumption or raising the level of domestic savings. This can be done by (i) cutting government expenditure, (ii) restricting domestic credit creation and expansion of the money supply, (iii) reducing the level of investment, (iv) domestic bond financing, and (v) increasing taxes.

Each of these measures affects domestic incomes, prices, wages and savings and creates serious economic, social and political problems for the debtor economies. For example, cutting public consumption expenditure will reduce the budgetary deficit and provide additional scope and incentive for the private sector to expand and stimulate growth and recovery in the domestic economy. It will also create additional domestic savings for debt servicing purposes. On the other hand, contraction in public expenditure will cause unemployment and a fall in incomes, given the size and importance of the public sector in most debtor countries. Further, cuts tend to fall disproportionately on social expenditure and the provision of social services for the poorest and most vulnerable groups in society. Therefore, while cutting public expenditure will help to streamline and improve the efficiency of the public sector and increase domestic savings, it will also impose an intolerable burden on the debtors' economies with serious social and political consequences for their governments.[9]

These are the dangers which Keynes foresaw when he addressed the problem of the reparation of Germany's war debts. They apply with equal force to SSA countries with their over-extended public sectors and huge budgetary deficits. Although some of them have streamlined public expenditure and cut budgetary deficits, there is still a long way to go before they can convert to a budgetary surplus. Domestic savings clearly need to be increased not only to finance the higher levels of domestic investment which are essential for recovery and long-term development, but also to provide a surplus for debt servicing purposes.

In the absence of an increase in net transfer of external resources, SSA countries will have to raise their marginal propensity to save by squeezing domestic consumption. This will cause immense hardship as consumption levels are already abysmally low, and lead to an increase in the number of people living in absolute poverty. Governments will also have to rely on their domestic monetary and banking systems to provide the necessary investment finance, for example by borrowing from the banks, domestic credit creation, increasing the money supply or domestic bond financing. As indicated in Chapter 1, the substitution of domestic credit for foreign capital inflows during the 1980s proved hugely inflationary and increased the budgetary burden of SSA countries. In addition, capital flight raised real depreciation requirements, resulting in a further increase in existing crippling foreign currency liabilities.

Alternatively, debtor countries can try to mobilise additional domestic resources by raising taxes, which gives rise to a different set of problems. In the case of SSA countries, the amount of additional revenue which can be raised in this way is very limited and cannot be increased significantly in the short-run. Taxation systems are weak, inefficient and poorly administered. The tax base urgently needs to be expanded, tax rates restructured and systems of administration updated and strengthened. But these measures take time to implement and involve many politically unpalatable decisions which their governments are reluctant to take. They prefer instead to rely on the traditional stand-by sources of agricultural production, exports and domestic financial assets for additional revenues.

(b) The Transfer Problem

International debts cannot be repaid in the debtor's own currency, unless, of course, that currency is an international medium of exchange or the debtor can issue such a currency. This was the problem which Germany faced in servicing its war debts. Its domestic currency (the deutchmark) was not acceptable to its creditors. Having mobilized the necessary domestic resources therefore, it had to convert or transfer them into foreign exchange or an international medium of exchange which was acceptable to its creditors. Keynes argued that the transfer process or the purchase of foreign exchange had 'the effect of causing the money in which the debt is expressed to be worth a larger quantity of German-produced goods than it was before or would have been apart from the payment of the debt: so that the population of the debtor state suffers a loss of purchasing power greater than the original equivalent of the amount of the debt'.[10]

In other words, the repayment of Germany's war debts necessarily entailed a depreciation of the German mark vis à vis the foreign currency accepted for payments. This, for Keynes, characterized the asymmetrical relationship between a debtor country and its creditors, when the former's domestic currency was not an international medium of exchange. It has also led Cencini and Schmitt to maintain that with no new capital inflows and additional export earnings, 'German economic agents were not only losing a part of their income equivalent to the amount of the external debt servicing but twice as much, since their country had to contact a new debt in the exact proportion of its external debt payment'.[11]

In terms of the internal dynamics of debt servicing operations, depreciation reduced the amount of domestic currency in circulation and caused domestic incomes and prices to fall, restraining imports and stimulating exports. The additional foreign exchange earned from the increase in exports would then be used to service its foreign debts. All of this is, of course, on the assumption that (i) the effects of depreciation in the domestic economy will not exceed the gains of an export surplus, and (ii) the debtor country receives new capital inflows. Neither of these assumptions held in the case of Germany during the inter-war years.[12]

The transfer problem is particularly acute in SSA countries. Their ability to increase their foreign exchange earnings depends primarily on the rate of growth of exports which, in turn, depends on such factors as the type of exports, market shares, levels of productivity, costs of production and their ability to compete in international markets. In addition, they have to overcome a number of trade restrictions, as well as marketing and institutional barriers imposed by the developed countries.

SSA countries clearly need to restructure their economies, increase levels of productivity and make their economies more competitive internationally. They need to recapture lost markets for their traditional exports as well as to develop new and additional non-traditional exports, if they are to earn a surplus for resolving the transfer problem. They need also to restructure their domestic tax systems, provide greater incentives for exporters, and streamline the vast array of disincentives which many of them impose on the production and export of agricultural commodities, the mainstay of their economies. These are very heavy demands to impose on fragile economies for which net capital inflows have stagnated.

For their part, creditor countries must increase their imports from SSA countries to enable them to earn the surplus to pay their foreign debts. Among other things, this will require them to reduce tariffs and other trade restrictions, liberalize and provide greater access and market opportunities for exports from SSA debtor countries. Also, they will have to reverse or moderate many of the economic and financial policies which proved particularly onerous for SSA debtor countries during the 1980s, and helped to precipitate the debt crisis. Finally, for the transfer problem to be smoothly and effectively accommodated, it requires a healthy and growing world economy to ensure that distortions to both debtor and creditor economies are minimized.

The immediate prospects of an upturn in the world economy are not good. Given the asymmetrical nature of the debtor/creditor relationship inherent in the transfer problem, this will not only increase the budgetary costs of adjustment but also pose a number of dilemmas for SSA debtors. For example, if by increasing exports they earn a surplus which is used to pay debts, then the benefits of export growth accrue to the creditors, and not to the domestic economy which bears the cost of adjustment. This raises the question, why should they increase the rate of savings at great sacrifice to themselves if the benefits accrue to their creditors? The dilemma is crystallized in the choice between paying foreign debts and jeopardising their long-term development prospects.

Or, to take another example, given the pervasive nature of the crisis, all SSA countries are required to increase exports at the same time. This means they have to compete with each other for dwindling markets which reduces the scope for expansion of inter-regional trade and the possibility of saving foreign exchange on intra-regional transactions. Effectively, therefore, they lose twice over. First by reducing the scope for inter-regional trade, and secondly by curtailing imports in order to generate a trade surplus. The economic and social costs of these policies cannot adequately be reflected by the usual statistics on the debt burden.

E. DEBT SERVICE PAYMENTS

Debt service payments are the most visible and immediate measure of the cost in foreign exchange of the crisis. Basically, these payments are determined by such factors as (a) the terms and conditions of past loans; and (b) the average terms of new loans and past debt consolidation exercises. In some instances, these factors counterbalance each other. In others, they reinforce and intensify the burden of debt service payments. In general, the average terms of new public lending have softened since the crisis, while private sector loans have hardened considerably. Repeated reschedulings have also increased the cost of servicing several countries' external debts. Table 2.4 shows total annual debt service payments of SSA countries by source and terms of lending between 1980 and 1988.

Of all service payments in 1988, 55 per cent were in respect of long-term debts to OECD countries and capital markets. Two developments in particular warrant attention. One is that service payments on export credits and obligations to financial markets, both of which rank as non-concessional lending, accounted for 95 per cent of all long-term service payments in 1988. The other is that service payments to multilateral financial institutions, or preferred creditors, increased threefold between 1982 and 1988. These provide clear evidence of the shift to non-concessional funding in the source and terms of lending since the crisis emerged.

The same pattern is evident in respect of the low-income SSA countries. Service payments on export credits and obligations to financial markets in 1988 amounted to \$4.9 billion, or 90 per cent of the group's total service payments on long-term debts. Also, their multilateral service payments in 1988 amounted to \$1.6 billion, more than three times the amount paid in 1982. Another significant point, in so far as these countries are concerned, is that they were responsible for 80 per cent of all SSA countries' service payments for the use of IMF credits.

For SSA countries as a whole, amortization or repayment of long-term debts peaked at \$6.5 billion in 1985. Over the next three years they fell away unevenly, and in 1988 stood at \$5 billion. This pattern was heavily influenced by repayments of export credits and obligations to financial markets and a fall in international interest rates. More significantly, perhaps, the current cost of servicing these debts has continued to rise, notwithstanding the number of reschedulings undertaken during this period. Interest payments on short-term debts have also begun to rise again.

Table 2.4 *Total annual debt service of Sub-Saharan African countries by source and terms of lending, 1980–88 ($ billion)*

	1980	1981	1982	1982	1983	1984	1985	1986	1987	1988
Long-term debt service payments										
I OECD countries and capital markets	4.8	5.4	5.6	5.7	5.8	6.3	7.7	6.2	5.5	6.1
A. ODA	0.3	0.2	0.2	0.3	0.3	0.3	0.3	0.4	0.4	0.4
B. Export credits	3.0	3.2	2.8	2.9	3.2	3.2	4.6	4.3	3.7	4.0
C. Financial markets	1.4	1.9	2.5	2.6	2.3	2.7	2.7	1.5	1.5	1.7
D. Other private	0.1	0.1	0.1	–	–	–	–	–	–	..
II Multilateral	0.5	0.5	0.6	0.7	0.7	0.9	1.1	1.6	1.9	2.1
of which: Concessional	0.1	0.2	0.2	0.2	0.2	0.2	0.4	0.5	0.5	..
III Non-OECD creditor countries	0.3	0.4	0.4	0.4	0.4	0.6	1.0	0.7	0.4	0.5
Sub-total: Long-term debt service	5.6	6.3	6.6	6.8	6.9	7.8	9.8	8.4	7.9	8.6
of which: Concessional	0.6	0.5	0.5	0.6	0.6	0.8	0.9	1.2	1.1	..
Total debt service excl. IMF credit	..	..	..	8.1	8.0	8.7	10.5	9.1	8.7	9.6
Amortization, long-term debt	..	..	..	3.5	3.9	4.9	6.5	5.6	4.6	5.0
Interest, long-term debt	..	..	..	3.2	3.0	2.9	3.3	2.9	3.3	3.6
Interest, short-term debt	..	..	..	1.3	1.0	1.0	0.7	0.7	0.8	1.0
Total debt service incl. IMF credit	..	..	..	8.7	8.7	9.7	11.5	10.5	10.1	11.1

Note:
.. Not available
– Nil or negligible
Source: *Financing and External Debt of Developing Countries, 1988 Survey*. Paris: OECD 1989, Table V.12, p. 59 (as amended).

The picture which emerges from this brief analysis should be tempered by several observations. First, almost 50 per cent of all amortization payments in 1987 were made by ten countries: Cameroon, Congo, Côte d'Ivoire, Ethiopia, Ghana, Kenya, Nigeria, Senegal, Zaire and Zimbabwe. There is an even greater concentration in respect of interest payments on long-term debts. Six countries (Cameroon, Côte d'Ivoire, Kenya, Nigeria, Senegal and Zaire) accounted for 55 per cent of total interest payments on long-term debts.

Secondly, debt service payments have to be adjusted to allow for valuation effects arising from changes in the value of the dollar, the currency in which at least 60 per cent of SSA countries' external debts are denominated. During the early 1980s, when the dollar appreciated, the cost, or the dollar equivalent in other economies, of servicing their external debts was reduced on average by 11 per cent per annum between 1981 and 1983. Similarly, when the dollar began to depreciate after 1985, the valuation effect of servicing their long-term debts increased on average by 9 per cent between 1986 and 1987.[13]

Thirdly, great care must be taken in interpreting and using data on debt service payments since it is not always clear whether such data represent scheduled (*ex ante*) or actual (*ex post*) payments. In principle, the data in Table 2.4 refer to actual service payments made. However, due to problems of data coverage and reliability – the range and variety of debts to be serviced, for example – it is not always possible to determine whether payments due were met in full, which debts were serviced, in what proportions, and so on. In many instances, scheduled payments due have been used as a proxy for payments actually made. The divergence between *ex ante* and *ex post* payments in the case of SSA countries is very substantial. For example, in 1985 Benin, Gambia, Madagascar, Mali, Sierra Leone, Somalia, Tanzania and Zambia actually met less than 50 per cent of scheduled service payments due on their outstanding external debts.

Finally, several SSA countries have fallen into arrears on their service payments. In 1987 Liberia's scheduled service payments amounted to $115 million, of which only $11 million were actually paid. In the case of the Sudan, scheduled service payments on long-term debts were estimated at $669 million, while actual payments amounted to $48 million. However, increases in arrears must be set against the substantial sums of new funding, principally in the form of grants and ODA loans, and debt relief which SSA countries have received. The picture is thus a lot more complicated than the aggregate data indicate.

The divergence between *ex ante* and *ex post* service payments clearly suggests that SSA debtors operate some sort of priority rating to decide who and what debts get paid, what proportion is rescheduled, and other related

Table 2.5 A summary of the structure of debt service payments in 1985

Creditor	Percent of total debt	Service payments Obligations	Payments
Bilateral	45	42	14
Multilateral	21	12	10
All private	22	36	16
IMF	11	9	9
Total[a]	100	100	50

Note:
[a] Totals do not add due to rounding
Source: Development Committee, Number 16, *Proposals for Enhancing Assistance to Low-Income Countries that Face Exceptional Difficulties*, Washington D.C.: World Bank, June 1988, p. 45.

matters. As Table 2.5 shows, in 1985 bilateral debts accounted for 45 per cent of all external debts and 42 per cent of debt service obligations, whereas actual payments amounted to 14 per cent of total payments. In other words, official creditors received only one-third of the amount due to them. Private creditors held 22 per cent of the total debt and 36 per cent of service obligations. They received 16 per cent of total payments. On the other hand, debts to the IMF amounted to 11 per cent of the total and 9 per cent of service obligations, which was paid in full. Meeting their IMF obligations in full and on time meant, in effect, that debts to other creditors, in particular bilateral creditors, either fell into arrears or had to be rescheduled.

The pressure to honour service payments to preferred at the expense of official creditors is particularly marked in the case of the low-income debt-distressed countries. For example, in 1985 Gambia's *ex ante* service payments to the IMF amounted to 13 per cent of total scheduled service payments. As it turned out, *ex post* payments to the IMF accounted for 37 per cent of all service payments made. By way of comparison, its *ex ante* payments on concessional bilateral debts were 16 per cent of total payments, whereas *ex post* payments ran to 4 per cent. The debt profile for individual SSA countries in 1989 is given in Table 2.6.

F. OTHER DEBT INDICATORS

There are several other indicators one can use to measure debt burdens. None of these on its own is a totally adequate measure, but taken together, they give a pretty good idea of the speed with which the crisis developed, its comprehensive and pervasive nature, and the ability of individual debtors to cope with it. Table 2.7 provides information on the principal ratios in respect of total external debts and public and publicly-guaranteed long-term debts between 1970 and 1987. Discussion will, however, be confined to (a) debt service ratios, (b) debts to GNP, and (c) resources and import cover: the three most commonly used ratios.

(a) Debt Service Ratios

Basically, this ratio shows the proportion of foreign exchange earnings on current account which has to be set aside each year to meet service payments. To the extent that foreign exchange is pre-empted for service payments, it is not available for financing essential imports and capital goods for development. The debt service ratio is thus a measure of the rigidity and short-term inflexibility which debtor countries face in their balance of payments. The higher the ratio, the greater the degree of inflexibility and vulnerability to balance of payments difficulties if foreign exchange earnings dropped suddenly or import requirements rose sharply in the short-term.

Conventionally, a ratio of 15 per cent or over has been considered the danger point, that is, the limit beyond which debtor countries would experience severe difficulties in servicing their foreign debts while maintaining existing levels of services domestically. However, this figure should be taken only as a rough rule of thumb, since several debtor countries have been carrying ratios well in excess of that figure for many years. An early postwar study on the capacity to service debts concluded that

> The degree of tolerance varies considerably from country to country, with the breaking point in most countries during the 1930s at 25 to 30 per cent. On the other hand, it was a sharp rise in the ratio resulting from the precipitous fall in export earnings that brought about the defaults.[14]

Significantly, this is the range which the World Bank uses to differentiate the debt-distressed SSA countries. In 1985 the debt service ratio for the group as a whole averaged 49.7 per cent, ranging from 17.7 per cent for Ghana to 105.6 per cent for Somalia.

However, too much should not be read into these figures since debt service ratios are essentially an index of liquidity, and do not take account of other major parameters such as changes in imports and new capital inflows. Nor do they give any indication of the debtor's foreign exchange reserves, structure of exports and potential for growth. They can, in fact, be quite misleading in the case of SSA countries with large foreign trade sectors,

Table 2.6 SSA countries' debt profile in 1989

Country	Total ($m)	Debt structure (%) Official Bi-lateral	Multi-lateral	Private[b]	Debt 1989 ($m)	Service actual[c] as % of exports	Debt Service 1990 obligation[c] ($m)	as % of exports	Debt/GNP ratio (%)	Debt per capita ($)	GNP per capita ($)
Angola	6,950[a]	n.a.	1	n.a.	1,322[a]	42.0	n.a.	n.a.	115.6[a]	716[a]	620
Benin*	1,177	28	37	35	26	6.7	77	20.0	71.9	256	356
Botswana	513	24	68	8	69	3.6	82	4.0	36.5	422	1,172
Burkina Faso	756	16	70	14	39	9.4	47	11.3	29.6	86	291
Burundi	867	22	70	8	38	33.0	49	42.6	81.9	164	200
Cameroon	4,743	39	26	35	365	19.4	691	36.7	42.2	412	972
Cape Verde	130	89	6	5	5	n.a.	11	n.a.	45.9	352	764
Central Afr. Rep.*	716	40	52	8	30	14.1	36	16.9	65.8	240	369
Chad*	368	21	69	10	12	5.3	10	4.4	36.7	67	190
Comoros	176	31	61	8	4	9.1	9	23.2	88.2	383	434
Congo	4,316	35	13	52	320	27.0	914	7.1	214.9	1,962	930
Côte d'Ivoire	15,412	19	16	65	1,358	40.9	1,912	57.6	182.2	1,316	722
Djibouti	180	29	44	27	15	n.a.	13	n.a.	n.a.	439	949[d]
Equatorial Guinea*	228	61	30	9	6	18.7	14	43.2	182.7	663	407
Ethiopia	3,013	48	36	16	280	38.7	322	44.5	50.6	62	121
Gabon	3,176	48	11	41	223	11.9	199	10.6	108.9	2,887	2,770
Gambia	342	25	64	11	18	10.9	20	11.8	172.9	403	223
Ghana	3,078	20	73	7	438	49.3	204	22.9	59.9	213	345
Guinea*	2,176	60	29	11	113	15.2	262	35.3	85.3	392	460
Guinea-Bissau*	458	43	46	11	12	43.0	20	74.1	276.3	477	174
Kenya	5,690	21	45	34	645	33.3	664	34.3	71.7	244	353
Lesotho	324	9	80	11	22	2.8	32	4.0	39.0	188	483
Liberia	1,761	27	41	32	5	n.a.	137	n.a.	176.3	712	404
Madagascar*	3,607	56	33	1	240	52.4	541	117.9	154.1	323	209
Malawi	1,394	19	73	8	95	28.0	76	22.4	89.4	169	189

Mali*	2,157	59	38	3	66	18.6	124	34.8	105.3	263	241
Mauritania*	2,010	60	30	10	102	20.1	170	33.4	213.2	1,029	474
Mauritius	832	29	42	29	143	9.8	106	7.3	41.0	783	1,911
Mozambique*	4,737	60	9	31	63	24.4	613	238.5	474.2	310	65
Niger*	1,578	27	43	30	122	33.0	155	42.0	79.4	211	266
Nigeria	32,832	37	10	53	1,796	21.3	4,802	57.0	119.3	289	242
Rwanda	652	18	74	8	29	18.5	25	15.7	30.2	95	312
São Tomé Príncipe	131	40	44	16	5	44.7	11	97.2	329.7	1,083	331
Senegal*	4,139	51	37	12	379	29.4	534	41.4	93.2	574	616
Seychelles	168	36	25	39	24	11.9	21	10.1	60.4	2,485	4,103
Sierra Leone	1,057	24	26	50	4	n.a.	33	n.a.	118.9	261	220
Somalia	2,137	52	39	9	32	34.0	118	124.2	202.8	351	173
Sudan	12,965	42	18	40	97	7.9	1,202	97.5	82.9	531	641
Swaziland	281	42	48	10	35	4.8	32	4.5	43.6	370	848
Tanzania*	4,918	55	34	11	87	16.6	365	69.1	186.1	192	103
Togo*	1,185	33	49	18	90	18.8	86	17.8	91.8	338	368
Uganda*	1,808	22	66	12	209	81.2	148	57.4	44.7	108	241
Zaire*	8,843	59	24	17	513	21.5	862	36.1	96.6	257	266
Zambia*	6,874	34	31	35	171	12.3	529	37.9	137.9	877	636
Zimbabwe	3,088	27	19	54	472	25.6	536	29.1	53.6	323	602

Notes
* Debt rescheduled on Toronto terms, 1988–90.
[a] Long-term debt only.
[b] Including all short-term debt.
[c] 1989 debt service covers actual payment on long- and short-term debt including IMF. 1990 debt service equals scheduled payments on long-term debt only. Ratio expressed as a % of 1989 exports.
[d] 1987.
n.a. = Not available.
Source: *Africa Recovery*, October–December 1990, vol. 4, no. 3–4. Dept of Public Information, United Nations (as amended), based on World Bank, *World Debt Tables, 1990–91* except for Angola (Bank data). Namibia not included because of lack of data. All debt totals refer to long- and short-term debt.

Table 2.7 Principal debt ratios for SSA countries, 1970–87 (%)

	1970	1975	1980	1981	1982	1983	1984	1985	1986	1987
Total external debt										
Total external debts/exports	n.a.	n.a.	97.5	136.3	182.7	222.3	209.9	241.4	329.7	362.3
Total external debts/GNP	n.a.	n.a.	28.2	33.6	37.2	44.0	46.1	52.8	75.2	100.1
Reserves/total external debts	n.a.	n.a.	26.8	12.4	7.6	6.1	6.4	6.9	6.3	6.0
Reserves/import cover (months)	2.5	3.3	2.9	1.5	1.1	1.2	1.4	1.8	2.0	2.0
Public and publicly-guaranteed debt										
Debts (outstand. & disb.)/exports	61.2	58.1	72.0	98.9	137.8	164.5	151.2	177.6	258.4	292.2
Debts (outstand. & disb.)/GNP	13.0	14.6	20.8	24.3	28.1	32.6	33.2	38.8	59.0	80.7
Total debt service/exports	5.4	5.5	7.1	9.6	13.1	15.8	17.8	20.9	17.7	14.7
Total debt service/GNP	1.1	1.4	2.1	2.4	2.7	3.1	3.9	4.6	4.0	4.1
Interest/exports	1.9	1.8	3.3	4.5	6.3	7.1	7.4	8.0	6.7	6.9
Interest/GNP	0.4	0.4	1.0	1.1	1.3	1.4	1.6	1.8	1.5	1.9
Reserves/debt (outstand. & disb.)	37.7	56.7	36.3	17.1	10.1	8.3	8.8	9.3	8.1	7.4

Notes
n.a. = Not available
outstand. & disb. = Outstanding and disbursed
Source: *World Debt Tables. External Debt of Developing Countries*. vol. I: *Analysis and Summary Tables, 1988–89 Edition*. Washington D.C.: World Bank, December 1988.

since foreign debt liabilities would appear small in comparison to their export earnings, but nevertheless, these countries experience severe debt difficulties. In other words, they do not differentiate the extent to which the debtor country has an export problem or a debt problem.

As an index of liquidity, debt service ratios give a photographic picture of the liquidity constraints which debtor countries face in any one year. They are particularly useful in cases where there is a 'bunching' of short-term maturities, as happened with the HICs. They are rather less helpful in respect of SSA countries where external debts are developmental in nature and have been accumulating over a long period, but which, more importantly, have been subject to considerable restructuring and relief in recent years. To quote a recent OECD study:

> in time series, past and present ratios may not be comparable owing to the importance of debt reorganisation and debt reduction: past years' ratios reflect effective service payments after debt relief (except for refinancing amounts). Projections for current or future years can only use estimated amounts 'due' after recent or estimated debt relief, but those estimates are extremely uncertain in cases of successive debt relief operations or fast changing trade arrears.[15]

The debt service ratios shown in Table 2.7 should not therefore be taken too literally. They do not give a true picture of the nature and development of the crisis over time. Similarly, the substantial improvement in the ratios since 1985 is due to the fact that SSA countries have either run into arrears or had their debts consolidated, and not to any fundamental improvement in their ability to service their external debts. For this, one must look to the interest/export ratio. This measures the proportion of export earnings which has to be set aside each year to pay interest charges on the current stock of debt. It also reflects the combined effects of changes in international interest rates and changes in the demand for, and supply of, exports from the debtor countries. As that table shows, this ratio increased from 1.9 in 1970 to 6.9 in 1987.

Debts can also be expressed either as a ratio of total debts (outstanding and disbursed) to annual export earnings, or in a more limited context of public and publicly-guaranteed long-term debts to annual export earnings. Whichever ratio one uses, SSA countries come out very badly. In 1987 their ratio of total debts (outstanding and disbursed) to exports was 362. The corresponding figure for the HICs was 357. For the developing countries as a whole the ratio was 212. In respect of public and publicly-guaranteed long-term debts, the ratio for SSA countries was 292 as against 272 for the HICs. For low-income SSA countries it was 415. Conventionally, a ratio above 250 is taken as an indication of severe debt problems.

(b) Debts to GNP

This ratio relates total external debts (the stock) to the debtor's GNP. It thus provides a reasonably good indication of the build-up of the crisis and a useful point of comparison with other debtor countries. As the figures in Table 2.7 show, this ratio rose from 28.2 in 1980 to 100.1 in 1987. The corresponding ratios for the HICs were 32.7 and 63.1, respectively. The latest data for individual SSA countries (given in Table 2.6) show that for 19 of them the ratio exceeded 100, in most cases appreciably so. In Mozambique it reached the staggering proportion of 474.2. Given the difficulty of estimating GNP accurately, particularly in SSA countries, these ratios could well underestimate the impact of the crisis.

Service payments may also be expressed as a proportion of GNP. Two such ratios are given in Table 2.7; namely, (i) total debt service/GNP, and (ii) interest/GNP. In both cases, the ratios virtually doubled between 1980 and 1987. There were obviously wide disparities between individual debtor countries, with ratios for the low-income SSA countries generally higher than for the group as a whole.

(c) Reserves and Import Cover

This is a measure of the adequacy of the level of international reserves, expressed in terms of months of import cover, which a country needs in order to avoid debt servicing difficulties. Traditionally, a period of three months was taken as the minimum cover needed to provide a safety margin. The choice of this level was largely determined by the standard 90-day letter of credit on most commercial and international trading transactions.

However, this level is clearly unrealistic in the case of SSA countries, for several reasons. First, they account for a very small proportion of the world's international reserves. Secondly, their holdings have in fact declined sharply in recent years. In 1980 they stood at $15 billion. By 1987 they were down to $8 billion. Thirdly, reserves are very unevenly distributed among the members. In 1987, for example, 25 per cent of the region's reserves were held by Botswana alone. Nigeria held a further 19 per cent, giving the two of them a combined figure of 44 per cent. Finally, their total import bill fell by almost $13 billion between 1980 and 1987, as a result of the severe compression of imports which they experienced. In 1982 reserves barely provided cover for one month's imports. Although there has been some improvement in the overall figures since then, the position in several members remains critical. In 1987 the import cover for Benin, Cameroon, Congo, Côte d'Ivoire, Equatorial Guinea, Gabon, Mali, Senegal, Somalia, Sudan and Seychelles was measured in days rather than months. In the case of Liberia, international reserves were virtually exhausted.

G. IMPACT AND OUTLOOK

The debt crisis, as measured by total debts outstanding and annual debt service payments, has worsened since 1982. That much is clear from the statistics. Its impact on SSA countries cannot, however, be as clearly or precisely determined. As a general proposition, it is true to say that foreign exchange which is used to pay debts cannot be used to finance development. To the extent, therefore, that service payments reduce the amount of foreign exchange available for development, they retard its progress. However, it requires a lot more statistical data and detailed analysis to establish the precise relationship between the two. The conventional assumption of complete substitutability or virement of expenditure, though convenient, is not totally sustainable. The foreign exchange which is saved could just as easily be diverted to non-developmental expenditure, such as arms procurement, defence and administration and capital flight. Each of these would have the same effect on the development process.

Although it is not possible to quantify precisely the impact of debt service payments on the growth and economic performance of SSA countries, few analysts will deny that they have pre-empted an increasing share of these countries' limited foreign exchange earnings and reduced their capacity to import essential capital goods for developmental purposes. Between 1973 and 1980 imports increased on average by 7.6 per cent per annum for the region as a whole. However, as a result of the debt crisis and the acute shortage of foreign exchange, imports fell on average by –5.3 per cent per annum over the period 1980–87. The worst cases of import compression occurred in Sierra Leone (–15.1 per cent p.a.), Nigeria (–14.0 per cent p.a.) and Liberia (–10.2 per cent p.a.).

The reduction in import capacity in turn affected the rate of growth of output, which, on a per capita basis, fell to –2.8 per cent per annum for the region between 1980 and 1987. In the case of Zambia, the fall in GNP per capita averaged –5.9 per cent per annum. For Liberia, it was –5.2 per cent per annum, –4.9 per cent per annum for Niger, –4.8 per cent per annum for Nigeria and –4.3 per cent per annum for Sudan. Gross domestic savings also fell sharply, with several SSA countries registering considerable dissavings in 1987. In Chad, for example, gross domestic savings averaged –12 per cent of GDP per annum. In Mozambique and Tanzania the proportion was –10 per cent and –6 per cent, respectively, while for Lesotho it reached 73 per cent.

The contraction in gross domestic savings had serious knock-on effects on the domestic economy. Gross domestic investment for the region dropped from 20 per cent of GDP in 1980 to 16 per cent in 1987. In the case of Niger, it fell from 37 per cent to 9 per cent. Other SSA countries for which gross domestic investment averaged less than 10 per cent in 1987 were Angola, Liberia and Sierra Leone. The resource balance, as measured by the difference between exports and imports of goods and non-factor services, also deteriorated markedly for most SSA countries. In 1987 it amounted to –31 per cent of GDP for Chad, –32 per cent for Mozambique, –34 per cent for Somalia, –50 per cent for São Tomé and Príncipe, and for Lesotho it ran to –99 per cent of GDP.

The combined effect of these developments on the balance of payments was absolutely disastrous. By 1987 the deficit on current account before official transfers (that is, excluding foreign aid) for Cameroon amounted to –$1112 million. Other major debtors for which the deficit exceeded $600 million were Côte d'Ivoire (–$642m), Kenya (–$639m), Mozambique (–$676m), Senegal (–$680m), Sudan (–$702m), Tanzania (–$605m) and Zaire (–$852m). However, the most striking case is that of Nigeria, which managed to convert an impressive surplus of $5299 million in 1980 to a deficit of –$380 million by 1987. The emergence of such massive deficits clearly convinced the World Bank that there was an urgent need for substantial sums of quick-disbursing finance to prevent the collapse of these economies.

One also has to take account of the social costs and consequences of the crisis. Here again, it is not possible, nor indeed is it necessary, to quantify precisely the relationship, but social conditions and the environment have clearly deteriorated as a result of the combined effects of the crisis in agriculture and the debt crisis. Poverty, ill-health, malnutrition and food insecurity – to mention a few social indicators – have all worsened. Severe food shortages are widespread throughout the region. The number of people facing food insecurity now exceeds 100 million, or roughly one-quarter of the region's population. Standards of public health have fallen. Two out of three persons do not have safe drinking water or proper sanitation facilities. Expenditure on the provision of basic needs and a whole range of social facilities has been severely cut in order to cope with the immediate economic and financial crisis. The World Bank summarizes the situation as follows:

> The crisis is taking a heavy toll in human terms. In several countries expenditure on social services is sharply down, school enrolments are falling, nutrition is worsening, infant mortality continues to be high. Open unemployment in the towns, especially of educated youth, is also on the rise. And, threatening Africa's long-term production capacity, population pressure on the land is accelerating desertification and deforestation; fuelwood is increasingly scarce, and soil fertil-

ity is being leached away, although none of these trends has been accurately measured.[16]

In addition, the debt crisis imposes a heavy cost in terms of the human and institutional resources which have to be devoted to debt crisis management. Consolidation exercises are expensive and time-consuming, and take up a lot of scarce resources that could be better used elsewhere. Also, having to deal with different bilateral and multilateral agencies and administrations, each with its own procedures and practices, imposes a severe strain on the limited administrative, managerial and institutional expertise and capacity available in SSA countries. Officials are overworked and/or inadequately trained to deal with the vast array of problems thrown up by the crisis and the need for closer aid coordination and debt relief programmes. Being tied down with the day-to-day details of the crisis, officials do not have time to work out a strategy for effective long-term debt management.

According to World Bank projections,[17] aggregate debt service payments for SSA countries are expected to fall to $5.2 billion by 1997, or less than one-third of its level in 1988. The virtual disappearance of private creditors as a result of the debt crisis itself is largely responsible for the contraction. Non-guaranteed debts are also expected to disappear by then, though it is not clear to what extent this is due to more effective management, control and accounting procedures, or the disappearance of this market following the onset of the crisis. This leaves official creditors as the main holders of SSA countries' debts. Service payments on these debts are projected to fall to $4.7 billion by 1997, after rising sharply to $8.7 billion in 1992. Effectively, therefore, what this means is that, despite repeated rescheduling and the various relief measures in operation, SSA countries will remain heavily indebted for the foreseeable future. The pattern of payment obligations will nevertheless remain the same as at present, with approximately 60 per cent of all service payments made by the principal debtor countries. Of this figure, about half will be contributed by Nigeria and Côte d'Ivoire.

NOTES

1. These include Argentina, Bolivia, Brazil, Chile, Colombia, Costa Rica, Côte d'Ivoire, Ecuador, Jamaica, Mexico, Morocco, Nigeria, Peru, Philippines, Uruguay, Venezuela and Yugoslavia.
2. See, for example, David F. Lomax, *The Developing Country Debt Crisis*. London: Macmillan, 1986; Peter Nunnenkamp, *The International Debt Crisis of the Third World: Causes and Consequences for the World Economy*. Brighton, Wheatsheaf Books, 1986; Stephany Griffith-Jones (ed.), *Managing World Debt*. Hemel Hempstead, Harvester Wheatsheaf, 1988; Robert Devlin, *Debt and Crisis in Latin America: The Supply Side of the Story*. Princeton, N.J.: Princeton University Press, 1989; Scott B. MacDonald, Margie Lindsay and David L. Crum, *The Global Debt Crisis*. London and New York: Frances

Pinter, 1990; and Alvaro Cencini and Bernard Schmitt, *External Debt Servicing: A Vicious Circle*. London and New York: Frances Pinter, 1991.

3. These are Burkina Faso, Burundi, Cape Verde, Central African Republic, Chad, Comoros, Djibouti, Equatorial Africa, Gambia, Ghana, Guinea, Guinea-Bissau, Liberia, Madagascar, Malawi, Mali, Mauritania, Rwanda, São Tomé and Príncipe, Senegal, Seychelles, Sierra Leone, Somalia, Sudan, Swaziland, Tanzania, Togo, Uganda, Zaire and Zambia.
4. These include Benin, Botswana, Cameroon, Ethiopia, Kenya, Lesotho, Mauritius, Mozambique, Niger and Zimbabwe.
5. The original list of debt-distressed SSA countries included Benin, Comoros, Equatorial Guinea, Gambia, Ghana, Guinea-Bissau, Madagascar, Mali, Mauritania, Mozambique, Niger, São Tomé and Príncipe, Senegal, Sierra Leone, Somalia, Sudan, Tanzania, Togo, Uganda, Zaire and Zambia. The other member, Liberia, is a middle-income country.
6. For the full classification, see World Bank, *World Debt Tables, 1989–1990*. Washington, D.C.: World Bank, 1990.
7. J. M. Keynes, 'The German Transfer Problem', *The Economic Journal*, Vol. XXXIX, March 1929.
8. See Keynes's articles on 'The German Transfer Problem' in *The Economic Journal*, Vol. XXXIX, March, June and September 1929. Bertil Ohlin, 'Transfer Difficulties, Real and Imagined', *The Economic Journal*, Vol. XXXIX, June 1929, and 'Mr Keynes' View on the Transfer Problem', *Economic Journal*, Vol. XXXIX, September 1929; J. Rueff, 'Mr Keynes' Views on the Transfer Problem. A Criticism by M. Jacques Rueff', *The Economic Journal*, Vol. XXXIX, September 1929.
9. For a detailed discussion of the budgetary problem, see Helmut Reisen and Axel Van Trotsenburg, *Developing Country Debt: The Budgetary and Transfer Problem*, Development Centre Studies, Paris: OECD, 1988, Part I.
10. J.M. Keynes, 'A Reply by Mr Keynes', *The Economic Journal*, Vol. XXXIX, September 1929, pp. 405.
11. Alvaro Cencini and Bernard Schmitt, *External Debt Servicing, A Vicious Circle*, London: Pinter Publishers, 1991, p. 32.
12. There is an extensive literature on the transfer problem. See, for example (i) A. C. Pigou, 'The Effect of Reparations on the Real Ratio of International Exchanges', *The Economic Journal*, Vol. XXXXII, pp. 532–43, 1932; (ii) Paul A. Samuelson, 'The Transfer Problem and Transport Costs: The Terms of Trade When Impediments are Absent', *The Economic Journal*, Vol. LXII, pp. 278–304, 1952; 'The Transfer Problem and Transport Costs II: Analysis of Effects of Trade Impediments', *The Economic Journal*, Vol. LXIV, pp. 264–79, 1954; 'On the Trail of Conventional Beliefs about the Transfer Problem' in Bhagwati, Jones, Mundell and Vanek (eds), *Trade, Balance of Payments, and Growth*, Amsterdam: North Holland Publishing Company, pp. 327–51, 1971; (iii) F. Machlup, *International Payments, Debts and Gold*, New York: Scribners, 1964; (iv) Helmut Reisen and Axel Van Trotsenburg, *op. cit.*, Part II; and (iv) Alvaro Cencini and Bernard Schmitt, *op. cit.*
13. For a fuller discussion of valuation effects, see Organization for Economic Co-operation and Development, *External Debt: Definition, Statistical Coverage and Methodology*. Paris: OECD, 1988, pp. 36–7; and *Financing and External Debt of Developing Countries: 1988 Survey*. Paris: OECD, 1989, pp. 75–7.
14. Dragoslav Avramovic, *Economic Growth and External Debt*, Baltimore, Md: Johns Hopkins University Press, 1964, p. 40.
15. Organization for Economic Co-operation and Development, *Financing and External Debt of Developing Countries: 1988 Survey*. Paris: OECD, 1989, p. 42.
16. World Bank, *Sub-Saharan Africa – From Crisis to Sustainable Growth: A Long-Term Prospective Study*. Washington, D.C.: World Bank, November 1989, pp. 2–30.
17. *World Bank Debt Tables, 1988/89 Edition. External Debt of Developing Countries*. vol. I: *Analysis and Summary Tables*. Washington, D.C.: World Bank, 1989.

3. Debt Relief Measures and Proposals

A. THE CONVENTIONAL APPROACH

The last decade has witnessed major changes in the attitude and approach of creditor nations to the problem of international indebtedness. To appreciate the significance of these changes and to trace the historical antecedents of present debt relief measures, it is necessary to outline briefly the essential characteristics and requirements of the conventional approach.

Traditionally, a country's foreign debts were regarded as contractual international financial obligations which had to be met in full and on time. If a country could not meet its service payments it was assumed to have mismanaged its economic and financial affairs. If it had exercised greater budgetary control and financial discipline, the problem would not have arisen in the first place. This approach not only blamed the debtor for getting into debt, it also put the responsibility firmly on it for getting out of debt. The creditors, by and large, showed little sympathy for, or appreciation of, the debtor's economic and financial situation. President Coolidge's pithy remark – 'Hell! They borrowed the money, didn't they?' – succinctly expressed the ruling philosophy and morality of the conventional approach.

Debt relief was not a feature of this scenario. It was only invoked in special and compelling circumstances, and was limited to critical cases, for example, when the alternative was default on existing claims. There were no groundrules or operating criteria. Each case for relief was treated on its own merits and without prejudice to other cases. There are, nevertheless, several features which characterize these early debt relief operations. First, they were essentially *'ad hoc'* in nature, with relief being regarded as a last resort. Secondly, relief was only given in exceptional cases, and limited to the minimum amount necessary to restore the debtor's credit-rating, enabling it to resume service payments as quickly as possible. Thirdly, losses to the creditor were kept to the absolute minimum necessary to safeguard its investment. Fourthly, the cost of postponement of amortization and interest payment was to be borne by additional interest charged at commercial rates. Finally, the amount of disruption to the international monetary and financial system should be minimal.

These criteria, justified no doubt by the rules of orthodox finance and banking, made good sense in the days of *laissez-faire* and free enterprise. Financial losses were private rather than public, and bankruptcy and ruin part of the inevitable price of efficiency, profitability and free enterprise. Within this scheme of things, the debt difficulties of individual countries were seen as an aberration of the world financial system, to be corrected as quickly as possible. Once the problem was put right, the system would continue to function as smoothly and efficiently as before.

Debt consolidation exercises were thus essentially 'short-leash' operations intended (a) to help the creditor country recover and/or safeguard its overseas investment, and (b) to deter the debtor from getting into a similar situation in future. To this end, they were invariably accompanied by a series of economic measures and reforms which the debtor country was required to implement in order to put its economy on a sound footing for the future. Short-leash operations were also regarded as one-off exercises. Consequently, the debts to be consolidated and the period of consolidation were kept to a minimum.[1]

Short-leash operations were clearly intended to serve and protect the interests of the creditors, namely, to ensure that they got paid and that normal market conditions were restored as quickly as possible. To the extent that they achieved these objectives, and/or they prevented a default or outright repudiation of external obligations by the debtors, one can say they were successful. However, they did little to restore the debtor's credit-rating or the viability of its domestic economy. Consequently, the brief respite which they provided was invariably followed by heavier debt burdens which, in turn, necessitated further rounds of debt consolidation.[2] They did not, in fact, take account of the underlying causes of the problem or of the debtor's ability to service its external debts on a long-term basis. As the Pearson Report remarked:

> These short-leash exercises involved heavy costs in terms of uncertainty, pre-emption of scarce management and professional skills, and the inability of the debtor to formulate long-term plans and policies.[3]

B. METHODS AND TECHNIQUES

Conventionally, the main methods and techniques of debt consolidation are (a) rescheduling, (b) refinancing, (c) moratorium and (d) cancellation. These are not mutually and/or operationally exclusive techniques. They allow for variants as well as combined forms. However, for purposes of elucidation, each will be discussed separately.

(a) Rescheduling

This is the most widely used technique. Basically, the repayment schedule of the existing debt is either amended or replaced by a new schedule extending the date of repayment, reducing the rate of interest and/or granting a grace period. Rescheduling is intended to reduce the country's debt profile and make its foreign debt burden more manageable. It is not intended to reduce the total debt outstanding. That remains unchanged. In fact, the stock of debt outstanding usually increases after rescheduling, due, among other things, to the capitalization of rescheduled interest payments.

Rescheduling is particularly appropriate when only individual debts are involved. It is also the usual procedure for providing temporary relief when debts are bunched over a period of two or three years, or when there is a temporary shortfall in foreign exchange earnings: the most usual causes of a liquidity crisis. On the other hand, it is unlikely to be of much use when the debtor's difficulties are chronic and deep-seated, as is the case with SSA countries. Nevertheless, most creditors rely to an overwhelming extent on rescheduling. It is, in a manner of speaking, the first and principal instrument in their armoury of debt reduction measures.

(b) Refinancing

Under this method the debtor is given a new loan or line of credit in order to meet existing service obligations, or to resume payment if this has been suspended. Alternatively, it may use its own reserves and foreign exchange balances, including short-term bank loans. It would then receive a refund from the creditor country for the consolidated portion of the debt. The latter, which is a more expensive technique, has been used more extensively in consolidation exercises.

Refinancing is suitable for long-term structural debts. By providing new loans on softer terms, it is particularly useful for a country that has substantial long-term obligations. But if that country is forced to refinance on commercial terms, the effect will be the same as if it had rescheduled its debt with a moratorium market rate of interest. Refinancing can thus be an expensive exercise if the new funds are raised on harder terms, which is invariably the case. Refinancing also often involves a heavy budgetary cost which many creditor countries prefer to avoid.

(c) Moratorium

This enables the debtor to suspend service payments on all or part of its external obligations, temporarily or for a longer period, depending on a whole range of factors affecting its ability to service its debts. As a holding operation it is not an end in itself, but rather a first step in an overall stabilization programme. It is particularly useful in a time of crisis, for example, when the debtor is under intense internal stress, or when there is a real danger of bankruptcy or default. It provides an opportunity for the debtor and its principal creditors to undertake an inventory of the former's external position. More importantly, it is an open admission that the problem cannot be solved by rescheduling or refinancing.[4]

There have been several instances of creditor countries declaring a moratorium on the repayment of outstanding debts. In 1919 the US government agreed to postpone interest payment on its Liberty Loans and other outstanding war debts, amounting to $475 million per annum, for a period of two to three years. But perhaps the best-known example is the Hoover Moratorium which postponed for one year all governmental debts, reparations and debt relief, both principal and interest, of foreign governments to the American government, conditional on a similar postponement for one year of all inter-government debts owed to other major credit countries.[5]

(d) Cancellation

This is the final stage in the process of debt consolidation. A creditor may decide to cancel or write off (either in part or whole) certain inter-governmental debts owed to it. The decision may be taken unilaterally, but more usually it requires the principal creditors to act multilaterally and in concert to ensure that losses are equitably distributed, and that relief given by one creditor is not used to pay the debts of another. It is used very infrequently and reluctantly – when all else fails and there is no hope of recovering one's investment, when the debtor's country economy is on the verge of collapse, or when a fresh start is considered desirable in the interests of international relations.

For example, as part of its new policy on colonial development, the British government decided in 1940 to cancel some £11.2 million owed by the colonies under the 1929 Colonial Development Act and earlier authorizations, in order to give them a fresh start on the urgent and intractable problem of colonial development. As Wicker put it:

> The British Government had decided to clear the decks on a substantial part of the colonial loans outstanding and to make an effort to reduce the amount of outstanding debts. Such debts acted as a sizeable drain on annual revenues and tended to inhibit economic development.[6]

All these measures depend on the mutual agreement of the creditor and debtor countries. There are instances, however, when debtors, for any number of reasons, have acted unilaterally and repudiated all (or part of) their foreign debts. This happened quite extensively during the years of the Great Depression. Debt repudiation is also likely to happen with a change of government when the incoming government refuses to accept responsibility for the external obligations of its predecessor, as happened in the case of Ghana following the overthrow of Nkrumah.

More recently, several debtor countries have unilaterally decided to limit the amount of foreign exchange for debt servicing purposes to a given proportion of annual export earnings. This is what García did when he became President of Peru in 1984. Brazil, to take another example, declared a temporary moratorium on all service payments in 1987. Both measures proved hugely counterproductive, mainly because they were seen as an attempt to renege on solemn international contractual obligations and a serious 'moral hazard' to the stability of the international economic and financial system. Both Peru and Brazil have since taken steps to revert to the conventional approach.

In brief, the conventional approach evolved in response to the problem of indebtedness between developed countries and was regarded as a temporary aberration of the system. Although there was a variety of measures and techniques for dealing with problem debtors, consolidation was confined to rescheduling and refinancing. Moratoria and debt cancellation were only considered in extreme cases. The widespread series of defaults and debt repudiations of the 1930s clearly questioned the assumptions and methodologies underlying this strategy. However, things were happening so quickly during this period – the Wall Street Crash, the Great Depression, the collapse and closure of international capital markets, to give a few examples – that it was difficult to differentiate cause and effect or to determine whether the strategy would have survived intact.[7]

C. THE POSTWAR SITUATION.

The postwar process of decolonization and the emergence of a growing number of newly independent nations added a new dimension to the problem of international indebtedness. The new nations were poor and underdeveloped and in a hurry to develop. As their own resources were clearly not up to the job, they needed additional inflows of external resources in order to achieve growth and accelerated development. However, various misconceptions and mis-specifications about the nature and process of development and the role and contribution of external capital to that process led to excessive external borrowing and the unproductive and inefficient utilization of these funds: the classic ingredients of a major debt crisis.

However, the postwar debt problems of the developing countries differed in two important respects from those of the earlier period. First, they were development-related, using that term in its widest sense to denote that the funds were intended to promote the long-term development and social transformation of the debtor countries. Secondly, the creditors were the rich (developed) countries of the North, and the debtors the poor (developing) countries of the South. This dichotomy gave rise to a new set of international economic and political considerations which took the debt problem beyond the confines of a straightforward commercial and financial transaction between creditor and debtor countries.

Notwithstanding these new and important features, the basic philosophy and techniques of postwar debt consolidation remained firmly rooted in the conventional approach. Of the 43 procedures which were negotiated between 1956 and 1974, no less than 27 of these were reschedulings and the rest refinancing. There were no cancellations, waivers or write offs. In other words, the process stopped at refinancing rather than utilizing the full range of options which the conventional approach allowed. In effect, the debt problems of the developing countries were regarded as a liquidity crisis for which the appropriate measures were rescheduling and refinancing. When these failed to respond, problem debts were again rescheduled. In all, nine countries shared the 27 reschedulings which took place.[8]

During the 1960s this approach was heavily criticized by various analysts and international studies, the most influential of which was the Pearson Report. It identified the indiscriminate proliferation of export credits as one of the major causes of the problem and concluded:

> The primary objective of debt refinancing or consolidation has been to 'bail out' the borrower by providing strictly short-run accomodation. The emphasis has usually been placed on speedy resumption of debt service payments rather than on re-establishing financial framework for orderly growth.[9]

It accordingly called for a new and more realistic approach which, among other things, avoided the need for repeated reschedulings. It also advocated that donor countries consider debt relief a legitimate form of aid and permit the use of new loans to refinance debt payments in order to reduce the need for full-scale debt negotiations.

UNCTAD extended the argument by stressing the contribution which cancellation would make towards reducing existing debt levels as well as partially offsetting the fall in the volume of new lending.[10] The case for cancellation was also made in a series of articles by the author; and in his book, *International Indebtedness and the Developing Countries*, he outlined an integrated scheme for using debt relief, principally in the form of debt cancellation, as an end in itself (to reduce the level of indebtedness) and as a means to a further end (to provide additional funds for development purposes).[11]

The common elements running through these studies were: (a) the creditor countries were faced with a completely different type of debt problem for which the conventional approach was inadequate and inappropriate; (b) the debts of the developing countries were not only development-related, but comprised of various types of debts carrying different terms and conditions; (c) the creditor countries bore some responsibility for the creation of the problem, as evidenced by the overwhelming preponderance of suppliers' credits. They should, therefore, adopt a more flexible and realistic approach in dealing with the problem; and (d) given the highly differentiated nature of the problem and the fact that the debtors were not a homogeneous group of countries, it was appropriate to consider cancellation a legitimate form of relief, particularly in respect of the poorer countries.

It soon became clear that there were in reality two main types of debtors among the developing countries. The first group was comprised of the traditional high-debtor nations of Latin America and the fast growing, or newly industrializing countries of Asia (NICs). The second included the low-income debtors: effectively, the rest of the developing countries. Although the debts of both groups were development-related, the economic performance and potential of the former group suggested *a priori* that their problems would respond to the conventional treatment of rescheduling and refinancing. The debt problems of the latter group were different. Their servicing capacity was severely constrained by low growth, poor investment opportunities and low credit-rating. These countries needed urgent and special consideration.

The case was finally accepted by the creditor countries at UNCTAD IV in May 1976, when they 'pledged themselves to quick and constructive consideration, within a multilateral framework, of individual requests to provide relief to developing countries suffering from debt service difficulties, in particular, the least developed and most seriously affected developing countries'.[12] This commitment was discussed extensively over the next two years and an outline proposal formally submitted to the Trade and Development Board at its Ninth Special Session in March 1978. At the end of its deliberations, the Board adopted Resolution 165(S-IX) which effectively formalized the concept of the Retroactive Terms Adjustment (RTA) and established its parameters.[13]

D. RETROACTIVE TERMS ADJUSTMENT

Resolution 165 (S-IX) called on donor countries to adopt measures to readjust the terms of past bilateral official development assistance to bring them into line with current ODA terms, or other equivalent measures, as a means of improving the net flow of official development assistance to the poorer developing countries. This would enhance their development effort in the light of internationally agreed objectives and conditions on aid.

Each creditor was free to decide whether, and to what extent, to participate in the scheme; what measures to adopt; which debtor countries would benefit, and by how much, as well as the role and relationship of RTA to its own aid policies and programmes. Other important details of the scheme were:

(a) it was to be reviewed at the fifth session of UNCTAD;
(b) any request for RTA was to be initiated by the debtor country seeking relief;
(c) such requests would be considered within a multilateral framework and involve all interested parties, including international institutions;
(d) the interests of both creditors and debtors should be equitably protected within the context of international economic cooperation.

The enormous flexibility and discretion which the scheme gave the creditor countries enabled them to employ a variety of terms and types of relief measures. These included:

(a) cancellation of all outstanding bilateral ODA loans;
(b) conversion of past loans to grants;
(c) cancellation of interst payments (either in whole or part) for a specified period of time on outstanding bilateral ODA loans;
(d) the provision of new funds on highly concessional terms, including grants to refinance existing service payments;
(e) the adoption of 'equivalent measures', a term which was not defined but which included principally local currency payments and local cost financing.

Between 1979 and 1985, when RTA was most active, the total nominal value of its operations amounted to \$6.2 billion, of which \$3.5 billion was for ODA debt cancellation, \$730 million for interest payment waivers and \$1.9 billion in equivalent measures, mainly in the form of conversion to local cost aid or local currency payments by the United States and Britain. RTA petered out after that, with West Germany accounting for about 34 per cent of the value of all relief granted. The United Kingdom was next, with 32 per cent, and the United States a long way behind, with 11 per cent. The other members of the DAC, the only creditor countries committed to the scheme, accounted for the rest.

RTA was not devised specifically for SSA countries, but given its terms of reference (that is, the least developed and the most severely affected countries) they did rather well out of it. Of the 58 beneficiary countries, 34 were SSA countries, and of these, 25 were least developed. In all, SSA countries received almost three-quarters of the total value of relief measures taken. Also, the majority of them received relief from multiple sources. Tanzania

Table 3.1 Summary of action taken under RTA in favour of the least developed SSA countries, up to September 1986 ($ million)

Beneficiary countries[a]	Action taken: Debt cancellation	Action taken: Interest payment waiver	Action taken: Equivalent measures	Number of creditors granting RTA
Benin	45.5	2.0		5
Botswana	119.4	2.3		5
Burkina Faso	112.4	10.5		5
Burundi	30.4	0.2		2
Central African Rep.	14.9	4.6		2
Chad	23.1	9.3		3
Comoros	5.0	3.0		1
Djibouti	14.5	3.4		1
Ethiopia	22.5	2.0		4
Gambia	21.9	n.r.s.		2
Guinea	33.8	1.0	27.0	4
Guinea-Bissau	9.8	0.7		1
Lesotho	12.6	0.2		2
Malawi	173.2	2.9	2.4	5
Mali	110.4	5.6		4
Niger	149.5	3.2		5
Rwanda	56.5	n.r.s.		3
Sierra Leone	71.2	13.2	10.1	3
Somalia	85.5	—	78.2	3
Sudan	299.5	8.5	175.0	8
Togo	114.0	22.0		2
Uganda	64.9	9.3		6
Tanzania	488.8	23.9	25.0	11
Total	2089.3[b]	127.8[b]	317.7	

Notes

[a] No debt relief operations have been reported for Cape Verde, Equatorial Guinea, Mauritania and São Tomé and Príncipe.

[b] Excluding amounts not allocatable by debtor country.

n.r.s. = Not recorded separately.

Source: Information abstracted from *Revitalising Development, Growth and International Trade: Assessment and Policy Options. Report to UNCTAD VII*. Geneva: UNCTAD, 1987, Annex Table 50.

topped the list with RTA from 11 different creditors, followed by Sudan with eight. Other major beneficiaries (five and over) were Benin, Botswana, Burkina Faso, Kenya, Malawi, Niger and Uganda. Table 3.1 gives a summary of the measures taken in favour of the least developed SSA countries up to September 1986.[14]

There were many things wrong with RTA. For one, the amount of relief provided was really too small to reduce debt levels to any great extent. Secondly, there was no uniformity in terms of creditor commitment or comparability of treatment of debtors' claims. The scheme was in fact beset with various anomalies and inconsistencies. Thirdly, the creditors made no real attempt to integrate RTA into their existing aid programmes and policies. They regarded it as a one-off operation, each request to be treated on its own. Consequently, RTA existed and operated as a separate programme on the periphery of the mainstream of the debt problem.[15]

E. BILATERAL RELIEF INITIATIVES

(a) OECD Creditor Countries

RTA did, nevertheless, perform an important function. It established debt cancellation as an essential and integral part of the overall strategy for reducing the debts of the poorer developing countries, and laid the foundation for subsequent relief initiatives by the OECD countries. In May 1986 Canada granted a moratorium on the repayment of the outstanding ODA loans of African countries for an initial period of five years, renewable for further periods of five years, up to the year 2000. The estimated value of this initiative was put at $250 million. Denmark cancelled the outstanding ODA debt of Tanzania. The Netherlands waived service payments, amounting to 200 million Dutch guilders, by low-income African countries for the period 1986–90. Relief was offered by Italy on its official debt in the form of multi-year stretch-outs over 20 years with a ten-year grace period at a highly concessional interest rate of 1.5 per cent. Donors, such as Sweden, went one step further, and authorized the use of ODA funds to alleviate debt service payments on commercial loans.

In addition, several creditors cancelled the concessional debt of a number of low-income countries. Belgium agreed to forgive about $180 million of bilateral official debt owed by 13 African countries – 70 per cent of this debt was owed by Zaire alone. The French government announced its intention to cancel the equivalent of $2.5 billion of ODA debt owed by 35 IDA-eligible African countries. Germany agreed to cancel about $1.4 billion of ODA debt of six low-income SSA countries implementing structural adjustment programmes. The US government decided to write off up to $1.3 billion of ODA loans made to SSA countries with adjustment programmes in place. The USSR also indicated its willingness to grant debt write offs, or 100-year moratoria, to least developed countries.[16] Finally, Japan said it would provide $1 billion in commodity grants to assist 17 least developed countries in Africa and Asia to service $5.5 billion of ODA loans granted between 1978 and March 1988. The cost of this initiative would be met from its aid budget which would increase to $50 billion between 1988 and 1992.

Cancellation is now, in fact, a major form of debt relief, particularly for the low-income SSA countries. Since 1988 all the major OECD countries have either cancelled or converted to grants the bilateral debts owed by the severely indebted low-income countries. Alternatively, some provide grants for debt service payment purposes. The total value of cancellations amounted to $5.4 billion between 1988 and 1990, which, when added to previous cancellations, brings the total value of ODA debt cancellation and conversion during the 1980s to $7.5 billion.

> Virtually all of the debt forgiven is concessional, arising from earlier ODA activities. The cash flow relief may help some countries avoid debt reschedulings in the future, while for other countries forgiveness slows the steady capitalisation of interest that results from repeated reschedulings. As a result of this ODA forgiveness, cash debt service is projected to be about $100 million lower in 1990, the equivalent of about 0.7 per cent of exports.[17]

Apart from small amounts to Bolivia ($5.4 million) and Myanmar ($42.4 million), the whole amount went to SSA countries. The principal beneficiaries were Gambia ($484.7 million), Kenya ($924.3 million), Madagascar ($502.1 million), Senegal ($812.5 million), Tanzania ($544.2 million) and Zaire ($710 million). Details are given in Appendix A.4.

(b) The Lawson Initiative

The principle of selecting the appropriate relief measure from a 'menu of options' introduced under RTA was further developed by Nigel Lawson, then British Chancellor of the Exchequer, in Washington in April 1987. His initiative, the so-called Lawson Initiative, was addressed specifically to the debt problems of SSA countries, and rested on a number of assumptions and preconditions. The most important of these were: (i) there was no way these countries could repay their debts; (ii) they could not return to economic viability by their own efforts; (iii) they would have to depend on concessional aid inflows for some considerable time; (iv) the creditor countries had a moral and economic responsibility to help these countries which were some of the poorest in the world; (v) SSA countries themselves needed to restructure their economies, to shift the emphasis back to agriculture rather than bolstering an inefficient manufacturing sector; and (vi) the facility should only be made available to countries which were implementing satisfactory economic reform policies. This last condition was in fact the *sine qua non* of the proposal.

The Initiative called for action on three fronts:

- First, the creditor nations should convert aid loans into outright grants.
- Second, longer repayment periods, with generous grace periods, should be allowed in rescheduling other official loans.
- And third, and of crucial importance, the creditor countries should reduce the interest rate payable on these debts to well below market rates.[18]

The proposal emphasized the need for quick and decisive action to be taken internationally to reduce interest rates on these countries' debts. The present practice of capitalizing unpaid interest charges increased the total burden of the debt and made it harder for them to meet their service obligations. The only way to break this vicious cricle was to reduce interest rates 'in an orderly way over a reasonable period of years'.

The Lawson Initiative was pursued at the Venice Summit of the G-7 Nations in June 1987.[19] The members recommended that:

> consideration should be given to the possibility of applying lower interest rates on their existing debts, and that agreement should be reached, especially in the Paris Club, on longer repayment and grace periods to ease the debt burden.[20]

The Paris Club responded quickly. Guinea-Bissau, Mozambique and Somalia, three debt-distressed countries, were given 20–21-year reschedulings with up to 11.5 years grace periods. Mauritania, Uganda and Zaire were granted up to 15.5 years reschedulings with a 6–7-year grace period. A 15-year maturity with nine years grace was agreed for Côte d'Ivoire. Previously, the standard Paris Club reschedulings for low-income SSA countries were ten years maturity with five years grace period.

F. THE TORONTO SUMMIT AGREEMENT

The Venice Summit not only built on the Lawson Initiative but paved the way for the major debt initiative agreed at the Toronto Economic Summit in June 1988. At this meeting, the G-7 nations announced that for the poorest developing countries undertaking internationally approved adjustment programmes, the members had

> achieved consensus in rescheduling official debts of those countries within a framework of comparability that allows official creditors to choose among concessional interest rates on shorter maturities, longer repayment periods at commercial rates, partial write-offs of debt service obligations during the consolidation period or a combination of these options ... consistent with their legal and budgetary constraints.[21]

The Paris Club was asked, as a matter of urgency, to work out the modalities of these options in order to ensure comparability. The benefits were expected to be additional to those already received from various bilateral and multilateral programmes. By September 1988 the Paris Club members had reached agreement on a 'menu of options' for softening rescheduling terms on non-concessional debt, mostly owed to export credit agencies. These were:

Option A – Partial write off
Cancel one-third of the debt service due during the consolidation period, and reschedule the remainder at market rates over 14 years with an 8-year grace period on principal payments.

Option B – Longer repayment terms
Reschedule debt service payments due during the consolidation period at market interest rates with a maturity of 25 years including a 14-year grace period.

Option C – Concessional interest rates
Reschedule debt service payments due during the consolidation period at reduced rates of interest – either 3.5 percentage points below or one-half of market rates, whichever is less – over 14 years and an 8-year grace period.

It was also agreed that for ODA loans, the maturity period would be the same as Option B and the interest rate as low as the original rate, regardless of the option chosen.

Option A and C are roughly comparable in terms of concessionality and the amount of net financial resources which they provide for the debtors. The degree of concessionality will depend on a variety of factors, for example, the amount and terms of the original loan to be rescheduled, the market rate of interest, as well as the rate of discount used. Piritta Sorsa has estimated that on a loan of $1 million with 7 per cent market rate of interest and a discount rate of 7 per cent (the figure used in the OECD Consensus definition of concessionality for mixed export credits), Option A is about 26 per cent lower than the conventional terms of Paris Club reschedulings. The grant element of Option C is 33 per cent, or about the same as for ODA loans. Option B, on the other hand, carries no concessionality, and is, in fact, some 28 per cent higher than normal Paris Club terms.[22]

Option C provides more resources up-front, though it becomes more expensive later. Option A reverses the process. It provides fewer resources during the grace period, but the debtors get more relief during the actual repayment period. Although the timing and the amounts will vary, Option A and C will generate additional cash flows to the debtors in the form of service payments saved. Option B will not. It is, in fact, the least costly to the creditors.

Option A, having the lowest repayment profile, should, *inter alia*, restore the debtor's credit-rating in the shortest period of time. Option B, on the other hand, is intended to provide relief over an extended period of time. However, its value to the debtors is limited by the facts that (a) it does not provide any additional resources in the short and medium term, which is when they are most needed; that is, to cope with the present crisis; and (b) it is not concessional. Also, it is riskier for the creditors, in the sense that repayment does not start until the other two options have been completed. As regards the stock of non-concessional debt, each option will obviously have a different impact, but generally speaking, Options A and C will reduce it by the end of the consolidation period. Option B will have the opposite effect, and could conceivably create additional 'bunching' problems for the debtors.[23]

An important precondition of the Toronto Summit menu of options was that, in order to become eligible for relief, a debtor country was first required to conclude a structural adjustment agreement with the International Monetary Fund (IMF) and the World Bank. Without the Fund's so-called 'seal of approval', the Paris Club, the body which deals with the actual negotiations, would not entertain an application for relief. On the other hand, having concluded an agreement with the IMF, a debtor would automatically become eligible for concessional assistance from the Fund's Structural Adjustment Facility (SAF) or its Enhanced Structural Adjustment Facility (ESAF). Additionally, SSA countries would be eligible for assistance from the Bank's Special Programme of Assistance (SPA), if (a) they receive only IDA credits; (b) have a debt service ratio of at least 30 per cent; and (c) have a structural adjustment programme in place.

Although the Toronto Summit menu of options was not designed specifically for SSA countries, they have been its principal beneficiaries. However, the condition that a debtor has to be 'in adjustment' before it can receive relief has divided SSA debtor countries into those with an adjustment programme (the so-called reformers) and those without (the non-reformers). The former are SPA-eligible. The latter are not. At the start of the programme there were 17 SPA-eligible SSA countries. The number has now increased to 30. Table 3.2 gives a summary of reschedulings on Toronto terms by the Paris Club up to July 1990. Full details are given in Appendix A.5.

With the single exception of Bolivia ($27 million), all the debts rescheduled on Toronto terms were in favour of SSA countries. In all, 17 countries benefited to the tune of $5.3 billion. Six of them (Central African Republic, Mali, Madagascar, Senegal, Tanzania and Togo) had their debts rescheduled twice. In virtually every case, both the principal and interest due on debts previously rescheduled by the Paris Club were included. Arrears were also included. On an annual basis, the net cash flow savings during the consolidation period, as compared with the savings under normal Paris Club arrangements, amounted to $97 million, less than 1 per cent of total export earnings. The net present value of service payments was reduced by $827 million, or about 20 per cent as compared with normal Paris Club terms.

As regards the different options, roughly 30 per cent of the reschedulings were under Option A, 36 per cent under Option B and 34 per cent under Option C. In other words, most creditors preferred Option B, which is the least concessional. It also increases the debtor's stock of non-concessional debt in the future. If these creditors had chosen either of the other two options, the present value of service payments would have been reduced by about 30–33 per cent, instead of 15–20 per cent as at present.

The Toronto Summit Agreement represents a major breakthrough in the search for a solution to the debt crisis in SSA countries. Among other things, it established the principle of granting relief for the reduction of the stock of official non-concessional debts. It also addressed the thorny problem of interest capitalization, a major contributory factor to the crisis. About 35 per cent of the long-term non-concessional debt of these countries in 1988 was interest capitalized through Paris Club reschedulings. According to the Development Committee, interest capitalization has been effectively about 20 per cent lower on debt rescheduled under the Toronto arrangement.[24]

Quite clearly the Toronto Agreement is a step in the right direction, but it does not go far enough. The amount of relief which it provides is limited both in scope and coverage. First, it covers only debts owed to Paris Club creditors which, on average, account for roughly 40 per cent of all bilateral non-concessional official debts of SSA countries and about one-third of their annual debt service payments. Secondly, the savings on moratorium interest payments are limited to the short-term. In 1989 these amounted to less than 2 per cent of total debt service payments due. Thirdly, the Agreement does not cover multilateral debts and arrears due to the IMF, the World Bank and other multilateral financial institutions. Consequently, SSA debtors have to honour their service obligations to these preferred creditors at the expense of their bilateral, creditors which largely defeats the purpose of the Agreement. Fourthly, only those SSA countries which have an adjustment programme in place (currently about half the number) are eligible for relief. The situation is gradually changing, but it takes time to get an adjustment programme off

Table 3.2 Summary of SSA countries which benefited under the Toronto Agreement, to July 1990

Beneficiary countries	Cut-off date[a]	PRD[b]	Arrears	Principal and interest (%)	Consolidation Amount ($m)	Consolidation Period (months)	Net cash flow savings[c] ($m)	Decrease in debt service[c] ($m)
1988								
Mali	1/1/88	No	Yes	100	56	16	...	3
Madagascar	1/7/83	Yes	Yes	100	265	21	4	34
Tanzania	30/6/86	Yes	Yes	100	341	6	4	68
Central African Rep.	1/1/83	Yes	Yes	100	30	18	1	4
Niger	1/7/83	Yes	No	100	43	12	1	11
1989								
Senegal	1/1/83	Yes	No	100	136	14	3	27
Uganda	1/1/81	Yes	Yes	100	90	18	3	16
Guinea	1/1/86	Yes	Yes	100	124	12	...	6
Mauritania	31/12/84	Yes	Yes	100	52	12	1	7
Togo	1/1/83	Yes	No	100	76	14.5	1	15
Benin	31/3/89	No	Yes	100	193	13	...	14
Zaire	30/6/83	Yes	Yes	100	1530	13	26	197
Chad	30/6/89	No	Yes	100	52	15	1	5
Guinea-Bissau	31/12/89	Yes	Yes	100	21	15	...	1
Mali	1/1/88	No	Yes	100	21	26	...	1

1990								
Senegal	1/1/83	Yes	No	100	158	12	2	34
Equatorial Guinea	1/7/84	Yes	Yes	100[d]	6	[e]	...	1
Tanzania	30/6/86	Yes	Yes	100	199	12	3	42
Mozambique	1/2/84	Yes	Yes	100	707	30	30	155
Central African Rep.	1/1/83	Yes	Yes	100	4	12	...	1
Togo	1/1/83	Yes	No	[f]	84	[g]	3	10
Madagascar	1/7/83	Yes	No	100	139	12	2	20
Zambia	1/1/83	Yes	Yes	100	965	18	14	136
Total/Average				100	5286	16	97	807

Notes

[a] Date before which debts must have been incurred in order to be eligible for rescheduling.
[b] Previously rescheduled debts by the Paris Club. In most cases these were included in the new rescheduling exercises.
[c] In relation to standard reschedulings with a 20-year maturity and a 10-year grace period. A discount rate of 9 per cent was used to calculate the present value of scheduled debt service payments.
[d] 100 per cent of arrears.
[e] As of December 1988.
[f] 100 per cent of 1981, 1983 and 1984 Paris Club reschedulings, and 100 per cent of principal of 1985 PRD.
[g] July 1990–June 1992 for 1981, 1983 and1984 PRD; and January 1991–June 1991 for 1985 PRD.
... less than $500,000.

Source: Information abstracted from *Development Committee Number 26, Development Issues*, Washington, D.C.: World Bank, Sept., 1990. Appendix Table B.2, pp. 56–9.

the ground. In addition, the consolidation exercise is a slow, time-consuming process which further reduces its impact and value. Finally, one of the main presumptions of the Agreement was that relief would be additional to existing aid disbursements. However, this has not happened. Most creditors have, in fact, financed debt reduction by transferring funds from their aid budgets to their export credit agencies (ECAs) to make good losses sustained on this account.

It would be wrong, though, to assess the achievements of the Toronto Agreement solely in terms of the amount of relief provided. It is, in fact, an integral part of the process of postwar North–South economic and financial relations which began at UNCTAD IV, when the creditors finally accepted the case for debt cancellation. It is thus the latest in a series of initiatives which reflects a changed attitude and approach to the debt problem of the poorer developing countries. As such, it stands alongside as well as builds on the foundations provided by other initiatives such as RTA and the Lawson Initiative. It has also provided the basis for more recent initiatives.[25]

G. POST-TORONTO INITIATIVES AND PROPOSALS

Since the Toronto Agreement, there have been several initiatives and proposals addressed to the debt crisis in Sub-Saharan Africa. Three in particular seek to capitalize on the momentum created by that Agreement. The first of these, the Pronk Proposal (after the Netherlands Finance Minister, Jan Pronk) was made at the Second UN Conference on Least Developed Countries held in Paris in September 1990. He proposed that the creditor nations collectively extend a complete forgiveness of bilateral official debt to the poorest developing countries facing severe debt problems, particularly the least developed countries and others belonging to the group of low-income countries. Only those debtors pursuing sound economic policies would be eligible for debt forgiveness.[26]

The second proposal was made by the then UK Chancellor of the Exchequer, John Major, at the Commonwealth Finance Ministers meeting in Trinidad in September 1990. Basically, its purpose was ‘to do more to bridge the long-term financing gap faced by some of the poorest debtor countries ... and the need to offer strengthened incentives to avoid default and continue the reform process’. To this end, it offered four proposals for improving the Toronto terms. These are:

(a) rescheduling should tackle the total stock of debt in a single, long-term operation rather than reschedule one year’s maturities at a time;

(b) the amount of debt written off should be increased to two-thirds of the total stock of eligible debt;
(c) interest payments occurring in the first five years should be capitalized, and repaid in a phased manner in which repayment of principal and interest increases as the debtor's capacity grows;
(d) the repayment period should be lengthened from 14 to 25 years.[27]

This proposal was also discussed at the annual meeting of the Fund and the Bank in Washington, and was favourably received. More recently, it was endorsed by the G-7 nations at their Economic Summit in London in July 1991. The modalities are presently being worked out by the Paris Club, and the signs are that these will be incorporated into the basic structure provided by the Toronto Agreement. If accepted, the so-called 'Trinidad Terms' will increase the grant element of debt and debt service reduction from its present level of 20 per cent (Toronto terms) to 67 per cent. This will provide a substantial increase in net cash flow savings for SSA debtor countries.

Finally, in 1989 the World Bank provided $100 million from its net income for the establishment of a Debt Reduction Facility to help IDA-only countries meet the cost of servicing their non-concessional debts to private creditors. This Facility is to be used by the recipient countries to buy back, swap or convert their commercial debts at substantial discounts so as to reduce future servicing costs. Each case will be considered on its own merits and assistance limited to a grant of $10 million per debtor country.

In order to qualify for assistance, each debtor country must have an appropriate medium-term structural adjustment programme agreed with both the Fund and the Bank. It must also have a debt management strategy which (a) includes a programme for resolving the country's commercial debt problem through funds provided by the facility and other sources; (b) provides for substantial debt relief from official bilateral creditors through an agreement with the Paris Club, preferably on Toronto terms; and (c) materially enhances the country's prospects for growth and development. The Facility will last for three years, after which any unexpended balance will revert to IDA's general operations account.

Up to September 1990 some 14 SSA countries with commercial debts of about $1.6 billion had applied for assistance. Of these, Mozambique is the most advanced in its negotiations with the commercial banks on a proposal for reducing some $280 million non-guaranteed commercial debt. Niger has also opened negotiations with its private creditors. However, there are two major problems with the scheme. First, the commercial banks are reluctant to participate, for fear of setting a dangerous precedent for countries in which their exposure is greater. Secondly, the facility will run out of time before it has managed to make an impact on the problem of commercial debts which, though small at present, are likely to increase significantly in the future. It is, nevertheless, an important step in the process of formulating a comprehensive debt management strategy for these countries.

H. PROPOSAL FOR REFINANCING AFRICAN EXTERNAL DEBT

This proposal, commonly called the Warburg Proposal, was put forward by the African Development Bank in November 1987, in consultation with S. G. Warburg, its financial advisers. It started from the premiss that the repeated short-term rescheduling at commercial rates of interest which African countries had undertaken aggravated rather than resolved the debt crisis. It accordingly proposed a refinancing arrangement which was based on the presumption that it is reasonable to expect that debts will be repaid eventually. Also, total annual service payments should not exceed a sustainable proportion of the debtor's export earnings, and the debtor country should seek to establish its creditworthiness. Creditors must be treated equitably and have a reasonable expectation of being repaid in full, and with interest due, within as short a period as practicable. Finally, they could expect to benefit from any economic improvement which the debtor country may achieve.

Its main elements were:

(a) all medium- and long-term external debts, excluding multilateral and concessional loans, should be converted into long-term securities of 20 years (or longer) single payment maturity carrying a fixed rate of interest;
(b) debt service payments over the medium term should be limited to a sustainable level of foreign exchange earnings to be negotiated between creditors and debtors;
(c) of this, a proportion, sufficient to retire these securities at maturity, should be paid each year, with a Redemption Fund set up to administer the scheme;
(d) the rest would be used to make interest payments;
(e) the fixed rate of interest to be paid on the securities would be mutually agreed between the creditors and debtors, and the amount set at the difference between the available foreign exchange over payments into the Redemption Fund;
(f) as an optional feature, these long-term securities could be converted into local currency or used for approved equity investment in the debtor countries, so long as the total cash flow cost to the debtor was not increased as a result.

The Redemption Fund would be managed (but not guaranteed) on behalf of the holders of the securities by a Board of Trustees drawn from the World Bank, the IMF, the African Development Bank, various classes of creditors and the debtor countries, and administered by the existing secretariat of the Paris Club. It would meet regularly to review the economic performance of the debtor countries. If their debt servicing capacity showed significant improvement beyond the original estimates, then the Board of Trustees could call for an increased rate of payment into the Redemption Fund. Conversely, if the debtor's servicing capacity deteriorated despite its adherence to agreed policies, the Board of Trustees could recommend that the rate of interest be reduced until its performance improved.[28]

Table 3.3 illustrates how the scheme would work for a hypothetical African country with a total external debt of $1 billion in 1987. Of this, $250 million are owed to multilateral institutions and $100 million are concessional bilateral loans, leaving a net total of $650 million. A Redemption Fund to accumulate to this amount at the end of 20 years on the basis of a medium-term interest rate of, say, 8.5 per cent per annum, would require payments of about $13.4 million per annum.

As the table shows, scheduled service payments due on the country's stock of debts over the previous five years (1983–7) are assumed to range between $130 and $150 million per annum, and the amount of debt relief

Table 3.3 An illustrative case of refinancing external debt ($ million)

	1983	1984	1985	1986	1987
Debt service payments					
Principal	70	70	70	80	80
Interest	60	50	70	70	80
Total debt service	130	120	140	150	160
Debt relief	(60)	(70)	(80)	(80)	(100)
Actual debt service	70	50	60	70	60
of which: Multilateral	10	10	10	20	20
Foreign exchange receipts	350	340	350	350	360
Debt service ratios (%)					
Scheduled	37	35	40	43	44
Actual	20	14	17	20	17

Source: African Development Bank, 'Proposal for Refinancing African External Debt', Financial Advisers, S.G. Warburg & Co Ltd, London, November 1987, Appendix 1.

following reschedulings from $60 to $100 million. Actual service payments thus ranged between $50 and $70 million per annum. The Proposal suggests that negotiations between creditors and debtor might conclude that this is a sustainable level of service payments which the debtor might reasonably be expected to make over the medium term. Assuming that service payments to multilaterals amounted to $20 million per annum and the cost of official bilateral concessional debt is negligible,

> the debtor country could afford to make interest payments on the issue of the new securities of between $36.6 million and $26.6 million, depending on whether the sustainable debt service level agreed in negotiation was $70 million or $60 million per annum. On the basis of a total issue of securities of $650 million, this amount of available debt service could cover a fixed interest rate on the securities of between 5.6 per cent and 4.1 per cent per annum.[29]

The Warburg Proposal has at least three features to commend it. First, it is home-grown in the sense that it is sponsored by the African Development Bank, one of the region's leading monetary and financial institutions. This goes a long way towards countering the claim that debtor countries have no proposals of their own but simply respond to other people's proposals. Secondly, it relates specifically to commercial debts which, though small in the aggregate and confined to a few countries, is perhaps the most intractable aspect of the whole crisis. The fact that Warburg had a hand in its preparation is a fair reflection of what the commercial banks might reasonably be expected to wear. Thirdly, it broke with the conventional approach of repeated reschedulings and/or the provision of new money. Commercial debt reduction through the issue of single maturity 20-year securities was not only a novel approach, but also based on a realistic perception of the nature of the problem and its effects on debtors and creditors alike. The former must be offered the prospect of eventually repaying their debts. Equally, the burden of granting relief must be equitably shared among the latter.

Although the Proposal was devised with Zaire in mind, clearly Nigeria and Côte d'Ivoire, the countries with most commercial debt in Sub-Saharan Africa, would benefit from its implementation. Unfortunately, it never really got off the ground and was quickly overtaken by events. However, the basic ideas and approach which it advocated have been adopted by Mexico and other debtor countries under the Baker and Brady Plans. A concerted effort should be made to reactivate this proposal in the specific context of Sub-Saharan Africa, since it (or variants of it) has been shown to be viable elsewhere, but more importantly, it would provide a useful complement to the IDA Debt Reduction Facility.

NOTES

1. The majority of debt re-arrangement exercises undertaken between 1956 and 1974 were for less than three years, usually 12–18 months. A few extended to four years or more. The longest period covered by any consolidation exercise was 5.5 years, in the case of Turkey in 1959.
2. For example, between 1956 and 1965 Argentina's foreign debts were renegotiated on four separate occasions. In the period 1959 to 1974, Brazil (1961 and 1964), Turkey (1959 and 1965) and Peru (1968 and 1969) each had two debt renegotiations, and Chile (1965, 1972 and 1974), India (1968, 1971 and 1973) and Pakistan (1972, 1973 and 1974) three each.
3. *Partners in Development: Report of the Commission on International Development* [commonly called the Pearson Report, after its Chairman, Lester B. Pearson]. New York: Praeger, 1969, p. 157.
4. A variant of this method of consolidation is the inclusion of a 'bisque' clause in the original loan agreement. This entitles the debtor to postpone service payments for limited periods of time when experiencing balance of payments difficulties. A number of postwar loans by Canada and the United States carried this provision. In December 1945, for example, the United States made a loan of $3,750 million to the United Kingdom to be repaid over 50 years. The agreement provided that under certain circumstances the interest would be waived. In 1957 the United Kingdom government decided, after agreement with the United States, to forgo its right to this waiver in exchange for the right to postpone up to seven instalments of principal and interest.
5. For details, see the *Annual Report of the Secretary of the Treasury.* Washington, D.C.: Government Printing Office, 1920; and Harold G. Moulton and Leo Pasvolsky, *War Debts and World Prosperity.* Washington, D.C.: Brookings Institution, DC, 1932.
6. E. R. Wicker, 'Colonial Development and Welfare, 1929–1957: the Evolution of a Policy', *Social and Economic Studies* (University of the West Indies), vol. 7, no. 4 (November 1958), p. 181.
7. For an evaluation of the conventional approach, see George C. Abbott, *International Indebtedness and the Developing Countries*. London: Croom Helm, and New York: M. E. Sharpe, 1979, pp. 189–94 and 206–20.
8. These were: Argentina (1956, 1961, 1962, 1965); Brazil (1961, 1964); Chile (1965, 1972, 1974); Ghana (1966, 1968, 1970, 1974); Indonesia (1966, 1967, 1968, 1970); India (1968, 1972, 1973); Pakistan (1972, 1973, 1974); Peru (1968, 1969); and Turkey (1959, 1965).
9. *Partners in Development*, pp. 156–7.
10. UNCTAD Secretariat, *Debt Problems of Developing Countries*. New York: United Nations, 1972, p. 17.
11. See George C. Abbott, 'Aid and Indebtedness – a Proposal', *National Westminster Bank Review*, May 1972, pp. 55–67; 'Debt Consolidation: the Case for Cancellation', *Intereconomics*, Hamburg: Verlag Weltarchiv July 1975, pp. 217–21; and 'What's Wrong With a Write-Off?', *Co-Existence – an International Journal*, vol. 13, no. 1, April 1976, pp. 34–48. Also, *International Indebtedness and the Developing Countries*, pp. 247–303.
12. For the full text of this commitment, see Resolution 94(IV) of the United Nations Conference on Trade and Development (UNCTAD), 31 May 1976, on *The Debt Problems of Developing Countries*, Nairobi, May 1976.
13. See Resolution 165 (S-IX), 'Debt and Development Problems of Developing Countries of the Trade and Development Board at its Ninth Special Session', 494th Meeting, UNCTAD, Geneva, 11 March 1978.
14. For a detailed breakdown of measures taken and beneficiary countries, see *Revitalising Development, Growth and International Trade: Assessment and Policy Options. Report to UNCTAD VII*, Geneva: UNCTAD, 1987, Annex Table 50.
15. For an evaluation of the scheme, see George C. Abbott, 'Retroactive Terms Adjustment', *Intereconomies*, Hamburg: Verlag Weltarchiv, July/August 1987, vol. 22, no. 4,

pp. 182–9; and 'Another Round of Retroactive Terms Adjustment', in *Third World Debt: How Sustainable are Current Strategies and Solutions?*, ed. Helen O'Neill, *European Journal of Development Research*, vol. 1, no. 2, December 1989, pp. 60–77.

16. These countries owe the Soviet Union over $220 million. This debt has an average grant element of 31 per cent and annual service payments amount to $50 million. It is concentrated in a few countries (Guinea, Madagascar, Mali and Tanzania). In 1986–67 repayments exceeded disbursements.
17. *Development Committee Number 26: Development Issues*. Presentations to the 39th Meeting of the Development Committee, Washington D.C.: World Bank, 24 September 1990, p. 44.
18. Speech by Nigel Lawson, Chancellor of the Exchequer, to an All Party Parliamentary Group on Overseas Development, House of Commons, 22 July 1988, pp. 4–5 (mimeo).
19. The Group of 7 major industrial countries includes Canada, France, Germany, Italy, Japan, the United Kingdom and the United States.
20. Communiqué of the Venice Summit of the G-7 Nations, Venice, June 1987.
21. Communiqué of the Toronto Economic Summit of the G-7 Nations, Toronto, June 1988.
22. Piritta Sorsa, 'Solving the Debt Problems of the Poorer Developing Countries: Issues and Options for Development Cooperation in the 1990s', OECD/DCD/REPD, October 1989, p. 8 (mimeo).
23. A useful comparative evaluation of the three options on the debt problems of those SSA countries which are eligible for relief under the Special Programme of Assistance (SPA) is given in Charles Humphreys and John Underwood, 'The External Debt Difficulties of Low Income Africa', Washington, D.C.: World Bank, September 1988 (mimeo).
24. *Development Committee, Number 26: Development Issues*, p. 45.
25. For an assessment of the Toronto Summit Agreement, see UNCTAD Secretariat, *Debt and Managing Adjustment: Attracting Non-Debt-Creating Financial Flows and New Lending*, Geneva: UNCTAD, 19 February 1990 (TD/B/C.3/24); UN Africa Recovery Programme, Briefing Paper, *African Debt: The Search for Solutions*, no. 1, New York: United Nations, June 1990; and George C. Abbott, 'The Toronto Summit and Sub-Saharan African Countries', *African Review of Money, Finance and Banking*, vol. 1, 1991 pp. 65–84.
26. See *World Bank Debt Tables, 1990–91*, vol. I: *Analysis and Summary Tables*. Washington, D.C.: World Bank, 1991, Appendix 6.
27. See *The Chancellor's Speech to Commonwealth Finance Ministers, Port of Spain, Trinidad, September 20, 1990*. London: UK Treasury, 1990 (mimeo).
28. See African Development Bank, 'Proposal for Refinancing African External Debt', London: S.G. Warburg and Co. Ltd, November 1987 (mimeo).
29. Ibid., Appendix 1, p. 2.

4. Structural Adjustment in SSA Countries

A. THE NEED FOR ADJUSTMENT

The macroeconomic imbalances experienced by SSA countries during the 1970s were clearly unsustainable and inimical to their long-term growth and development. The rate of absorption was greater than the supply of domestic resources and the amount of external funding which they could raise on appropriate terms. There were also chronic inefficiencies, considerable capacity under-utilization, serious distortions and rigidities in factor markets, as well as institutional inadequacies. Although there was much controversy as to whether the region's problems were self-inflicted or the result of its vulnerability to unfavourable external factors, most analysts agreed that the region was in serious decline, and that major policy changes and economic reforms were urgently needed to restore balance and stability and to promote long-term sustainable growth and development.

This was the message which the World Bank stressed in a series of reports published during the 1980s. The first of these, *Accelerated Development in Sub-Saharan Africa: An Agenda for Action*[1] (the Berg Report), called on SSA countries to utilize their resources (internal as well as external) more efficiently and to provide a more effective system of incentives and institutional support for production, particularly agriculture which it identified as the key to the region's recovery. It called for the systematic and long-term neglect of agriculture to be reversed and for major policy changes and reforms to be implemented in order to improve the sector's performance. These included higher producer prices and incentives to increase production for home consumption as well as exports; the liberalization of markets; more efficient marketing and distribution systems; and more resources for agricultural research.

It also called for major changes in trade and exchange rate policies in order to remove the bias against agricultural exports in order to make them more competitive internationally and to recapture lost export markets. It singled out the correction of over-valued exchange rates, improved price incentives for agricultural exports, lower levels of taxation, the removal of subsidies, lower and more uniform protection for industry and less use of direct controls as the most essential changes needed for accelerated growth and sustainable long-term development.

The report considered the public sector clearly over-extended, given the present scarcities of financial resources, skilled manpower and organizational capacity. It recommended, therefore, that SSA governments should urgently examine ways in which the sector could be reorganized and made to operate more efficiently:

> for example, by improving government policy making institutions and procedures; by giving the public sector's development-related agencies – 'parastatals' – clearer mandates and greater management autonomy; by giving wider responsibilities to the small-scale indigenous private sector; by allowing greater scope for decentralised cooperatives; and by defining an appropriate role for larger-scale private capital, domestic and foreign.[2]

It accepted that several SSA governments had already moved in this direction, but more needed to be done to reduce the widespread over-commitment of the public sector, and to develop and utilize the managerial capacities of private individuals and firms, particularly in small-scale industry, marketing and service activities.

Finally, the Berg Report underlined the need for increased donor assistance to enable SSA countries to implement the necessary structural changes and policy reforms. It accordingly recommended that the level of aid should be doubled in real terms by the end of the 1980s – from $4.9 billion to $9.1 billion – and the additional funding should (a) be targeted to improve efficiency of resource use in the short and medium term, and (b) take the form of quick-disbursing balance of payments support. It reckoned that the programme of reforms along with the increased aid flows would increase per capita incomes of the oil-importing countries by about a quarter over the decade.

In 1983 the World Bank issued a progress report[3] on the implementation of the programme of reform recommended in the Berg Report. This report noted that the economic crisis facing SSA countries had deepened and that the world trading and financial system had deteriorated. The need for structural adjustment and major domestic policy reforms was thus even more urgent. Most SSA governments recognized this, and a modest start had in fact been made, but progress was slow:

> the review of experience over the past few years shows that despite widespread improvements in agricultural producer prices and often in exchange rate policies, limited headway has been made in restructuring the incentive structure. Similarly, institutional changes, including changes in the respective roles of the private and

> public sectors, have been introduced only slowly. Political opposition to change is undoubtedly a major obstacle to more rapid adoption of efficient policies and institutional arrangements, but in addition, administrative, technical, legal and other delays must be recognised.[4]

It reiterated the point that for adjustment to be successful, SSA countries needed increased and sustained external financial support for bridging the gap between the adoption of policy reform and its impact on the availability of resources. Finally, it outlined the various programmes and operations which the World Bank had set in train to assist these countries with their structural adjustment programmes.

In the following year, the World Bank published another report on the deepening crisis in Sub-Saharan Africa and the need for policy reforms to promote accelerated growth.[5] This report (the Please Report) reiterated the conclusions and recommendations of the Berg Report, in addition to making a number of its own. Among other things, it emphasized the need for appropriate levels and types of external assistance to support domestic economic reforms. It singled out the need to make better use of investment resources, internal as well as external, as the key to effective reform. It called for a greater role for non-governmental institutions and the private sector, and it analysed the debt problem of SSA countries in the context of their overall requirement for foreign exchange. It outlined a joint programme of action, the main features of which were:

(a) the formulation of national rehabilitation and development plans by African Governments;
(b) more explicit and monitorable commitments by recipient governments and donors to implement their respective responsibilities under an agreed programme;
(c) provision of adequate, timely, and sustained external financial assistance to programmes of major economic reforms, in particular, agriculture which is essential to restore Africa's economic growth;
(d) public expenditure programmes should give greater emphasis to the rehabilitation and maintenance of existing infrastructure in support of policy reform rather than investment in new capacity. The change of emphasis should be reflected in donors' aid programmes.
(e) the formulation of low-cost, efficient, and well-targeted programmes in education, health, population, agricultural research and forestry; and
(f) at a minimum, net capital flows should be maintained at their 1980–1982 level in real terms, in order to provide adequate support for those countries undertaking the necessary policy reforms and restructuring their development and investment programmes. About $2 billion additional bilateral and multilateral disbursements would be required each year. These funds were to be placed in a special assistance facility to be used only when required to support reform programmes.[6]

B. APPER AND UNPAAERD

Various declarations, policy statements and outline programmes during the 1970s and 1980s make it clear that SSA countries not only accepted the need for reform but had, in fact, committed themselves to specific strategies for achieving recovery and the long-term development of their economies. For example, the Monrovia Strategy adopted by the heads of states and governments of the Organization of African Unity (OAU) in 1979 emphasized self-reliant and self-sustained development as the appropriate strategy for African countries.[7] The following year they adopted the Lagos Plan of Action which set out a series of targets for implementing the Monrovia Strategy. These included: the alleviation of mass poverty; improvement in standards of living; the attainment of food self-sufficiency; and the provision of various critical goods and services. The Lagos Plan of Action remains the official blueprint for Africa's long-term development.[8]

Both documents proclaimed unequivocally that the responsibility for Africa's development rested with the African countries themselves. However, given the enormity of this undertaking, they required the support and assistance of the international community in order to strengthen and promote the long-term structural transformation of their economies, the basic strategy for which was set out in the OAU's 'Africa's Priority Programme for Economic Recovery 1986–1990 (APPER)'.[9] This Programme called for a new spirit of cooperation and genuine and equal partnership between African countries and the international community, in which the former pledged themselves to implement various national, regional and sub-regional programmes in order to secure the medium- and long-term development of their economies, and the latter to support and complement these efforts.

At the national level, various sectoral priorities were identified with the emphasis placed firmly on the revitalization of the food and agriculture sector. An extensive range of measures was specified for (a) combating food emergencies, both now and in the future, and (b) increasing productivity and output in the medium term. These covered virtually every aspect of the sector's activities, and were to be applied in a combination relevant to the circumstances of each country. The total investment required to implement the various programmes for this sector alone was put at $57.4 billion, or about 44.8 per cent of the full cost of APPER.

Additionally, a high priority was accorded to the rehabilitation and development of agro-related industries (for example, the processing of raw materials and intermediate inputs) and other sectors in support of agriculture, such as transport and communications. In the field of trade and finance, the measures included improving distribution channels for domestic trade, and providing price incentives for agricultural products. For financial cooperation, greater use was to be made of existing clearing arrangements. Domestic financial markets and institutions were to be coordinated, and efforts intensified for the establishment of the African Monetary Fund. The cost of these programmes was estimated at $60.1 billion.

A further $3.41 billion was envisaged for various measures to stem and control the effects of drought and desertification on both the ecological environment and the development process. Finally, policies for the efficient development, planning and utilization of human resources and the full and effective participation of the people in development were estimated at $7 billion. APPER also contained measures for improving the management of the domestic economy and the rationalization of public sector investment policies and expenditure, while the role of the private sector was to be encouraged through well-defined and consistent policies.

Other priority measures were identified at the sub-regional and regional level, bringing the cost of implementing APPER to $128.1 billion. African countries committed themselves to providing $82.5 billion through the mobilization of domestic resources. This left a gap of $46 billion to be filled by external resources, or approximately some $9 billion per annum over five years.

In 1986 the United Nations convened a Special Session to discuss the critical economic situation in Africa, following the devastation of the 1984 drought and famine, and to mobilize support and additional resources for the implementation of APPER. The Session concluded by adopting the United Nations Programme of Action for African Economic Recovery and Development 1986–1990 (UNPAAERD).[10] This new programme incorporated and expanded the priorities and objectives of APPER. It reaffirmed the determination and commitment of African states to push on with the necessary reforms for long-term sustainable growth and development. The international community in turn, recognized that African countries needed additional external resources, and committed itself

> to making every effort to provide sufficient resources to support and supplement the African development effort; it also appreciates that the realisation of Africa's development efforts would be greatly eased if the flows of external resources were predictable and assured.[11]

That, apparently, was as far as the donor countries were prepared to go in terms of concrete commitments to UNPAAERD.

A variety of desiderata for improving the quality and modality of external assistance and cooperation was specified, for example, greater emphasis on programme support; speedier disbursement of funds; increased concessionality; more effective coordination methods; local cost financing of programmes, and so on. UNPAAERD also called on the international community to improve the external environment by removing many of the factors which aggravate the African situation. It singled out such matters as the elimination of protectionism in the developed countries, greater market access for African exports in these markets and the early implementation of the Common Fund to deal with the problems of commodity prices.

It listed a number of measures which the donor countries agreed were necessary to support African policy reforms. However, their commitment to provide the necessary support and financial resources to underwrite these reforms was expressed in very general terms and did not extend beyond what had already been done to help African countries. A comprehensive set of proposals for increasing South–South cooperation and promoting collective self-reliance among developing countries was outlined. Finally, UNPAAERD called for the establishment of effective follow-up and evaluation machinery to monitor and coordinate progress at national, regional, sub-regional and international levels. The Programme also called for a mid-term review and appraisal to be presented at the 43rd Session of the UN General Assembly.

This Review[12] concluded that the majority of African countries had made a courageous and commendable effort to adopt policy reforms and structural adjustment measures. However, some had done nothing and others were not pursuing them with vigour. As for the international community, it accepted that some important initiatives had been taken, but more needed to be done, particularly in the interrelated problems of financial flows, commodities and debt.

More specifically, it listed a range of immediate measures which African governments had taken to combat food emergencies, and concluded that about half of them now had national emergency preparedness mechanisms; 18 had early warning systems and many had set up national food security arrangements. As regards medium- and longer-term measures, the Review reported that

> more than 90 per cent of African countries accord the highest priority to the food and agriculture sector in their development programmes. Approximately 6 in 10 of the responding countries reported that 20 to 25 per cent of public investment was allocated to agriculture, as called for in the Programme. The most recent development plans indicate the following investment allocations to the agricultural sector: Cameroon, over 26 per cent; Congo, 24 per cent; United Republic of Tanzania, 24 per cent; Tunisia, 32 per cent; Morocco, 19 per cent; and Zambia, 14 per cent.[13]

Additionally, producer prices for groundnuts were raised in Gambia and Senegal, while Ghana and Nigeria increased prices for cocoa. Other countries such as Cameroon, Côte d'Ivoire and Mali banned imports of food, or subjected them to heavier taxes and duties in order to give greater incentives to domestic producers. Other countries adopted policies to remove or reduce subsidies on inputs, to rationalize public sector intervention, increase the role of the private sector in input procurement and distribution and rationalize interest rates. Efforts had also been made to improve the overall level of capacity utilization of agro-related industries as well as to develop Africa's human resources. Table 4.1 gives a summary of some of the reform measures undertaken by African governments under UNPAAERD.

Although the information in this table is illustrative rather than definitive, it is instructive in a number of important respects. First, virtually all SSA countries have undertaken some type or measure of policy reform. This in itself is indicative of their commitment to the Programme. Secondly, more than half of them have adopted public enterprise reforms. It has been repeatedly emphasised that the public sector is badly 'out of synch' with the rest of the economy and urgently needs reforming. The message finally seems to have got through. Thirdly, SSA countries are seriously concerned about the need to improve productivity and output in the agricultural sector. A decade ago the sector received, on average, less than 10 per cent of public investment expenditure, which partly explains why its performance deteriorated. Finally, several of them have been persuaded to pursue explicit population policies.

Although the Review considered that the economic performance of SSA countries between 1986 and 1988 was generally disappointing, it urged them to redouble their efforts, as there was evidence to suggest that the reforms were beginning to take effect. It also stressed the basic incompatibility of the short-term perspectives of the Programme with the longer-term objective of sustainable growth and development. In its words:

> Structural adjustment programmes need to be designed as an integral part of a long-term development strategy and the human dimension needs to be made a central concern of both the shorter-term adjustment programmes and the longer-term strategies.[14]

The response of the international community was reviewed under a variety of headings, the most important being resource flows, trade and commodity issues and debt relief. On the question of resource flows, it noted that these had increased in 1986 and 1987 in nominal terms, but fell in real terms, as compared with 1985. It accepted that SSA countries enjoyed preferential treatment in developed country markets and that there were various international mechanisms for stabilizing and for compensating them for loss of export earnings, such as STABEX, SYSMIN and the Compensatory Financing Facility. But it argued that their scope and use were not commensurate

Table 4.1 Summary table of selected reform measures taken by SSA countries under UNPAAERD, 1986–8

	Policy reforms	Early warning systems	Public enterprise reforms	Share of agricultural investment in total public investment (20–25%)	Explicit population policies
Angola					
Benin	*		*		*
Botswana	*	*	*		
Burkina Faso	*				*
Burundi	*		*	*	*
Cameroon	*		*		*
Cape Verde	*	*		*	*
Central African Republic	*		*	*	
Chad	*				
Comoros	*			*	*
Congo	*		*		*
Côte d'Ivoire	*		*	*	*
Djibouti					
Equatorial Guinea	*				*
Ethiopia	*	*	*	*	*
Gabon	*				
Gambia	*		*	*	
Ghana	*	*	*		*
Guinea	*		*		
Guinea-Bissau	*	*	*	*	*
Kenya	*		*		*
Lesotho	*	*			*
Liberia	*		*	*	*
Madagascar	*		*	*	*
Malawi	*	*	*		
Mali	*	*	*	*	*
Mauritania	*		*		
Mauritius	*		*		*
Mozambique	*				
Niger	*	*	*	*	*
Nigeria	*		*		*
Rwanda	*		*		*
São Tomé and Príncipe	*	*		*	*
Senegal	*	*	*	*	*
Seychelles					
Sierra Leone	*		*	*	*
Somalia	*	*	*	*	*
Sudan	*		*	*	*
Swaziland	*				*
Tanzania	*	*	*	*	
Togo	*		*	*	*
Uganda	*		*	*	*
Zaire	*		*		*
Zambia	*	*	*		
Zimbabwe	*	*		*	

Source: ECA 1987 and 1988 surveys on the implementation of the Programme of Action and data collected by the UNDP/World Bank/ECA project on development programmes and aid flows, reproduced in UNPAAERD Mid-term Review, UN Doc. A/43/500, 10 August 1988, pp. 26–8 (as amended).

with the scale of the problem. They needed to be strengthened and liberalized. It also acknowledged the initiatives taken to reduce the debt problem. But, again, it argued that these did not go far enough or provide a durable solution to the problem.

However, the Review adopted a more positive approach to the efforts and contributions of the various specialized agencies and organizations within the UN system. It highlighted the work which the World Food Program (WFP) and the FAO had done in combating food shortages as well as their longer-term programmes for promoting the recovery and development of the agricultural sector. ECA's contribution to land use policies and farming systems was mentioned. So, too, was the work of the United Nations Development Programme (UNDP), and both UNCTAD and UNIDO were commended for their work in SSA countries.

UNPAAERD, like APPER before it, was billed as a major cooperative effort between African countries and the international community, in which the former committed themselves to implementing a vigorous and comprehensive set of economic reforms, and the latter to support and supplement their efforts. The Mid-term Review applauded the effort and energy which SSA countries had put into getting the Programme off the ground, but admitted that there was little by way of solid achievement. Nevertheless, it urged them to persist with UNPAAERD. A more recent study has reviewed UNPAAERD's achievements, and comes to the same conclusion.[15] However, having admitted that 'in terms of *concrete results* the Programme has by and large not worked', it looks forward to UNPAAERD II to provide tangible effects during the 1990s. Whether or not there will be an UNPAAERD II is a moot point. One rather suspects not. UNPAAERD has served its purpose which, principally, was to demonstrate internationally the earnest commitment of African states to economic reforms and structural adjustment.

C. THE WASS REPORT

Following the UN Special Session on Africa, the Secretary-General appointed an Advisory Group of Eminent Persons with particular competence in the field of international finance to assess Africa's critical financial situation and to make practical recommendations. The Group was headed by Sir Douglas Wass, former Permanent Secretary to the UK Treasury, and the members participated in their individual capacities rather than as representatives of governments. Their report, entitled *Financing Africa's Recovery*[16] (commonly called the Wass Report), came to the conclusion that Africa was in a critical situation and that there was a real danger that without increased support from donor and creditor countries, many SSA governments would not be able to carry through the economic reforms on which they had embarked. 'The consequences of failure, in both political and economic terms could be incalculable', to use its own words.

The Wass Report continued the momentum developed by APPER and UNPAAERD. It detailed the causes of the crisis and what needed to be done in the short-term to put SSA countries back to where they were in the early 1980s. It estimated that their net external position, excluding Nigeria, had deteriorated by about $6.5 billion per annum, between 1979–81 and 1985–87, due to the combined effects of terms of trade losses, increased debt service payments and reduced capital inflows. The basis of this calculation is given in Table 4.2.

Table 4.2 Consolidated change in external position of SSA countries,[a] *1979–81 to 1985–7*

Item	$ billion per annum
Terms of trade losses	2.9
Increased interest payments	2.1
Reduced net credit flows	2.4
Reduced direct investment	0.2
Total deterioration	7.6
Increased official grants	1.1
Net deterioration	6.5

Note:
[a] Excluding Nigeria.
Source: Department of International Economic and Social Affairs of the United Nations Secretariat, based on data and estimates of IMF, *World Economic Outlook*, October 1987, and published in *Financing Africa's Recovery*. New York: United Nations, February 1988, p. 14.

The report admitted that this figure was subject to a wide margin of error. Nevertheless, it estimated that for the next few years SSA countries needed an extra $5 billion external resources per annum, over and above what they were expecting to receive for the rest of the decade. This was necessary to restore growth to pre-crisis levels, ease the severe import strangulation and underpin the economic reforms and structural adjustment programmes which the majority of them had adopted.

Although this was considered a conservative estimate, it was also broadly consistent with other estimates of these countries' external financing needs.

The World Bank, for example, estimated that 14 low-income, debt-distressed SSA countries with adjustment programmes in place, needed an extra $1.5 billion per annum between 1988 and 1990 to ensure their programmes stayed on track. These countries accounted for about one-quarter of the economy of Sub-Saharan Africa.

> If the same assumptions about export prospects and import requirements are applied to the rest of the region, excluding Nigeria, the financing gap rises to over $5 billion per annum.[17]

Another estimate, based on the external financing gap for each SSA country, and produced by the ECA, put the total gap for all SSA countries, excluding Nigeria, at $21 billion for the period 1986–90, or $4.2 billion per annum.

All these estimates were based on the assumption that there would be no significant improvement in the growth performance of the world economy. If, however, there were a general pick-up in world economic activity, then the size of the external financing gap would be reduced. Whether or not this happened, the gap would remain large, and the transitional costs of reforms could not be borne by SSA countries alone. Although African governments had contributed greatly to their own predicament through misguided and inappropriate policies and mismanagement, they were now committed to a process of reform, and it was incumbent on donor countries to facilitate and expedite that process.

The Wass Report argued that the gap of $5 billion per annum could be financed through a combination of debt relief measures and the provision of new funds. Briefly, its recommendations in respect of debt relief were:

(a) concessional ODA loans to low-income SSA countries that were unlikely to become creditworthy should be converted to grants;
(b) those with no prospects of becoming creditworthy in the foreseeable future, but which had an agreed medium-term structural adjustment programme in place, should have all principal and interest payments due over the next three years (that is, 1988 to 1990) rescheduled at rates of interest comparable to IDA credits and the Fund's Structural Adjustment Facility (SAF);
(c) the debts of those with better prospects of regaining creditworthiness should be rescheduled annually at below market rates of interest so as to bring future debt burdens into line with their capacity to pay;
(d) low-income countries without any prospects of becoming creditworthy should have their existing World Bank loans refinanced on highly concessional terms;

(e) low-income countries unable to service their debts on market-related terms, should have access to the Enhanced Structural Adjustment Facility (ESAF) to refinance IMF repurchases;
(f) commercial banks should, on a case-by-case basis, take special relief measures along the lines of the Warburg Proposal.

The Report estimated that these measures could provide up to $1 billion annually towards filling the gap. The rest would come mainly from various international initiatives already in hand which, if fully implemented, could provide an additional $3 billion annually. It also recommended that:

(g) the Eight Replenishment of IDA and the Fifth Replenishment of the African Development Fund should be implemented as soon as possible;
(h) the World Bank Special Programme of Assistance (SPA) for IDA-eligible SSA countries should be implemented without delay;
(i) individual donor countries should provide a substantial increase of bilateral assistance to Africa as quick-disbursing balance of payments support; and
(j) the IMF should create a facility to finance balance of payments shortfalls among low-income countries due to unforeseen circumstances. This facility, akin to its Compensatory Financing Facility (CFF) should be available as low conditionality, on a relatively automatic basis and carry concessional rates of interest.

It was anticipated that the remaining gap of $1 billion would be met through a further increase in bilateral flows.

The achievements of the Wass Report cannot be measured in practical terms. Rather, they are essentially psychological and attitudinal, though no less real for that. For one, its impartial and authoritative analysis of the crisis greatly influenced the attitude and approach of both sides. It stressed the highly differentiated nature of the crisis, and proposed a variety of options and strategies for different debts and/or categories of debtors. Secondly, it spelled out the duties, responsibilities and prerequisites of the debtors for resolving the crisis and promoting the recovery and growth of their economies – that is, their obligation to ensure that additional funds would be used effectively within a well-articulated programme of structural reforms. Thirdly, its dualistic approach of debt relief and new money provided the basis for formulating an integrated debt/development strategy in which structural adjustment programmes played a central role.

D. STABILIZATION AND IMF-SUPPORTED PROGRAMMES

Since their inception, both the IMF and the World Bank have provided various forms and levels of assistance to help SSA countries stabilize their economies and to promote long-term growth and development. It is not necessary to review the course and extent of this involvement, except to say that over the years both institutions have increased substantially the amount of resources and their involvement in the economic and financial management of these countries.

This increased involvement has not always led to an amiable or amicable relationship. It has, nevertheless, persisted and these two institutions are now the largest source of external resources to SSA countries. They also play a central role in the stabilization and the reform process. This section discusses the efforts and contribution of IMF programmes to that process.

Stabilization is traditionally the domain of the IMF, being part of its responsibility to provide funds for members facing balance of payments difficulties. Its resources are available under a variety of facilities and policies, depending on the member's balance of payments needs, the strength of its adjustment policies and the degree of conditionality attached to them. For example, members can draw automatically up to 25 per cent of their quota entitlement under its first credit tranche for minor balance of payments problems. All they have to do is demonstrate that they are making reasonable efforts to overcome their problems. Performance criteria and purchase instalments are not required, and repurchases are made in 3.5–5 years. Beyond this low conditionality funding, members enter the Fund's upper credit tranches which consist of different short-, medium-term and special facilities. Their quota entitlement, repurchase periods and operational requirements are shown in Table 4.3.

Short-term financing is provided principally under its Stand-By Arrangements (SBA) for members with temporary balance of payments difficulties. In order to qualify for assistance, members are required to have a strong and viable stabilization programme for overcoming their difficulties. They can then draw from the Fund up to specified amounts during a given period of time once they satisfy the performance criteria and other requirements outlined in the SBA. Most SBAs run for 12 to 18 months, though many of them have been extended to three years. Drawings usually take place in instalments; and repayments to the Fund are made 3.5–5 years after each purchase.

The Fund's medium-term or Extended Financing Facility (EFF) was introduced in 1974 to assist members whose balance of payments problems are structural and macroeconomic in origin. It provides funds for longer periods and in larger amounts than allowed under the usual credit tranches. EFF

Table 4.3 IMF financing facilities and arrangements

Facility	Period (years)	Quota entitlement (%)	Repurchase (years)	Principal conditions
Stand-By Arrangements (SBAs) (short-term) [a,b]	(i) 1–1.5 (ii) 3 (max)	90–110 annual 270–330 400–440 (cumulative)	3.5–5	Performance criteria; disbursement by instalments (phased payment)
Extended Financing Facility (EFF) (medium-term)[a,b]	3 4 (max)	140 p.a. 440 (cum.)	4.5–10	Performance criteria; disbursement by instalment. Comprehensive stab. prog; detailed outline for first 12 months.
Enlarged Access Policy (additional)	Additional to SBA and EFF. Apportioned between members' ordinary quotas and market funds.		3.5–7	Market rate of interest dependent on Fund's cost of borrowing.
Compensatory and Contingency Financing Facility (CCFF)	Based on a formula.			Show willingness to co-operate with Fund to find appropriate solution to balance of payments problem. Temporary; beyond member's control.
export shortfall[c]		40	3.5–5	
excess cereal import costs[c]		17	3.5–5	
contingency financing[d]		40	3.5–5	
optional tranche[c,e]		25	3.5–5	
combined[f]		122	3.5–5	

Buffer Stock Financing Facility (BSFF)			45	3–5	
Structural Adjustment Facility (SAF)[a]	3	1st 2nd 3rd	20 (70) 30 20	5.5–10	Provided on concessional terms to low-income countries; PFPs. Detailed annual prog. prior to disbursement; performance criteria; phased payments semi-annually.
Enhanced Structural Adjustment Facility (ESAF)[a]	3		250	5.5–10	As above.

Notes

[a] Disbursements may exceed the limits in exceptional circumstances.
[b] Lower limits temporarily suspended from November 1990 to 31 December 1991.
[c] Until end of 1991, access for export shortfalls, cereal import excesses and the optional tranche may alternatively be used to compensate an excess in oil import costs.
[d] A sub-limit of 35% applies on account of deviations in interest rates.
[e] May be used to supplement the amounts for export shortfalls, excess in cereal import costs or contingency financing.
[f] When a member has a satisfactory balance of payments position (except for the effect of an export shortfall or an excess in cereal costs) a joint limit of 105% of quota applies.

Source: *IMF Survey*, Washington, D.C.: IMF, September 1991, p. 16.

usually runs for three years (four in exceptional circumstances) and must be supported by a comprehensive stabilization programme outlining the objectives and policies for the whole period. In addition, a detailed statement of the policies and measures to be followed during the initial 12-month period is required. Members have to meet certain performance criteria and drawings are by instalments. Repurchases are made in 4.5–10 years.

Funding provided under SBA and EFF is supplemented by the Fund's Enlarged Access Policy. This facility enables members whose balance of payments needs exceed their quota entitlement to have access to additional funding. They are raised by the Fund specifically for this purpose, and attract a higher rate of interest which is related to the Fund's own cost of borrowing, and must be repaid 3.5–7 years after purchase. The Fund's Enlarged Access Policy is reviewed annually.

The Fund's Compensatory and Contingency Financing Facility (CCFF) is comprised of two main elements. The first (compensatory) provides resources for members facing an export shortfall or an excessive increase in cereal import costs due to factors beyond their control. The second element (contingency) helps members with a Fund-supported adjustment programme in place to maintain the momentum of their adjustment efforts in the face of unanticipated adverse external shocks, such as a fall in export prices. Drawings under this Facility are additional to those allowed under the Fund's regular credit tranches. Repurchases are made in 3.5–5 years.

The CCFF is clearly of major significance to SSA countries, given their increasing dependence on cereal imports. It was revised in April 1990, mainly to increase its flexibility to suit the particular needs of members. However, they have made limited use of it so far. The Fund also operates a Buffer Stock Financing Facility (BSFF) to help members meet the cost of their contribution to approved international commodity buffer stock schemes, provided they can demonstrate balance of payments needs, and are prepared to cooperate with the Fund in seeking appropriate solutions to balance of payments problems.[18]

In order to obtain an SBA, a member has to sign a letter of intent agreeing to undertake a specific set of policies and reforms. Typically, these include measures to control the money supply, restrict domestic credit, reduce the budgetary deficit by imposing strict limits on government spending and raising additional revenues, cut subsidies, decrease real wages, devalue the domestic currency and liberalize markets.

These measures are intended to reduce aggregate demand and return the economy to more sustainable levels of spending. Government policy-induced distortions will be eliminated, allowing relative prices to reflect the scarcity value of factor endowments. Credit and money supply control will reduce inflation, as will lower levels of public expenditure and increased taxation.

Lower real wages will reduce costs and raise profits, leading to greater private sector investment and growth.

Table 4.4 *Use of SBA and EFF arrangements by SSA countries up to 30 April 1990*

Country	Number of arrangements	Amount approved (SDR m)
Burundi	9	54.00
Cameroon	1	69.53
Central African Republic	7	70.40
Congo	4	31.10
Côte d'Ivoire	6	1003.25
Equatorial Guinea	3	14.70
Gabon	3	190.69
Gambia	6	38.99
Ghana	11	999.80
Guinea	3	49.60
Kenya	8	946.08
Liberia	18	285.95
Madagascar	9	252.93
Malawi	8	166.24
Mali	12	137.34
Mauritania	6	94.41
Mauritius	7	244.23
Niger	4	57.59
Nigeria	2	1125.00
Rwanda	5	17.00
Senegal	8	500.43
Sierra Leone	8	277.68
Somalia	13	204.91
Sudan	11	1023.50
Tanzania	4	254.30
Togo	8	135.28
Uganda	5	252.50
Zaire	10	1063.56
Zambia	9	1797.30
Zimbabwe	2	337.50

Source: *IMF Annual Reports*, Washington, D.C.: IMF, various issues.

Devaluation will improve the trade balance, while the removal of price controls and higher producer prices will encourage increased production of domestic foodstuffs. The liberalization of financial and money markets will lead to higher interest rates reflecting the relative scarcity of capital. Higher interest rates will also encourage the retention of higher savings in the domestic financial system and increased capital inflows. Finally, the lifting of foreign exchange controls, combined with devaluation and the removal of export taxes, import subsidies and licences, will encourage and stimulate the growth of exports.

It is clear from Table 4.4 that SSA countries have made extensive use of SBAs and EFF arrangements. Liberia topped the list with 18 arrangements, followed by Somalia (13) and Mali (12). However, the sums approved were small by comparison with the really big users – Côte d'Ivoire, Nigeria, Sudan, Zaire and Zambia, each of which exceeded 1 billion SDRs. Disbursements against these amounts were made by instalments, and depended on the implementation and/or achievement of specific reforms and targets incorporated in each arrangement. If a member failed to satisfy the requisite performance criteria, the arrangement could be extended, terminated or cancelled, depending on the circumstances, and it became ineligible for further assistance from the Fund. This happened in many cases.

Sierra Leone, which is not a large user of the Fund's facilities, had three programmes (1981, 1983 and 1987) cancelled after drawing the first tranche, mainly on account of its failure to meet the requisite performance criteria. Negotiations for a new arrangement in 1988 foundered, and Sierra Leone was declared ineligible for further IMF funding. On the other hand, Zambia relied heavily on IMF funding between 1976 and 1986 to stabilize its external position; the last SBA (230 million SDRs) and a Compensatory Financing Facility (69 million SDRs) being approved in February 1986. However, it was unable to meet most of the performance criteria, and the programme was cancelled in May 1987, when only the initial tranche of 35 million SDRs had been drawn. Also, having built up massive arrears on previous obligations, Zambia was declared ineligible for further funding from the IMF in September 1987.

Other examples can be cited. The point is that, despite having used these facilities extensively, Fund-sponsored stabilization programmes have not improved the external position of SSA countries. Indeed, many observers argue that they have been counterproductive. Given the structure of these economies, the time period was clearly too short to accommodate the changes specified by the performance criteria. Also, the IMF programmes emphasized the need for macroeconomic balances, monetary restraint and more efficient demand management, without taking account of the serious social and political costs domestically. For example, the reduction of budgetary deficits has had to be achieved mainly through cuts in public expenditure (rather than increases in tax revenues), given the short-term nature of the programmes and the need for quick results. This has led, among other things, to a loss of essential services and benefits for vulnerable groups. Also, many governments financed their budgetary deficits by borrowing from the domestic banking system, thereby fuelling domestic inflation. The excess liquidity generated went into informal activities, including the black market for foreign exchange where rates were pushed up by the pressure to transfer wealth out of the country.

(a) Structural Adjustment Facility

The Structural Adjustment Facility (SAF) was introduced in March 1986 to provide balance of payments support for low-income IDA-eligible countries with protracted balance of payments problems. The existence and operation of SAF are based on the fundamental notion that structural adjustment and growth must be mutually reinforcing. Its basic purpose was, therefore, to provide concessional, medium-term assistance to low-income countries to enable them to restore and maintain balance of payments viability while undertaking the necessary structural reforms which would enable them to achieve a high and sustainable rate of growth, and to facilitate orderly relations with creditors and a reduction in trade and payments restrictions.

SAF was created with about 2.7 billion SDRs drawn mainly from repayments on loans from the Trust Fund. It operated within a medium-term perspective of three years, and was to be available until 1991. Originally, support was limited to 47 per cent of members' quota, but this was later increased to 70 per cent. Funds are disbursed in three annual instalments, repayable semi-annually over ten years, with a five year grace period and interest at the rate of one-half of 1 per cent.

To be eligible for a SAF, a member must provide a Policy Framework Paper (PFP). This is a comprehensive three-year policy document which is prepared by the member's national authority with the joint assistance of the Fund and the World Bank. It sets out the macroeconomic and structural policy objectives and priorities for the next three-year period, the policy strategy and measures that will be adopted, estimates of the financial requirements of the adjustment programme and possible sources of funding. It is also intended as a means of catalysing and coordinating financial and technical assistance in support of the adjustment programme.

In particular, the PFP identifies the principal macroeconomic and structural constraints to higher growth and an improved external payments position. It also describes and assesses the public investment programme, its financial requirements and the role of the major aid donors. Finally, it analyses the social implications of the programme and the measures to be taken to ameliorate the adverse short-term effects on vulnerable groups within the country. It is updated at the beginning of each programme year, which provides a framework for consistent policy implementation and analysis.

The reforms outlined in the PFP are intended to increase growth, output, domestic savings and investment and mobilize additional resources; remove structural constraints and rigidities; and improve the efficiency and performance of the economy. On the external front, it contains measures to liberalize trade and exchange regimes, introduce tariff reforms, and improve the country's debt management strategy. Detailed measures are also included to deal with inflation and the domestic money supply; to reduce public expenditure; and to close, divest or rehabilitate public enterprise. In the agricultural sector, it incorporates measures to provide better infrastructure, introduce and improve ancillary services and better agronomic practices, eliminate restraints and controls on marketing and distribution, and provide better incentives and higher producer prices. Within this overall mix of policies, attention has invariably been focused on the fiscal and financial sector, closely followed by the agricultural sector.

In addition to the broad objectives and priorities, the PFP must outline the specific objectives and policies to be pursued during the first 12 months of the programme. Performance is monitored by means of a series of financial and other benchmarks which reflect the programme's key elements. Although disbursement does not directly depend on observance of these benchmarks, non-compliance would call for policy readjustments in respect of later periods in the programme.

Of the 62 members currently eligible for SAF loans, the two largest – China and India – have indicated that they do not intend to use the facility. As at 30 June 1991, a total of 35 SAFs, totalling approximately 1.97 billion SDRs, had been approved. Of these, 27, amounting to 57 per cent of total approvals, were in respect of SSA countries, making them the principal beneficiaries. Zaire alone received 203.70 million SDRs.

(b) Enhanced Structural Adjustment Facility

SAF got off to a slow start. By the end of its first year of operations only 327 million SDRs had been committed. However, it was generally felt that its resources were not enough and that additional concessional funds would be needed to help the poorest members undertake the necessary structural reforms to achieve long-term sustainable growth. Accordingly, the Enhanced Structural Adjustment Facility (ESAF) was created in December 1987, with an additional 6 billion SDRs financed partly with funds from SAF's undisbursed balances, but mostly with grants and special loans from a variety of sources including several middle-income developing countries. This brought the Fund's total concessional resources to 9 billion SDRs, to be used to help the poorest members undertake strong three-year macroeconomic and structural programmes to improve their balance of payments and encourage growth.

ESAF became operational in April 1988. Its objectives, eligibility and basic procedural features, including the role of PFPs, are virtually the same as for SAF. Differences between the two facilities relate mainly to access, monitoring and funding. In addition, the measures supported by ESAF are geared towards achieving a substantial strengthening of the member's balance of payments position over the three years of the programme. The same 62 low-income members are eligible for ESAF loans. However, China has again indicated that it does not intend to apply for ESAF, unless its balance of payments position deteriorates markedly. Eligible members can request assistance under either facility, but not under both at the same time. Originally, requests for ESAF resources had to be approved before the end of November 1989. This has now been extended to November 1992 to take account of the new four-year ESAF arrangements.

ESAF operates on a case-by-case basis, with particular emphasis being placed on the borrower's balance of payments needs and the strength of its adjustment efforts. Each ESAF arrangement is financed by the member's unused access to SAF and its quota entitlement under ESAF. The latter is subject to a maximum of 250 per cent of quota which may be increased to 350 per cent in exceptional circumstances. The terms of repayment are identical to those of SAF. The same basic monitoring procedures apply to both facilities, though additional performance criteria are required under ESAF, for example, a mid-year review of policies and performance. However, unlike SAF, disbursements are made semi-annually.

Again, SSA countries have been the principal beneficiaries of ESAF. Up to the end of June 1991, 15 arrangements with a total value of 1.83 billion SDRs were approved. Twelve of these, amounting to 1.35 billion SDRs, or 70 per cent of total drawings, were in favour of SSA countries, with Ghana (388.55 million SDRs) and Kenya (241.40 million SDRs) being the main recipients. Table 4.5 gives the details of drawings under SAF and ESAF by SSA countries since these two facilities were instituted.[19]

Three points emerge from this brief review. First, the IMF has extended the scope of its activities beyond the conventional role of providing short-term, temporary balance of payments finance for stabilization purposes. It now provides medium- and extended term financing for promoting economic reforms and structural adjustment programmes as well. While, conceptually, it is possible to differentiate the two roles in terms of their respective functions and time-frames, these differences become blurred and largely artificial in practice. Both programmes are not only mutually supportive,

Table 4.5 Use of SAF and ESAF arrangements by SSA countries up to 30 June 1991

Facility	Arrangement dates Approved	Expiry	Amount approved (SDRs million)	Unused balance
SAF				
Benin	16.6.89	15.6.92	21.91	15.65
Burkina Faso	13.3.91	12.3.94	22.11	15.80
Burundi	8.8.86	8.7.89	29.89	–
Central African Rep.	1.6.87	31.5.90	21.28	6.08
Chad	30.10.87	29.10.90	21.42	6.12
Comoros	21.6.91	20.6.94	3.15	3.15
Equatorial Guinea	7.12.88	6.12.91	12.88	9.20
Gambia	17.9.86	23.11.88	11.97	–
Ghana	6.11.87	9.11.88	143.15	–
Guinea	29.7.87	28.7.90	40.53	11.58
Guinea-Bissau	14.10.87	13.10.90	5.25	1.50
Kenya	1.2.88	15.5.89	99.40	–
Lesotho	29.6.88	28.6.91	10.57	3.02
Madagascar	31.8.87	15.5.89	46.48	–
Mali	5.8.88	4.8.91	35.56	10.16
Mauritania	22.9.86	24.5.89	20.34	–
Mozambique	8.6.87	7.6.90	42.70	–
Niger	17.11.86	12.12.88	23.59	–
Rwanda	24.4.91	23.4.93	30.66	21.90
São Tomé & Príncipe	2.6.89	1.6.92	2.80	2.00
Senegal	10.11.86	21.11.88	54.04	–
Sierra Leone	14.11.86	13.11.89	11.58	–
Somalia	29.6.87	28.6.90	30.94	22.10
Tanzania	30.10.87	29.10.90	74.90	–
Togo	16.3.88	31.5.89	26.88	–
Uganda	15.6.87	17.4.89	69.72	–
Zaire	15.5.87	14.5.90	203.70	58.20
ESAF				
Gambia	23.11.88	22.11.91	20.52	3.42
Ghana	9.11.88	8.11.91	388.55	48.00
Kenya	15.5.89	14.5.92	241.40	60.47
Lesotho	22.5.91	21.5.94	18.12	15.86
Madagascar	15.5.89	14.5.92	76.90	25.63
Malawi	15.7.88	14.7.91	55.80	–
Mauritania	24.5.89	23.5.92	50.85	33.90
Mozambique	1.6.90	31.5.93	85.40	61.00
Niger	12.12.88	11.12.91	47.18	23.59
Senegal	21.11.88	20.11.91	144.67	25.53
Togo	31.5.89	30.5.92	46.08	15.36
Uganda	17.4.89	16.4.92	179.28	39.84

Source: *IMF Annual Reports*, various issues, and updated by *IMF Survey*, 12 August 1991.

they often operate simultaneously in the same country. Also, the performance criteria are virtually the same for both programmes. It is difficult, therefore, to know where one stops and the other takes over.

Secondly, the creation of the additional lending facilities has significantly changed the role and relationship of the Fund with its members. It now plays a more active role in the formulation and implementation of their domestic policy reforms. It sets the economic and financial objectives and targets to be achieved; establishes the priorities and parameters for reform and recovery; assesses their performance and progress and provides a major share of the necessary funding. Its participation and/or cooperation are thus crucial to the success of their stabilization and adjustment programmes. On the other hand, its increased involvement in the determination and management of their domestic affairs has led to a deterioration in its relationship with many members. Some of them have refused to accept the Fund's conditionality, and consequently, are not eligible for its assistance.

Thirdly, the Fund has several facilities specifically earmarked for its low-income member countries. Although these started as *ad hoc* measures to deal with specific situations, they have gradually been liberalized and extended in scope, access and other operational respects. They have, in fact, become an integral and increasingly important part of its on-going activities in these countries. The IMF has thus made a major contribution to the conduct and course of structural adjustment in SSA countries.

E. WORLD BANK ADJUSTMENT PROGRAMMES

(a) A Brief Overview

Structural adjustment loans (SALs) or policy-based lending was introduced by the World Bank in 1980 in response to the massive macro-imbalances and external shocks experienced by its members. These non-project loans provide medium-term funding (up to five years) to finance a programme of reforms and institutional changes which members agree to implement in order to eliminate external imbalances and stabilize their economies, improve the management and utilization of domestic resources, raise the level of domestic savings, promote recovery and put their economies on a path of sustainable long-term growth and development.

Basically, SALs are intended to achieve the same macro-goals of stabilization and structural reform as the IMF's adjustment facilities. There is thus a considerable amount of overlap and complementarity in terms of objectives and policy instruments of both sets of measures. The stabilization elements of SALs, for example, require the recipient countries to adopt more or less the same expenditure-reducing and expenditure-switching measures as SAFs and ESAFs, such as reducing the rate of domestic absorption, cutting subsidies and increasing public revenues, switching expenditure from non-tradables to tradables and exports, and improving domestic economic management.

The structural adjustment requirements of SALs include a variety of policy reforms designed to increase the mobilization and effective utilization of resources; raise the level of domestic savings and investment; rationalize and improve efficiency in the public sector, including deregulation, divestiture, privatization and other measures to reduce the government's share and control of productive activities; liberalize trade and exchange rate regimes in order to increase exports and international competitiveness; and strengthen the country's institutional capacity for reform and recovery and put the economy on a path of sustainable growth and development.

To achieve these ends, the World Bank structural adjustment programmes require the borrowing countries to adopt specific reforms in pricing policy, trade and exchange rate regimes, marketing and distribution systems and institutions. These include:

(i) the reduction and/or elimination of price controls;
(ii) deregulation of markets and the introduction of an appropriate structure of price incentives: 'getting prices right', as it is called;
(iii) the removal of subsidies on commodities and services and/or targeting them to the appropriate groups;
(iv) the reduction of tariffs and other restrictive measures on imports;
(v) appropriate incentives for export promotion and expansion;
(vi) devaluation in order to improve the balance of payments position and make exports more competitive;
(vii) reform of the budgetary and taxation system;
(viii) control of domestic inflation and the money supply;
(ix) positive real rates of interest;
(x) wage controls and the shedding of surplus labour in the public sector, including parastatals;
(xi) improved efficiency in the public sector along with switching resources to the private sector;
(xii) institutional and human resources capacities.

Table 4.6 shows the various types of policy measures requested in return for SAL finance between 1988 and 1991. The need to reduce both the budgetary deficit and the balance of payments deficit is heavily underscored. Without exception, all the loans made during this period required the recipients to improve export incentives and to reform budgetary and fiscal systems

in order to reduce external imbalances and improve the manag
domestic economy. Also, they emphasize the need to 'get pri

Table 4.6 *Types of policy measure requested in return for adju finance, 1988–91*

Measure	Percentage of policy-based operations[a] subject to conditions in this area
Trade policy	
Remove quantitative restrictions on imports	86
Reduce tariffs	43
Improve export incentives, etc.	100
Resource mobilization	
Macro framework; reform budget or taxes	100
Positive real interest rates	79
Improve financial performance of public enterprise/privatization	64
Raise aggregate public investment rate	14
Efficient use of resources	
Revise priorities of public investment programme	57
Raise agricultural prices	36
Dissolve or reduce powers of marketing boards	36
Reduce or eliminate some agricultural input subsidies	50
Energy pricing and conservation	43
User charges for social services	21
Institutional reforms	
Development bank reform	50
Improve support for agriculture (marketing, etc.)	14
Improve support for industry	21
Abolish/reduce price controls	71
Distribution of income	
Minimum levels of specific social expenditures	14

Note

[a] Policy-based operations denotes all Structural Adjustment Financial sector, and Trade Policy/Export Development, and Sectoral Adjustment Loans.

Source: ALCID Index, World Bank Country Policy Department, Washington, D.C.: World Bank (data provided by Paul Mosley (mimeo)).

for example, abolishing price controls, liberalizing domestic markets and introducing positive real rates of interest.

Two other points of significance are (i) the overwhelming emphasis on agricultural prices which characterized the early SALs has been reduced. A study by Mosley covering the period 1980–86 showed that 73 per cent of all SALs were subject to conditions in this area.[20] As Table 4.6 shows the proportion is now down to 36 per cent; (ii) SALs now require specific conditions in respect of the distribution of income. This is a major change which goes some way towards meeting the criticism that the earlier SALs lacked a social dimension.

SALs were introduced as a purely temporary facility to provide quick-disbursing finance for general balance of payments support and import cover to enable the recipients to maintain the appropriate level of investment and growth envisaged in their reform programme. The four SALs approved in 1980 amounted to $370 million, or 3 per cent of total World Bank commitments. However, they quickly established themselves as a permanent instrument of the Bank's lending operations, and throughout the 1980s both the members of SALs and the total amount of resources committed rose dramatically. In 1991 the World Bank committed some $5.9 billion, or 26 per cent of its total lending commitments, to 46 SALs. This was an increase of about $1.7 billion on the previous year's operation. Most of this was due to increased adjustment lending to countries in Eastern and Central Europe (Poland $780 million, Czechoslovakia $450 million and Hungary $250 million).

In addition to SALs, the World Bank provides sector adjustment loans (SECALs). Although the distinction between the two is not always clear-cut, generally speaking, SECALs support more narrowly focused programmes of reform and restructuring. These range from major changes in macroeconomic policies and institutions in sectors such as agriculture, trade, industry and finance to the establishment of an appropriate framework for investment in energy and education. SECALs may be disbursed over a five year period.

Being less comprehensive in scope, SECALS can be targeted on specific activities. This makes them suitable for countries which, on account of their limited institutional and human resources capacities, cannot effectively implement a full SAL. Many SSA countries fall into this category. In Ghana, for example, two Reconstruction Import Credits (1983 and 1985) and an Export Rehabilitation Credit (1984) were followed by a SAL in 1986. They are also suitable for situations in which a country's structural adjustment programme runs into difficulties, and has to be abandoned in favour of a more limited approach. Bolivia is a case in point. Notwithstanding the failure of its first SAL in 1980, the Bank supported two further Reconstruction Import Credits. In other cases, such as Turkey and Korea, SECALs have been used to strengthen and complement the adjustment process initiated by SALs. Finally, being less intrusive in the internal affairs of the recipient country, SECALs are often more politically acceptable than SALs.

Additionally, the World Bank provides hybrid loans in support of an on-going structural adjustment programme which itself is financed by a SECAL or an SBA from the Fund. These loans are used to finance investment in specific sectors or a time-slice of a sectoral investment programme. They are also used to finance recurrent expenditure if the member experiences temporary budgetary problems, or where there are significant start-up costs associated with a reconstructed sectoral strategy. In 1986, for example, a hybrid loan of $34 million was used to finance part of the education budget of the Ghana Education Sector Credit.

In terms of the type of loans disbursed, there has been a marked preference for SECALs, with the result that both the number and value of these loans have risen sharply over the years. They are now the principal form of the Bank's policy-based lending programme. Twenty-five SECALs with a total value of $3.4 billion, or 15 per cent of all the Bank's lending commitments, were made in 1991. Ten of these SECALs went to SSA countries. They also received 11 of the 21 SALs disbursed in 1991.[21]

(b) The Special Facility for Sub-Saharan Africa

This facility was created by the World Bank in May 1985 in response to the recommendations of the Please Report which, inter alia, called for a special facility to support reform programmes in SSA countries.[22] It was administered by IDA which was authorized to receive contributions from two main sources: (i) direct contributions from donors, and (ii) resources for special joint financing. It began operations in July 1985 and lasted three years.

During that time it mobilized almost $2 billion, of which $1.2 billion were direct contributions from 14 donor countries. The principal contributors were France ($244 million) and Italy ($222 million). The Bank itself contributed $150 million. Six countries contributed some $791 million to the Special Joint Financing Facility. Of these Japan ($338 million), Germany ($168 million) and the United Kingdom ($128 million) were the main contributors.[23]

These funds were used to provide 'African Facility Credits' and Special Joint Financing to IDA-eligible SSA countries, which had already undertaken, or were committed to undertaking, appropriate medium-term structural adjustment programmes and institutional reforms. Eligibility was determined in a flexible manner, taking into account the specific circumstances of each country. The African Facility Credits were disbursed on the usual IDA terms (50 years maturity, including a ten-year grace period, and subject to an annual 0.75 per cent service charge and a yearly 0.50 per cent commitment charge), and used to help finance quick-disbursing lending operations in support of structural and sectoral adjustment as well as economic rehabilitation and emergency reconstruction programmes.

By the end of June 1988 just over $1 billion Special Facility Credits had been disbursed, with a further $786 million as Special Joint Financing. In addition, IDA provided credits to the value of almost $1.6 billion to finance its own projects, making an overall total of $3.4 billion, or 43 per cent of all the World Bank's concessional funding disbursed between 1985 and 1988. These credits were used to finance projects for structural adjustment, road rehabilitation and maintenance, economic recovery credits, agriculture sector adjustment and rehabilitation, transport and industrial sector assistance. Of all disbursements, 11 per cent went on projects related to the agricultural sector, reflecting the Bank's wish to reverse the systematic and long-standing bias against agriculture and the rural areas. In all, some 49 projects in 25 SSA countries were supported. Ghana did best with five projects. Guinea, Madagascar, Niger and Zaire each had three, and the rest either one or two.[24]

(c) The Special Programme of Assistance

The case for a Special Programme of Assistance (SPA) to low-income debt-distressed countries in Africa which face exceptional difficulties was outlined in a joint paper by the World Bank and the IMF.[25] Basically, this paper argued that these countries needed additional external assistance beyond what they were presently getting in order to enable them to pursue and intensify creditable medium-term structural adjustment programmes. It identified a number of financing options for increasing the volume and effectiveness of external resources and for providing additional concessional debt relief. Based on a sample of 14 of the largest low-income debt-distressed countries with structural adjustment programmes in Sub-Saharan Africa, it estimated that in order to maintain manageable debt service levels and to restore per capita imports, these countries needed an extra $1.5 billion per annum over the three years 1988–90.[26]

The SPA was endorsed by the Development Committee in September 1987, and later launched at a multi-donor conference in Paris in December 1987. At that meeting a number of donor countries and international organizations pledged themselves to provide a total of $6.4 billion in highly concessional, quick-disbursing finance between 1988 and 1990 to low-income debt-distressed SSA countries with severe debt problems and which were pursuing growth-oriented policies backed by structural adjustment programmes. These extra funds were to be provided as grants or concessional loans on terms which were no harder than IDA credits (or a combination of both). More than 50 per cent were to be in support of adjustment, and disbursed under formal co-financing agreements with the Bank, with the rest as highly coordinated financing. Most donors agreed to provide their contribution as untied assistance. In all, about two-thirds of the total was untied assistance. The programme was to be administered in a flexible manner and on a case-by-case basis. Details of individual donor commitments are given in Table 4.7.

For a country to be eligible for assistance, it had to satisfy three basic criteria. First, it had to be poor, in the sense of being eligible for IDA credits rather than IBRD loans. Secondly, its projected debt service ratio for 1988–90 must exceed 30 per cent; and thirdly, it must actually be pursuing a

Table 4.7 Individual donor commitments for financing the SPA, 1988–90

Donor governments and institutions	Adjustment financing under the Programme (3 yr) ($US millions)	(annual)	Terms	Tying Status
Afr. Dev. Fund	360	120	IDA	untied
Austria	85	28	concessional loan	mostly tied
Belgium	30	10	mostly grant	partial
Canada	355	118	all grant	some untied
Denmark	150	50	all grant	partial
European Community[a]	600	200	all grant	mostly untied
Finland	194	65	mostly grant	partial
France	800	267	concessional loan	mostly untied
Germany	275	92	mostly grant	untied
Italy	700	233	all grant	tied
Japan[b]	500	250	grant/concessional loan	untied
Netherlands	300	100	all grant	partial
Norway	210	70	all grant	untied
Spain	30	10	concessional loan	mostly tied
Sweden	675	225	all grant	mostly untied
Switzerland	150	50	all grant	mostly untied
United Kingdom	450	150	all grant	tied
United States	570	190	all grant	mostly untied
Total	6434	2228		

Notes

[a] Including the European Investment Bank.

[b] Japan's contribution covered only the first two years of the programme.

Source: World Bank.

structural adjustment programme which required quick-disbursing finance. When the programme started, 19 SSA countries were eligible, of which all but one had a SAF or an ESAF with the IMF. By mid-1989 the number had grown to 22. Since then, there have been several changes as other SSA countries have become eligible while some existing members have been declared ineligible. In 1991 the following SSA countries were eligible for the SPA: Benin, Burundi, Central African Republic, Gambia, Ghana, Guinea, Guinea-Bissau, Kenya, Madagascar, Malawi, Mali, Mauritania, Mozambique, Niger, São Tomé and Príncipe, Senegal, Tanzania, Togo, Uganda and Zambia. Somalia and Zaire became ineligible in 1990 because of weakened reform efforts. In 1991 Burkina Faso, Comoros and Rwanda were declared eligible.

The financial requirements of the SPA were based on estimates of the financing gaps of the original 19 members, and put at $13.3 billion for the

Table 4.8 Composition and projected disbursements for SSA countries eligible for the SPA[a]

Item	1988–90 Total ($US bill.).	1988–90 %[b]	1988 preliminary ($US bill.)
External financing gap	13.3	100	3.2
SPA-financing and reduction in debt service			
Additional IDA-8 disbursements	0.7	5	0.1
Increased co-financing operations	3.8	29	1.0
already committed	2.6	20	1.0
to be provided	1.2	9	–
Supplemental IDA credits	0.2	1	0.0
ESAF[c]	1.4	10	0.2
Debt relief (including on arrears)	7.2	54	1.9

Notes

[a] For the original 19 SSA countries – Burundi, Central African Republic, Gambia, Ghana, Guinea, Guinea-Bissau, Kenya, Madagascar, Malawi, Mali, Mauritania, Mozambique, Niger, São Tomé and Príncipe, Senegal, Tanzania, Togo, Uganda and Zaire.

[b] Figures do not add to total due to rounding.

[c] Projections for the ESAF are illustrative. As at the end of 1988, $0.8 billion had been committed from the ESAF. Projected disbursements from the ESAF are taken into account in estimating the external financing gap. SAF disbursements were $0.3 billion in 1988.

Source: Development Committee no. 21, *Progress of Initiatives to Benefit Sub-Saharan Africa*, Washington D.C.: Development Committee. Table 4, p. 15 (as amended).

three years. This extra funding was to come from five main sources, namely (a) additional IDA-8 disbursements; (b) increased co-financing and coordinated financing operations; (c) supplemental IDA credits; (d) additional IMF resources from ESAF; and (e) greater debt relief. The Bank monitors progress under each component semi-annually, though only the first three are under its direct management. Table 4.8 shows the composition and projected disbursements of the SPA for the original 19 eligible SSA countries.

Additional IDA-8 disbursements were to be financed by the Eighth Replenishment of IDA, at least 50 per cent of which was earmarked for SSA countries. This would provide an additional $1 billion, of which $700 million would go to the original 19 eligible countries. About 60 per cent of these funds would be quick-disbursing to allow IDA to step up its disbursement rate, assuming, of course, that the recipients' adjustment programmes stayed on track.

Increased co-financing operations were the linchpin of the SPA. It called for an extra $1.2 billion for (i) co-financing operations linked to specific IDA adjustment projects, and (ii) providing highly concessional, quick-disbursing coordinated finance not linked directly to a specific adjustment project but which, nevertheless, is crucial to the success of the recipient's adjustment programme; for example, the formulation, implementation and monitoring of programmes, closer coordination of procurement procedures and timely disbursements.

Supplemental IDA credits (the so-called Fifth Dimension) were intended to alleviate the debt burden of IBRD loans on the debt-distressed countries which had ceased to qualify for World Bank lending and become eligible only for IDA credits. Basically, the scheme involved using a proportion of IDA repayments on earlier credits to supplement adjustment credits to IDA-eligible countries with outstanding loans that were pursuing adjustment programmes and were current on their payments to the Bank. The amounts available annually were to be distributed among eligible countries in proportion to the interest due on IBRD loans when the debtors were creditworthy.

Fifty-four per cent of funding for the SPA was to come from increased debt relief on concessional terms. It was estimated that this would provide $7.2 billion, or about 40 per cent of the projected debt service obligations between 1988 and 1990 of the 19 eligible countries. The modalities of this component have been articulated and operationalized by the Paris Club as the so-called Toronto Terms. The amounts of relief received by individual SSA countries are given in Appendix A.5.

The SPA was supported and supplemented by three other initiatives. The first of these, the Regional Project Facility, provided a total of $10 million for identifying, appraising and monitoring programmes aimed at alleviating poverty and for financing studies on the social dimensions of adjustment in the recipient countries. Secondly, a World Bank Task Force on Food Security was set up in order to help SSA countries achieve the goal of food security by the end of the century; and thirdly a Council of African Advisers was appointed to provide, among other things, independent and objective advice on the role of the Bank in Africa.

In its assessment of the SPA, the World Bank reported that although several SSA countries had experienced severe problems, there were clear signs of progress on many fronts. Additional external resources had been mobilized, gross disbursements were up and the external balances of most recipient countries had improved. It produced a variety of statistics to show that, in the aggregate as well as at the sectoral level, countries with strong reform programmes had outperformed those with weak or no reform programmes. Between 1988 and 1990 the eligible countries received about $17.5 billion in adjustment support, of which gross disbursements from the donors came to $7.5 billion. The rest was due to debt relief and rescheduling operations. Nevertheless, the Bank argued that most of these reforms were of a tentative nature and needed to be followed up with more comprehensive changes.[27]

This, no doubt, helped to convince the donors that the SPA should continue beyond 1990, the date when it was due to expire. Consequently, a second phase (SPA II) was inaugurated in October 1990, when 18 donors pledged a further $7.4 billion in co-financing and coordinated finance in support of structural adjustment in SSA countries for another three years (1991–3).[28] IDA credits, including resources from its Ninth Replenishment, were expected to provide a further $2.9 billion, and contributions from the IMF under its various adjustment financing facilities were estimated at between $1 and $2 billion. No figures were put on the amount of debt relief to be provided under SPA II, but it was expected that, after relief and rescheduling on Toronto Terms, the debt service payments of active SPA countries would average about 25 per cent of their expected export earnings between 1991 and 1993. Taken together, these funds were considered sufficient to cover the financing needs of all the eligible SSA countries. According to the World Bank, 'the task, then, is to commit, manage, and disburse the resources of SPA II in a way that facilitates their efficient use'.[29]

F. THE AFRICAN ALTERNATIVE FRAMEWORK

While SSA countries accept the need for structural adjustment, many argue that the World Bank–IMF model is inappropriate for Africa because it is based on conventional economic theory which assumes, *inter alia*, the existence of well-structured economies and perfect markets. This is not the case with African economies which are characterized by weak and disarticulated production structures and imperfect markets. Policies which are geared, therefore, to eliminating macro and financial imbalances rather than tackling fundamental structural weaknesses are unlikely to succeed.

They also dispute the assumption that Africa's external imbalance stems from excess domestic demand, over-valued exchange rates, trade controls, high and unsustainable budgetary deficits and an over-extended public sector. They blame external factors: the collapse of primary commodity prices, rising debt burdens and falling net flows of external resources. Policies which are geared, therefore, to cutting public expenditure and reducing both the budgetary and balance of payments deficits, liberalizing trade and payments regimes and privatizing large sections of the domestic economy aggravate the problem.

Further, cuts in public expenditure fall mainly on health, education and other social expenditure, with the result that the most vulnerable groups in society (that is, women and children) bear the social cost of adjustment. Also, by concentrating on short-term macro-imbalances, the World Bank–IMF model ignores the long-term goals of African countries and ultimately makes it more difficult and costly to transform their economies. This, briefly, is the background against which the ECA developed the African Alternative Framework to Structural Adjustment Programmes for Socio-economic Recovery and Transformation (AAF-SAP).[30]

According to Adedeji:

> The main thrust of AAF-SAP is its holistic nature in which the macroeconomic framework, the policy directions and measures, and the implementation strategies take into account the dynamic relationships existing among all major elements related to adjustment with transformation. Thus, the dichotomy between structural adjustment and long-term development is eliminated. The alternative framework also puts great emphasis on the full mobilisation and effective utilisation of domestic resources and the need to establish an enabling environment for sustainable development and to adopt a pragmatic approach between the public and private sectors. Above all, at the centre of the alternative framework is the human dimension – the recognition that it is only through the motivation and empowerment of people as well as the ensuring of the equitable distribution of income that development can take place on a sustainable basis. An adjustment programme that marginalises people is doomed to failure.[31]

AAF-SAP is based on the following macro-entities: (a) operative forces, (b) available resources, and (c) the basic needs and services for 'human-centred' development. The first module specifies the operative forces which influence total output, and is expressed as

$$Y = f(F1, R) \qquad (1)$$

where Y represents total output of goods and services, $F1$ is a set of parameters representing the different forces affecting the level and pattern of total output and the rate of development (for example, technology, weather, research and organizational infrastructures), and R is the available resources, domestic as well as external.

The second module defines the distribution of output and the allocation of factor incomes as

$$I = f(F2, Y) \tag{2}$$

where I represents the incomes of the various groups (households, enterprises, and so on); $F2$ is a set of parameters affecting the level and pattern of income distribution (rural–urban terms of trade, patterns of land ownership, and so on); and Y is as defined in module (1).

The third module specifies the operative forces which interact with the level and pattern of income distribution to determine the degree of domestic satisfaction of basic needs:

$$N = f(F3, I, E) \tag{3}$$

where N represents individual and collective needs, $F3$ is the index of forces determining the different needs (consumption, degree of poverty, etc); I is as defined in module 2; and E represents the gap between production and needs (imports, debts, and so on).[32]

AAF-SAP is intended to be interactive and dynamic over time and space as well as sufficiently broad and flexible to be adopted to individual country needs and requirements. Also, it claims to integrate the social and economic interactions which conventional programmes often marginalize.

Each module has its own policy objectives. For the first module these are:

(a) enhanced production and efficient resource use;
(b) greater and more efficient domestic resource mobilization;
(c) improving human resource capacity (with a recommendation that at least 30 per cent of total government outlays should be devoted to the social sector);
(d) strengthening the scientific and technological base;
(e) vertical and horizontal integration.

The policy objectives of the second module are:

(a) establishing a pragmatic balance between the public and private sectors;

(b) creating an enabling environment for sustainable development;
(c) shifting of resources;
(d) improvements in the pattern of income distribution among different socio-economic groups.

And for the third, the following are regarded as basic:

(a) food self-sufficiency;
(b) lessening import dependence;
(c) realignment of consumption patterns with production patterns;
(d) managing debt and debt servicing.

Appendix A.6 gives a summary of the policy instruments and measures to achieve what AAF-SAP calls 'the goals of adjustment with transformation'. Additionally, some measures currently in place will have to be modified or scrapped as being inconsistent with the attainment of these goals. These are shown in Appendix A.7.

Figure 4.1 Sequencing of adjustment under AAF-SAP

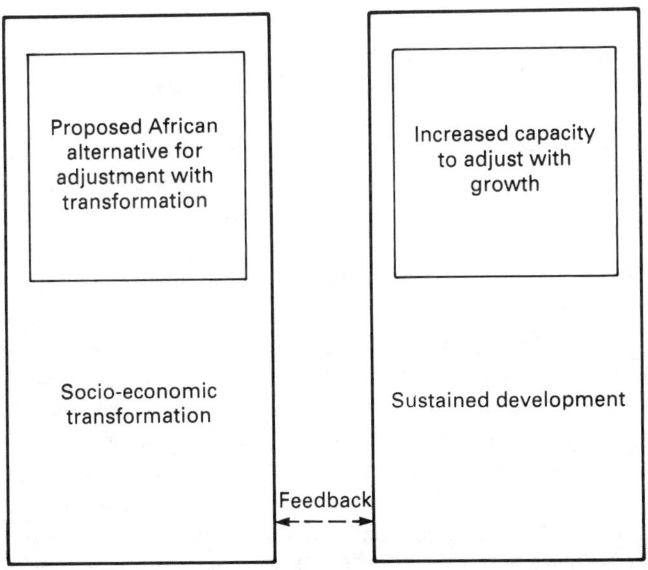

Source: African Alternative Framework to Structural Adjustment Programmes for Socio-economic Recovery and Transformation (AAF-SAP). Addis Ababa, Ethiopia: UN Economic Commission for Africa, July 1989, (Doc. E/ECA/C.M.15/6/Rev.3), Figure 4.2, p. 29.

Each country will have to choose the particular combination of policy objectives, instruments and measures to suit its own circumstances and needs which will change over time. This, in the context of sequencing outlined in Figure 4.1, it is argued, will lead to a simultaneous improvement in its capacity to adjust and transform its economy.

Finally, AAF-SAP calls on the international community to cooperate and help create the conditions necessary for the successful implementation of the African Alternative. Multilateral and bilateral donors are asked to show greater flexibility and provide additional funding during the transitional period and to support the new programmes. No estimates of the cost of AAF-SAP are given, however. It will be up to individual governments to design and cost their own programmes and to mobilize the necessary internal and external resources, though AAF-SAP does identify a variety of sources which can be tapped effectively. These include attracting additional remittances from nationals living abroad, preventing the flight of domestic capital and limiting the amount to be spent on debt servicing.

G. STRUCTURAL ADJUSTMENT IN PERSPECTIVE

Ever since the World Bank and the IMF got into structural adjustment in a systematic way, their programmes have attracted criticism from a variety of sources, but particularly the developing countries for whom these programmes were devised. In a way, this is not surprising, given (a) the nature of the relationship between the developing countries and these institutions, and (b) the efforts of both the Bank and the Fund to devise and apply a general model of policy reform requirements to fit all debtor countries' circumstances. What is surprising is the extent to which the focus of criticism has shifted between the two institutions. In the past, this was concentrated mainly on the role of the IMF and conditionality attached to its lending facilities. The operations of the World Bank were regarded on balance, as sympathetic and supportive of the development needs and aspirations of developing countries. However, with the introduction of policy-based lending, the focus of criticism has shifted to the Bank's structural adjustment programmes which are regarded by many developing countries as anti-development.

While this has served to deflect some of the heat from the Fund, it portrays a fundamental misunderstanding of the role and responsibility of each institution for implementing and administering structural adjustment and the new relationship which exists between them. They now cooperate in the coordination and administration of their lending policies and facilities for financing stabilization and structural adjustment in recipient countries. Further, their lending operations are underpinned by a system of cross-conditionality which complements each other's activities. In effect, therefore, structural adjustment is an integrated process involving both the Bank and the Fund.

Within this process, the Fund's role is absolutely crucial. Its so-called 'seal of approval' is really what activates adjustment. Unless a country is prepared to commit itself to a programme of reforms or adopt a series of stabilization measures approved by the Fund, it is unlikely to secure a structural adjustment programme with the Bank, receive additional funding from donors, or gain and maintain access to international capital markets. Basically, therefore, the distinction between adjusting and non-adjusting countries is determined by the simple criteria of whether or not a country accepts the Fund's conditionality and the extent to which it complies with them.

This not only puts the Fund in the driving seat, so to speak, but gives rise to some spurious divisions and comparisons. For one, the distinction between adjusting and non-adjusting countries is largely artificial and cannot be justified by either needs or the superior performance of the recipient countries. All SSA countries, for example, need a substantial injection of external assistance to meet the immediate economic crisis facing them as well as to finance their recovery and long-term growth. However, only the adjusters, or those who accept conditionality, qualify for and receive external funding for structural adjustment, although the evidence on their superior economic performance is, at best, patchy and open to question.

Secondly, making the IMF's 'seal of approval' a *sine qua non* of structural adjustment financing could well encourage countries to enter into adjustment for the wrong reasons. Given that this is the only way to gain access to additional external funding, countries may over-commit themselves or agree to various reforms in order to win the approval of both the Fund and the Bank, only to find that things start going wrong once they are in adjustment. For example, their programmes may be blown off course through no fault of their own. They may under-perform, fail to comply with specific policy requirements, or they may simply abandon the programmes at the first sign of trouble. It does not then greatly matter whether they entered negotiations in good faith and subsequently had a run of bad luck, or whether they had no intention of complying with the conditions and requirements of adjustment, the results are the same: (i) many abandoned programmes, (ii) several false starts, (iii) low compliance rates, (iv) wasted resources, and (v) an indifferent record of performance.

One can, of course, argue that these results are inevitable, given (a) the nature and scope of structural adjustment, (b) mis-specification of the problems of adjustment, stereotyping of conditions in developing countries and the blanket application of conditionality, and (c) the price of learning to adapt to new roles and respond to situations and challenges which were not foreseen when these institutions were established. One can also argue that there has been a considerable improvement in the design and implementation of structural adjustment programmes over the last decade, and that the second generation of adjustment programmes are more flexibly administered and responsive to the needs of the recipient countries. They also include a social dimension, something which the first generation lacked, and which made them particularly sensitive to criticism.

Basically, this is the view of the Fund and the Bank. They accept that mistakes have been made in design and implementation, the poverty impact and social costs of adjustment neglected or under-estimated, that progress has been slow and indeterminate and results difficult to quantify. Nevertheless, they argue that adjustment is necessary for the recovery and long-term development of the recipient countries, and on balance, the reformers have outperformed the non-reformers. Consequently, notwithstanding its indifferent record, developing countries should persist with adjustment. For their part, both institutions were more exercised with such questions as the ability of countries to sustain adjustment in the face of external stocks; the variability of performance between countries; why recipient countries abandoned structural adjustment programmes; the reasons for low compliance rates; institutional rigidities and supply responses in low-income performing countries; and, government commitment and popular support for reforms.

These issues were addressed by the Bank in an extensive evaluation of its experience with adjustment lending over a ten year period.[33] The study compared the relative performance, in terms of growth and resource balance, of a group of 30 countries which had received adjustment loans before 1985, in order to establish whether there was a trade-off between an increase in growth rates and a reduction in the resource balance (goods and non-factor services) in the balance of payments. Its calculations were based on changes in the average value of the two variables over a period of three years after and three years before adjustment lending. Its analysis indicated a very variable experience among the group. In 12 countries, the resource balance (adjusted for the terms of trade) was reduced at the cost of growth (for example, Malawi, Côte d'Ivoire and the Philippines). In five, an increase in growth was accompanied by a higher resource gap (for example, Ghana, Senegal and Yugoslavia). In another 12 countries, there was an increase in GDP growth and a reduction in the resource gap (for example, Korea, Turkey and Uruguay) and for Uganda, there was both a decrease in GDP and an increase in the resource gap.

The study also compared the performance of the reformers with that of non-reformers, and concluded that, on balance, the former out-performed the latter. Within the reforming group, middle-income countries did better than low-income countries. The below average performance of SSA countries was explained by the legacy of deep-seated structural problems. In its own words,

> Inadequate infrastructure, poorly developed markets, rudimentary industrial sectors, and severe institutional and managerial weaknesses in the public and private sectors have proved unexpectedly serious as constraints to better performance – especially in the poor countries of SSA.[34]

On the question of sustainability, it argued that sound economic policies, a strong export drive, consistency of effort, credibility and commitment to reform, as well as adequate funding, were all crucial to the success of sustaining reforms. For example, inadequate funding and lags in export drive contributed greatly to Zambia's inability to sustain its reform programme in contrast to Ghana, where there was no shortage of funding and the government was fully committed to designing and implementing a very difficult programme.

Although progress was slow and variable across policy areas and individual countries, the report concluded that considerable success had been made in implementing conditionality. Data on 51 SALs and SECALs in 15 countries indicate that about 60% of all conditions were fully implemented during the loan disbursement period. In the case of SSA countries, the proportion was down to 52%. The report did however express concern over the number of waivers and delayed tranche releases due to insufficient progress in fulfilling conditions affecting close to three-quarters of all adjustment loans. This, it felt, could compromise credibility with the Bank's conditionality. It accordingly called for a tighter approach combined with greater realism and simplicity of conditions.

In their recent study of World Bank policy-based lending, Mosley, Harrigan and Toye take a different view of conditionality and its effects on adjustment.[35] They regard conditionality as a bargaining process between the Bank and the adjusting country, in which the former provides funding in exchange for a commitment by the latter to undertake a programme of reforms in accordance with agreed conditions, procedures and performance criteria. The Bank's main objective is to maximize compliance with the conditions attached to its loans so as to ensure the success of the programme. The adjusting country on the other hand, seeks to obtain the maximum amount of funding in exchange for the minimum number of reforms. It also seeks to safeguard its national sovereignty and minimize the short-term political cost of adjustment.

Notwithstanding the conflict of aims and objectives, both sides share a common interest in ensuring that the programme continues. The Bank faces internal pressure to continue to fund structural adjustment operations, and the borrowing country needs the funds. Consequently, a deal is struck. However, the parameters of negotiations are not determined by economic needs and circumstances, but by the relative bargaining strengths and power relationship of both parties.

Clearly some countries are able to strike a better deal than others. Or, to put it another way, the weaker the bargaining position of the borrower, the more conditions are likely to be attached to its adjustment programme. The authors argue, though, that even weak countries have managed to circumvent compliance with politically unacceptable conditions or the implementation of a difficult programme, since non-compliance has seldom been punished or a second tranche of funding withheld. The Bank's need to meet its lending target and avoid what they call its 'disbursement dilemma' invariably ensures that the programme will continue, although overt slippage on conditionality exceeded 40% in many cases. They conclude therefore that conditionality is not a collateral but a bargaining chip which has proved largely ineffectual.[36]

Their study uses basically the same methodology as the World Bank's, although it is based on a smaller sample of countries. It accepts that it is difficult to assess the results of structural lending, but argues that these are disappointing in relation to what was expected. Like the World Bank, it concludes that on balance, adjusting countries have done better than non-adjusters. More specifically, it shows that adjustment lending has been moderately successful in promoting growth and exports, but has had a negative effect on investment, which fell during the adjustment period in adjusting countries. Also, adjustment lending does not seem to have any effect one way or the other on the net inflow of financial resources.

Volume 2 of their study contains detailed case studies of Turkey, the Philippines, Thailand, Ghana, Malawi, Kenya, Jamaica, Guyana and Ecuador. The vast disparity of these countries' experiences in designing and implementing adjustment programmes and meeting the Bank's conditionality range from Turkey which was not only fully committed to adjustment but also did everything that was required of it, and whose adjustment programme is generally regarded as a success, to Guyana and Ecuador where the opposite was the case, and in every respect, adjustment a singular failure. Other useful comparisons emerge from their analsyis, but in the main, their conclusions are broadly in line with those of the Bank's more comprehensive study. Also, their proposals for improvement are commonsensical rather than original, and would probably be regarded by the Bank as 'work in progress'.

Although the two studies start from different perspectives, they agree that structural adjustment is here to stay. The debate is no longer whether or not to adjust but rather how to adjust; what is the most appropriate sequencing of reforms; how to improve compliance rates, indigenize adjustment and induce greater local commitment, participation and accountability; and how to sustain adjustment in the face of major external shocks and intractable problems such as the debt crisis. These problems will have to be tackled regardless of which model of adjustment is adopted. The African Alternative offers no guidance on these points. They also agree that, apart from one or two notable exceptions, SSA countries have under-performed and lagged behind other adjusters. The severe economic crisis which the region faced during the 1980s was not only largely responsible for their poor performance but strengthened the case for the introduction of the SPA, the umbrella programme under which adjustment is now devised and implemented in their case.

NOTES

1. World Bank, *Accelerated Development in Sub-Saharan Africa: An Agenda for Action* (Berg Report), Washington, D.C.: World Bank, October 1981.
2. Ibid., p. 5.
3. World Bank, *Sub-Saharan Africa: Progress Report on Development Prospects and Programs*. Washington, D.C.: World Bank, September 1983.
4. Ibid., p. 12.
5. World Bank, *Towards Sustained Development in Sub-Saharan Africa. A Joint Program of Action* (Please Report). Washington D.C.: World Bank, September 1984.
6. Ibid., pp. 3–8, *passim*..
7. See Economic Commission for Africa (ECA) Resolution no. 332 (xiv), *Development Strategy for Africa for the Third Development Decade* (E/1979/50, E/CN. 14/725); the so-called Monrovia Strategy adopted at the Fourteenth Meeting of the Conference of Heads of State and Ministers of the OAU, held in Rabat, Morocco, March 1979.
8. *The Lagos Plan of Action for the Economic Development of Africa, 1980–2000*, adopted by the Heads of State and governments at a Special Summit Conference of the Organization of African Unity in Lagos, Nigeria, April 1980.
9. 'African Priority Programme for Economic Recovery 1986–1990 (APPER)', in *Africa: United Nations Programme of Action for African Economic Recovery and Development, 1986–1990, (UNPAAERD)*. New York: United Nations Department of Public Information, Division for Economic and Social Information, June 1986.
10. *Africa: United Nations Programme of Action ... (UNPAAERD)*, pp. 14–20.
11. Ibid., p. 15.
12. See United Nations General Assembly, Document A/43/500 dated 10 August 1988: *Critical Economic Situation in Africa: United Nations Programme of Action for African Economic Recovery and Development, 1986–1990*. Mid-term review of the implementation of the United Nations Programme of Action for African Economic Recovery and Development, 1986–1990: Report of the Secretary-General.
13. Ibid., para. 61.
14. Ibid., para. 112.
15. Jan Isaken, *What Did UNPAAERD Accomplish? A Review of Development in African Economies, 1986–1990*. Norway: Fantoftvegen 38, Ch. Michelsen Institute, Department of Social Science and Development, November 1990.
16. *Financing Africa's Recovery. Report and Recommendations of the Advisory Group on Financial Flows for Africa* (Wass Report). New York: United Nations, February 1988.
17. Ibid., p. 15.
18. For a fuller discussion of these Special Facilities, see *IMF Annual Report 1990*. Washington D.C.: IMF, 1990, pp. 40–1, and *IMF Survey*, September 1991, pp. 17–18.

19. See IMF *Annual Reports* and *IMF Survey, passim*, for details of individual loans. See also Development Committee no. 26, *Progress of Initiatives to Benefit Sub-Saharan Africa*. Washington D.C.: World Bank, December 1989, pp. 21–4, for a good general review of the operation of these facilities.
20. Paul Mosley, 'Conditionality as a Bargaining Process: Structural Adjustment Lending, 1980–1986', in *Essays in International Finance*, Princeton University Series no. 168. Princeton, N.J.: Princeton University Press, October 1987, p. 5.
21. For a fuller discussion of the World Bank policy-based lending programmes, see Vittorio Corbo, Morris Goldstein and Moshin Khan (eds), *Growth-oriented Adjustment Programs*. Washington, D.C.: International Monetary Fund and the World Bank, 1987; Fahrettin Yagci, *et al.*, 'Structural Adjustment Lending: An Evaluation of Program Design', *World Bank Staff Working Paper*, no. 735, Washington, D.C.: World Bank 1985; Elliot Berg and Alan Batchelor, 'Structural Adjustment Lending: a Critical View', *World Bank CPO Discussion Paper*, no. 1985–21, Washington, D.C.: World Bank, 1985; Gerald Heillener, 'Policy-Based Program Lending: a Look at the Bank's New Role', in *Between Two Worlds: The World Bank's Next Decade*. Washington, D.C.: Overseas Development Council, 1986; 'Lending for Adjustment: an Update, *World Bank News*, Special Report, April 1988; *Adjustment Lending: An Evaluation of Ten Years of Experience*, Policy and Research Series. Washington, D.C.: World Bank, Country Economics Department, 1989; Development Committee no. 23, *Problems and Issues in Structural Adjustment*. Washington, D.C., April 1990; and *World Bank Annual Reports*.
22. See note 6.
23. For details, see *The World Bank Annual Report 1988*. Washington, D.C., World Bank, 1988, Box Table 3.1a, p. 36.
24. For details, see ibid., Box Table 3.1b, p. 37.
25. Development Committee no. 16. *Proposals for Enhancing Assistance to Low-income Countries that Face Exceptional Difficulties*. Washington, D.C., June 1988.
26. The 14 countries, representing about 35–40 per cent of the global financing requirements of SAF/IDA-eligible countries, were Gambia, Ghana, Madagascar, Mali, Mauritania, Niger, Senegal, Sierra Leone, Somalia, Tanzania, Togo, Uganda, Zaire and Zambia. For details of the methodology used and detailed estimates of individual countries, see ibid., Appendices C and D, pp. 59–113.
27. For a fuller discussion of achievements of the SPA, see *The World Bank Annual Report 1988*, pp. 86–9; Development Committee, no. 16, *Proporsals*, pp. 12–28, and *The World Bank Annual Report 1991*. Washington, D.C.: World Bank, 1991, pp. 109–14.
28. Pledges were made by Belgium, Canada, Denmark, Finland, France, Germany, Italy, Japan, Kuwait, The Netherlands, Norway, Spain, Sweden, Switzerland, the United Kingdom, the United States, the African Development Fund and the European Community.
29. *World Bank Annual Report 1991*, p. 46.
30. *African Alternative Framework to Structural Adjustment Programmes for Socio-economic Recovery and Transformation*, (commonly referred to as AAF-SAP). Addis Ababa, Ethiopia: United Nations Economic Commission for Africa, July 1989 (Doc. E/ECA/C.M.15/6/Rev.3).
31. Ibid., p. iii.
32. For a general formalization of the model, see ibid., Annex 1, pp. 55–6.
33. World Bank, *Adjustment Lending. An Evaluation of Ten Years Experience*, Washington DC; Country Economics Department, Policy, Planning Research, The World Bank, December 1988.
34. The World Bank, ibid., p. 3.
35. Paul Mosley, Jane Harrigan and John Toye, *Aid and Power. The World Bank and Policy-Based Lending, Vol. 1, Analysis and Policy Proposals*, and *Vol 2, Case Studies*, London and New York: Routledge, 1991.
36. See ibid., ch. 3 for a fuller discussion.

5. Towards Sustainable Development

A. STRATEGIES OF THE 1980S

Basically, the various proposals, initiatives and policy reforms of the 1980s fall into two main categories, reflecting the dual or two-track approach to the region's problems. In the first track were the measures which dealt specifically with the debt crisis. These were short-term, temporary, immediate and *ad hoc*. More importantly, they were expected to benefit both the debtor and the creditor countries. The former would regain their creditworthiness and access to international financial markets, and the loss and inconvenience to the latter would be minimized. This can be called the fast-track approach.

The second, or slow-track, contained an extensive array of medium- and long-term policy reforms and institutional requirements which were intended to stabilize the debtors' economies, promote recovery and put their economies on a path of sustainable long-term growth and development. The essential characteristics of this approach were, first, that the responsibility for and the cost of implementing these reforms devolved mainly on the debtor countries. Secondly, that the benefits were long-term and sustainable, and while they were slow to materialize, they would result in a more efficient and properly managed domestic economy. Thirdly, that the benefits to the creditors were long-term and indirect, and would manifest themselves in due course in a stable and more prosperous world economy, from which debtors and creditors alike would benefit.

The international dimensions of these externalities meant that the slow-track approach had to be multilateralized. No single country had the incentive or resources to finance the reforms and institutional changes required to bring about sustainable development in the debtor countries. The legitimacy and international responsibility for financing as well as monitoring progress towards this goal thus passed to the international monetary and financial institutions, principally the IMF and the World Bank. They were the only institutions with enough funds to tackle the job, but also, more importantly, they represented the collectivity of the international community of nations.

A different set of considerations dictated the pace of the fast track. On the one hand, the nature of the debt crisis required bilateral negotiations between the debtor and the creditor countries, and on the other, the outcome of these negotiations rested on such considerations as equity, balance and burden-sharing among creditors. Effectively, therefore, bilateral negotiations had to be conducted within a multilateral framework which enabled the creditors to proceed as fast and as flexibly as the most reluctant member allowed. It also enabled them to keep relief to a minimum and to concentrate on short-term, emergency situations and measures.

Although the two systems were clearly interrelated, they developed as separate and self-contained strategies, dictated largely by the practical considerations and priorities of international economic and foreign policy relations on the one hand, and the internal problems of the debtor countries on the other. The debt crisis, for example, was treated as a separate phenomenon, rather than as an integral part of the more generalized problem of economic mismanagement and the need for policy and institutional changes to sustain long-term growth and development in SSA countries. Similarly, although the link between structural adjustment and the debt crisis was recognized, policy reforms geared to the former usually ignored the impact of the latter on the debtor's economy.

This compartmentalization of policies meant that neither the debt crisis nor structural adjustment was adequately or effectively addressed. Vital linkages were ignored, discontinuities and diseconomies of scale developed, and frequent reversals of policy contributed to the general ethos of crisis management and *ad hoc*ery. Consequently, notwithstanding the substantial amount of relief which they received, SSA countries were more heavily indebted at the end of the 1980s than at the beginning. Total debts outstanding in 1989 exceeded $152 billion, almost three times their 1980 level.

The basic pattern of indebtedness has also not changed. Debts are still heavily concentrated in a few principal countries. In 1980, ten countries (Cameroon, Côte d'Ivoire, Ghana, Kenya, Nigeria, Senegal, Sudan, Tanzania, Zaire and Zambia) accounted for 62 per cent of the region's total external debts. By 1989 their share had risen to 65 per cent. Besides these principal debtors, there are several countries, such as Congo and Madagascar, for which debt totals increased threefold. In fact, no single SSA country managed to reduce the level of its external indebtedness over the decade.

Other indicators confirm that the debt crisis has worsened. By 1989, for example, scheduled debt service payments of the severely indebted low-income countries had risen to $7.5 billion, not including amounts due on IMF repurchases and charges, interest due on short-term debts, and interest on these countries' stock of $6 billion of interest arrears on long-term debt. Against this, actual service payments amounted to $2.5 billion. The rest was either rescheduled on Toronto Terms or fell into arrears.

More revealing than the growth in aggregates is the difference between scheduled and actual payments. In 1989 service payments on bilateral official debts amounted to $4.3 billion or 56 per cent of all scheduled service payments. The amount actually paid was $700 million, roughly 17 per cent of what was due. On the other hand, scheduled payments on multilateral debts amounted to $1.5 billion, whereas actual payments ran to $1 billion, 66 per cent of the amount due. Similarly, scheduled payments to private creditors was estimated at $1.8 billion (24 per cent of the total), and actual service payments to private creditors amounted to $800 million, or 44 per cent of all payments made in that year.

In other words, SSA countries honoured their obligations to multilateral financial institutions (principally the IMF and the World Bank) and private creditors at the expense of their bilateral official creditors. This repayment strategy was determined by (a) the preferred creditor status of the multilateral financial institutions whose debts cannot be rescheduled, and (b) the need for the debtors to re-establish their creditworthiness and regain access to international capital markets. Both prerequisites meant that obligations to these creditors were accorded priority over bilateral official debts.

This strategy has clearly been counterproductive. First, as debts to multilateral creditors cannot be rescheduled, they introduced a strong and increasing element of inflexibility in the debtor's ability and scope for devising an effective debt management strategy. Secondly, a debtor which fell into arrears on multilateral debts automatically ceased to be eligible for further use of these institutions' facilities. It faced enormous pressure therefore to continue to service these debts, regardless of what happened elsewhere in the domestic economy. Thirdly, it created a serious dilemma for the debtors. They had to choose between honouring their international obligations and remaining upright members of the international financial community, or concentrating on achieving long-term sustainable growth and development, thus incurring the censure of these institutions. They invariably chose the former.

SSA countries have not regained their creditworthiness and access to international capital markets, nor has the net flow of private capital increased. Indeed, the opposite has happened. Private capital flows dried up overnight and have not returned. Private creditors seem to have decided to get out and stay out. In 1988, when the secondary market was most active, Nigerian debt sold at 26 cents in the dollar. Even at this huge discount there were few takers. Also, the Warburg Proposal failed to win the support of the commercial banks, and other major debt reduction schemes such as the Baker and Brady Plans bypassed SSA countries. The Toronto Summit Agreement went some way towards remedying the situation, but by the end of the 1980s these countries attracted less private capital than at the beginning.

Their economic performance and prospects also suffered as a result of the two-track approach. Development was relegated to the slow-track, and the priority given to servicing multilateral debts and private credits left them short of foreign exchange to finance their long-term development: the means by which they were expected to grow out of debt ultimately. As the servicing costs of these debts mounted, they exercised an increasingly repressive effect on growth and development, and virtually ensured that SSA countries would not resolve their debt crisis or achieve sustainable development.

Data published by the World Bank show that, although the economic performance of SSA countries improved towards the end of the 1980s, most of the gains have since been wiped out. In 1990, for example, GDP grew by 1.1 per cent which, when converted to a per capita basis, shows that output for the region as a whole fell by –2.1 per cent. A similar deterioration can be traced in respect of gross domestic investment and savings rates. The former declined from 20.6 per cent of GDP in 1981 to 15.8 per cent in 1990, and the latter from 14.3 per cent to 12.8 per cent over the same period.[1]

SSA countries have also failed to reduce the level of domestic inflation or to raise real interest rates. Notwithstanding their commitment to domestic price stability and the implementation of strict monetary and financial policies, the rate of inflation for the region averaged 21.6 per cent per annum between 1986 and 1989. The corresponding rate for 1980–85 was 19.4 per cent per annum. The initial success of countries like Ghana, Nigeria and Tanzania in reducing inflation was, in fact, overshadowed by the performance of Somalia, Zambia, Zaire and Sierra Leone where inflation got completely out of control. In Zaire and Sierra Leone it averaged 81 per cent and 88.7 per cent per annum, respectively, between 1985 and 1989.

The same picture holds in respect of central government deficits. Some countries, notably Ghana, Gambia, Senegal, Tanzania and Madagascar, improved fiscal management by raising taxation revenues and cutting public expenditure, while in others (Ethiopia, Zaire and Mozambique) fiscal deficits increased substantially. For the region as a whole, central government deficits increased from –5.7 per cent of GDP per annum between 1982 and 1985 to –7 per cent of GDP for 1986 to 1989. Clearly, a lot more needs to be done to reverse this worsening trend and to improve the efficiency of fiscal systems. The level of military expenditure is the most obvious candidate for cuts in public expenditure. Ethiopia and Mozambique, for example, spent more than 10 per cent of GDP per annum on military expenditure over the period 1972–88. These are perhaps extreme examples. A more representative figure is provided by Daniel Hewitt, who shows that over the same period SSA countries as a group spent on average 12.8 per cent of central government expenditure on military expenditure.[2] A drastic reduction in these levels would release substantial additional resources for financing growth and development.

Notwithstanding the fall in aggregate growth and output, many SSA countries did, in fact, record major improvements in the performance of specific sectors and policy reforms. The massive over-valuation in exchange rates of the early 1980s has been substantially reduced. In the case of IDA-eligible members, real effective rates of exchange fell by almost 50 per cent between 1983 and 1989. Some countries (Ghana, Gambia, Mozambique, Nigeria, Tanzania and Uganda) also made substantial progress in reducing the gap between parallel market rates and the official exchange rate. In addition, many countries complemented the adjustment of exchange rates with various trade and exchange liberalization measures in order to improve their international competitiveness and to enable their domestic economies to function more efficiently.

Progress in agricultural prices and marketing reforms has been, at best, patchy. Most governments still set producer prices, control the sale of export crops and run internal marketing and distribution systems. On the other hand, several have attempted to reform and improve the efficiency of their agricultural sectors by investing more in the rehabilitation, upgrading and creation of new capacities. A few countries, notably Mali and Sudan, have made no progress towards modernizing their agricultural sectors. On the whole, though, the majority of SSA countries have made some attempt to implement several of the reforms to which they were committed under UNPAAERD. Those which have made the most progress include Burundi, Central African Republic, Gambia, Mozambique and Senegal.[3]

Reforms in other sectors, such as the industrial, financial, public enterprise and public institutions, and regulations have been slow and lacking in conviction. Progress in some countries has been more than counterbalanced by lack of progress, stagnation and even decline in others. To quote UNCTAD:

> Progress has been uneven and insecure. Many countries in Africa have been unable to reconcile the objectives of external balance, price stability and economic growth and development. For them, policies geared primarily towards quickly achieving external balance and internal price stability have either failed or recorded success only by sacrificing employment, growth and distributional objectives, and even then improvements tended to be ephemeral. In many cases, adjustment associated with financial stringency had drastic effects on rates of investment, living standards and levels of economic activity generally, comprising the countries' capacities for serving their external debts in the longer term.[4]

In brief, failure on the fast track has been compounded by stagnation and deterioration on the slow. Despite substantial debt relief operations and additional net resource inflows, SSA countries are still characterized by weak agricultural growth, declining industrial output, poor export performance, mounting debt burdens and rapidly deteriorating social conditions.

B. THE ROLE OF RELIEF

Given the level of international commitment and resources devoted to the debt crisis and the promotion of economic recovery and reform in SSA countries, the lack of a breakthrough on either front raises questions about the strategies adopted during the 1980s.

As indicated in Chapter 3, debt relief was essentially an *ad hoc* operation. Creditor countries strongly resisted any attempt to formalize procedures and establish a system of groundrules. Consequently, there was no basis for evaluating or comparing the effectiveness of individual relief negotiations, nor, more importantly, their impact on the domestic economy of the debtor countries. The primary objectives of these exercises were (a) to minimize losses and the disruption to the world's monetary and financial system, (b) to ensure that the burden of relief was shared equitably and fairly among creditors, and (c) to uphold the sanctity and enforceability of international legal contracts and obligations.

This approach allowed creditors to employ a diversity of criteria and requirements for relief, and to compartmentalize the crisis by treating debtors, and types of debts, differently. Some creditors concentrated on specific debtor countries and types of debts and excluded others, while some debtors received relief on similar types of debts and others did not. Ostensibly, the purpose of this approach was to give the creditors greater flexibility and room for manoeuvre to deal with the crisis. What it did, however, was to enable them to introduce a number of extraneous considerations in order to secure for themselves the maximum mileage, economically, politically and strategically.

This distortion of priorities reduced the contribution of debt relief exercises, and in many cases rendered them counterproductive. No attempt was made to deal with the crisis as a whole. Rather, attention was focused on its minor and residual features as these provided the greatest scope for flexibility. It also enabled the creditors to keep relief to the minimum consistent with their own preferences and priorities. Consequently, whatever relief was received was soon swallowed up by the rapid growth and expansion of other debt-creating flows not covered by, or eligible for, consolidation. In other words, as the tail of the dog got smaller, the dog itself got larger and more unmanageable!

Further, debt relief measures were essentially *post eventum*. They dealt with the past. More importantly, they represented a belated acceptance of the reality of the situation; namely, that the debts could not be repaid without seriously jeopardizing international economic and political relations between the rich (creditor) nations and the poor (debtor) countries. It was therefore a case of damage limitation. Consequently, no attempt was made to look to the future or to deal with such questions as: was the amount of relief enough? how, and in what ways, would the relief measures contribute to the economy of the debtor country? what happened after consolidation? would the debtor be able to avoid a repetition of the situation? and would it be able to resume or achieve sustainable growth and development?

These questions would have required a degree of commitment to debt consolidation as an on-going process which the creditor countries were not prepared to make. It was more convenient, therefore, to assume that once relief was granted, growth would be resumed and the necessity for a repeat exercise avoided. However, subsequent events have shown that this is not the case. Debt levels in SSA countries have continued to rise and arrears to accumulate, despite repeated reschedulings. Indeed, the countries which under-performed during the 1980s were precisely the ones whose debts were repeatedly rescheduled.

There are several reasons for this, but two in particular stand out. First, debt relief operations dealt with the symptoms rather than the root cause of the crisis, and secondly, they were essentially freestanding, one-off operations. Each consolidation exercise stood on its own. It was not related to, or contingent upon, other measures. Debt relief was, in fact, regarded as an end in itself. Also, there was no coordination among the various creditors. Each creditor did its own thing, in its own way. Consequently, there was a series of negotiations taking place simultaneously, with no attempt to coordinate their activities, integrate them into domestic economic management or measure their collective impact on the domestic economy of the debtor country.

Finally, these relief operations concentrated on the expenditure side of the debtor's external accounts. This was obviously based on the assumption that debts which were cancelled, written down or reduced by other measures would release additional foreign exchange for expenditure on capital imports for development purposes. Relief would thus ease the debtor's foreign exchange constraint and facilitate a straightforward switch of expenditure to development, thereby accelerating its progress towards sustainable long-term growth and development.

This clearly has not happened, not because the amount of relief was too small (though this was undoubtedly a factor), but principally because there is no automatic relationship between the two items of public expenditure. In reality, the switch from one item to the other depends on a combination of factors reflecting the debtor's economic, social and political priorities, the stance and effectiveness of its monetary and fiscal policies and overall domestic economic management. It also depends on whether or not creditors attach conditions to the use of resources provided by their relief packages. This last condition did not, in fact, apply in the case under consideration, so that SSA countries were free to spend the additional resources as they saw fit, which is what they did.

The rapid growth and expansion in military expenditure, defence and administration witnessed during the 1980s suggest that most of the additional resources were spent on these items. Very little seems to have gone on providing general balance of payments support, easing the severe import compression of the early 1980s, or financing productive investment and income-generating projects, all of which were crucial to the development effort. In fact, the various income-generating possibilities of debt relief were ignored. It is not surprising, therefore, that the results were not commensurate with the international effort that went into these exercises.

C. THE CURRENT PARADIGMS

All the reports and the programmes for reform and recovery in SSA countries stressed the role and relationship of debt relief to that process. UNPAAERD, for example, identified the heavy burden of debt and debt servicing obligations as one of the main constraints on Africa's prospects for economic recovery and growth, and called on the international community to take steps to alleviate this burden.

The Wass Report, *Financing Africa's Recovery*, was more specific. It estimated that Africa needed an extra $5 billion per annum beyond what it received in 1987 in order to restore the prospects for growth and development which it enjoyed in the early 1980s, and to implement the appropriate reforms for promoting its long-term growth and development. This gap was to be financed by a combination of new funds and debt relief, of which the latter was expected to contribute about $1 billion per annum. However, in order to be eligible for debt relief and the new funds, the debtors had to agree to undertake a programme of structural reform (if they did not already have one) with the IMF and the World Bank, both of which were expected to provide a substantial proportion of the extra funding. Effectively, therefore, the Wass Report not only accepted the interrelationship of debt relief and reform, but envisaged an integrated approach to the dual problems of debts and development.[5]

Although the World Bank accepts that there is a direct relationship between debts and development in SSA countries, it regards the primary role of relief as supplementing the total amount of external resources for financing the necessary reforms for their recovery and long-term sustainable development. In 1986 it estimated that they faced a total resource gap of $2.5 billion per annum over the next four years (1986–90), in order to stop their economic decline and to restore import capacity. This gap was to be filled by a combination of new inflows of concessional assistance and debt relief, of which the latter was expected to contribute about $1 billion per annum.[6]

In a later study, it reiterated its commitment to the three-pronged approach of additional inflows of concessional assistance, debt relief and structural adjustment reforms, as the appropriate strategy for achieving the target rate of growth of 4–5 per cent per annum projected for the 1990s for SSA countries. Although it did not anticipate that the resource gap faced by them would be appreciably smaller than that of the 1980s, it argued:

> the external resource requirements of Sub-Saharan Africa during the 1990s could be met if donors achieved two related targets. First, during the 1990s gross ODA continues to increase at about 4 per cent in real terms. Second, relief mechanisms are put in place so that the actual debt service payments for countries with strong reform programs are kept within manageable limits.[7]

The mechanisms to which it referred were, of course, the so-called menu of options which allows creditors to decide which debts to consolidate and what measures to take.

This three-pronged approach, in fact, underpinned its own Special Programme of Assistance (SPA) for SSA countries. Increased debt relief on more concessional terms from a menu of options was expected to contribute 54 per cent of the additional external resources for financing the resource gap of the 19 core countries (that is, those IDA-eligible countries which either had a structural adjustment programme already in place or had agreed to implement one). Additional new funding, also on concessional terms, was to be provided by the aid donors and international institutions from a variety of sources, new facilities and special arrangements. And, more importantly, the implementation of the whole programme turned on the single criterion of whether or not the debtor country was in adjustment.

The reformers received more debt relief and new funding than the non-reformers. This was clearly an inducement to sell the programme and to speed up the process of recovery and reform. On the basis of numbers alone, the policy seems to have worked, as the number of reforming countries now exceeds 30. However, both the programme and the process of structural adjustment have engendered an enormous amount of controversy. The World Bank, for example, has repeatedly argued that the reforming countries have outperformed the non-reformers since embarking upon structural adjustment.

Its preliminary report was decidedly upbeat. It argued that although structural adjustment would take time to show results, there were clear signs that it was beginning to work. Many governments had implemented the necessary reforms to increase efficiency, regain their international competitiveness and markets and improve domestic fiscal and financial management. On the basis of a variety of statistical indicators of policy reforms and economic performance it concluded: 'The evidence of the past three years leaves room for optimism. These encouraging signs, though still preliminary, augur well for the future.'[8] It accordingly exhorted SSA countries to press on with their reforms, and pleaded with the donor countries and international institutions to continue to support and provide additional funding for the extension of the programme.

However, the ECA took a less sanguine view. It accused the World Bank of (a) one-dimensionality and selectivity in compiling and presenting data, and (b) adopting a simplified approach to Africa's crisis. Using data from the World Bank, it showed that the non-reformers in fact outperformed the reformers between 1980 and 1987, the period covered by the Bank's analysis. Although not explicitly stated, the implication of the ECA's line of argument was that not only had the Bank's reform programme failed, it had held back those countries which had implemented it. This was reinforced by its criticism of the Bank's simplified approach which, it argued, completely misunderstood, and consequently misrepresented, the nature, causes and requirements for structural adjustment and social transformation in SSA countries.[9]

Its own version (the AAF-SAP) adopted a holistic approach in which everything hung together in an ill-defined and rather loose way. It called for a limit to be set on the amount of foreign exchange used for debt servicing each year, on the grounds that this would release more resources for financing the adjustment process. Other external sources of additional funding included a reduction in the level of IMF repurchases, increased private and public sector inflows and the repatriation of capital. The actual process of adjustment was left indeterminate and open-ended, on the assumption that each country would decide its own policy objectives, priorities, reforms and means of financing the process. Consequently, no estimates were given of the cost of adjustment or the amount of resources to be mobilized internally or externally.

Attempts to reconcile the two models have proved inconclusive, and claims that their respective premisses and strategies have been synthesized into a coherent long-term strategy for sustainable development in SSA countries are largely illusory. They are, in fact, competing paradigms which reflect fundamental conceptual and ideological differences in their perception of the nature and functioning of the world economic system and the role of SSA countries in it.[10] However, for a variety of reasons, the World Bank model remains the only realistic option for recovery and reform open to these countries. Not only is it fully operational, it enjoys the support and financial backing of the donor countries and international institutions who have endorsed its extension (SPA II) to 1994.

Table 5.1 shows that, in the main, SPA core countries out-performed the non-SPA countries, and that the former group entered the 1990s better placed

Table 5.1 Sub-Saharan Africa: selected performance indicators, 1980–90

Indicator and country group	% p.a. (unless otherwise stated) 1980–84	1985–7	1988–90
Gross Domestic Investment (GDI)			
SPA core countries	–6.3	12.5	8.5
non-SPA countries	1.9	1.2	3.5
Export volume			
SPA core countries	–0.6	3.2	5.7
non-SPA countries	1.3	2.0	2.4
Import volume			
SPA core countries	–1.3	2.6	4.1
non-SPA countries	2.0	0.5	3.0
Consumption per capita			
SPA core countries	–0.7	–0.8	–0.1
non-SPA countries	0.7	–0.7	–0.6
GDI/GDP ratio (%)			
SPA core countries	18.4	16.7	19.3
non-SPA countries	23.9	21.2	19.6
GDS/GDP ratio (%)			
SPA core countries	2.9	4.0	4.9
non-SPA countries	8.9	9.3	8.8
Terms of trade (1987=1.000)			
SPA core countries	1.055	1.064	0.939
non-SPA countries	1.208	1.058	1.024

Notes
Non-SPA countries include Somalia, Zaire and Zambia, and exclude Angola, Comoros, Djibouti, Equatorial Guinea and Swaziland because of incomplete data (Zambia is now an SPA country).
GDS = Gross domestic savings.
Source: *The World Bank Annual Report 1991*. Washington D.C.: World Bank, August 1991, Table 3.2, p. 46.

to achieve long-term sustainable growth and development. Within this group, the Bank singled out Ghana, Madagascar, Malawi and Togo as countries in which the standard of domestic economic management was well above average. Also, the fact that the number of countries entering into adjustment had virtually doubled since the programme began was cited as an indication of the superiority of its own model. No doubt, the better performance of the

SPA core countries, particularly in 1990, was largely responsible for the implementation of SPA II.

However, the Bank warned against complacency. To quote:

> The overall economic situation in Sub-Saharan Africa (SSA) remains difficult. For many countries, the external environment continues to be hostile, as reflected by the adverse effects of debt overhang, capricious weather, sluggish growth in export demand, and steady declines in terms of trade. A few countries are even suffering internal strife and famine conditions.[11]

In other words, notwithstanding the effort, special programmes and facilities of the international community, the region faces essentially the same economic, social and political problems as it did a decade ago. In addition, a series of adverse international events, in particular the Gulf War and the current world recession, has exacerbated their existing problems. It is difficult, therefore, to see how they will be able to achieve the targets which the World Bank regards as essential for their long-term survival and development.[12]

Most of the gains made between 1988 and 1990 have, in fact, already been eroded. SPA II will have, therefore, to concentrate on recovering lost ground rather than on consolidating and building on the progress made under SPA I. In addition, being an extension of SPA I, its scope for action and innovation is determined by the parameters and operational procedures of that programme. Given the loose structure of the three-pronged strategy adopted under SPA I, its achievements are likely to fall short of expectations. It could well end up trying to prevent reforms from slipping by throwing money after them. There is clearly a need for a tighter and better integrated strategy.

D. AN INTEGRATED DEBT–DEVELOPMENT STRATEGY

The general principles and basic framework of such a strategy already exist in SPA II, which is essentially a multilateral system based on a loose and indirect relationship between its three principal components of debt relief, new funding and domestic economic reforms. Although debt relief is an integral part of this system, relief negotiations are conducted bilaterally, with both the measures and the amount of relief determined unilaterally by the creditors. It is assumed that relief provides additional free foreign exchange which is then used to pay for imports of capital goods and other essential items in support of the development effort. However, there is no mechanism to ensure that this happens, with the result that the additional free foreign exchange is often diverted to non-developmental expenditure.

Secondly, the system is activated and driven by the debtor country's commitment to a programme of reform. Once this is agreed multilaterally (that is, between the IMF, the World Bank and itself), the debtor becomes eligible for funding from a variety of sources within SPA II. The total amount and the timing of the release of these new funds are directly dependent on a set of performance criteria and/or the achievement of specific targets and policy reforms. Although debt relief is one of the sources of finance within SPA II, its role and relationship to reforms are loose and indeterminate. The amount of relief which a debtor country receives is not determined by the size or success of its reform programme (which are essentially long-run oriented), but by a complex mixture of short-run economic, political and foreign policy considerations. The system is thus characterized by a set of asymetrical relationships in which debt relief, designed as one of its three pillars, has been marginalized. This needs to be reversed.

One way of doing this is to reverse the role of debt relief and make it central to a new set of relationships in which it performs a dual function. First, it would continue to perform its present role of debt reduction. Secondly, the free foreign exchange released from debt service obligations would be used to finance specific reforms within the debtor's overall reform programme. This would require that the present tenuous assumption that free foreign exchange is used for developmental purposes be replaced by a set of binding conditions regarding their release and utilization. These would also have to be backed up by a system of sanctions in order to ensure that undertakings are honoured, resources used effectively and productively, and the scheme administered fairly and efficiently.

The modalities of these provisions will be determined by the main thrust and focus of the scheme, which is to ensure that debt relief is actually used to finance reforms. A commitment to reform is not enough. This must be substantiated and supported by positive and quantifiable results, such as the introduction and implementation of identifiable and agreed reforms, or the achievement of specific policy reforms. The success of a debtor's reform programme would, in turn, render it eligible for additional debt relief and new funding (again, on agreed criteria and conditions) to finance more reforms and so accelerate its progress towards achieving its long-term goal of sustainable growth and development.

The proposal is thus essentially performance related, in the sense that the size and success of a debtor's reform programme are directly related to (a) its effective utilization of debt relief, and (b) the extent to which these resources are integrated into its overall debt/development strategy. Clearly, those countries that utilize debt relief more effectively (that is, to finance reforms) will outperform those that use it for other purposes. The superior performance of the former will increase their eligibility for additional relief and new funding which, in turn, will have the 'ratchet effect' of enhancing their performance and lifting them on to a higher level from which the process begins once more.

Debt relief is thus the key to the whole process. This would be negotiated as at present (that is, within the existing institutional framework and applying the same procedures and mechanisms). Once a package of relief measures is agreed, the uses to which the resources are put and their impact on the debtor's own reform programme and progress towards long-term sustainable growth and development become the driving force of the system. In order to ensure that this happens, the debtor countries would have to give a binding commitment to use the resources for the purposes for which they have been granted. For their part, the creditors including the international institutions, would have the authority to exercise surveillance over the scheme, and/or, in the final analysis, to impose some sort of sanctions for non-compliance.

Although these conditions are crucial to the success of the scheme in practice, they are very difficult to enforce. It is one thing for the creditors to stipulate that debt relief resources should be used for one purpose and not another. It is another matter for them to ensure that their stipulations are observed. Given the fungibility of resources, the recipient countries can, for example, switch funds from one use to another, or as is more generally the case, use their own resources to finance non-productive activities and projects that they would not otherwise have been able to finance, thereby frustrating the basic purpose of the scheme.[13]

Similarly, the imposition of sanctions (even as a last resort) would create much international ill-will and mistrust, and could well cause the scheme to collapse. It would require, therefore, great diplomatic skill, administrative expertise and a lot of goodwill and international cooperation to ensure that the system works fairly and efficiently. Fortunately, the foundations for such a system already exist. The extension of SPA and UNPAAERD, to take two obvious examples, is clear evidence of the desire to strengthen and develop the programmes, procedures and mechanisms of international cooperation established over the last decade for dealing with the critical economic situation facing SSA countries.

(a) Outline and Operation

Drawing on the immense goodwill generated by this new ethos of international commitment and cooperation, the integrated strategy for achieving the twin goals of debt reduction and sustainable development is based on the assumptions that:

(i) both debtors and creditors are committed to achieving the same goals, which, explicitly stated, are, first, to reduce existing debt burdens to more manageable levels in the short-run; and secondly, to implement the necessary reforms for recovery and sustainable development in the long-run;

(ii) they share the responsibility for achieving these goals. This, among other things, requires the debtor countries to utilize debt relief resources and all new funding productively and efficiently in order to achieve realistic and quantifiable targets and policy reforms;

(iii) the creditors and international institutions would discharge fully their commitment and obligations to provide adequate resources so that the reform programme is not blown off course or curtailed for lack of external funding;

(iv) adequate provisions are included to safeguard and promote the interests of debtors and creditors alike. These include, for example, appropriate procedures and powers of surveillance and sanctions, and, more positively, various incentives to encourage participation and reward performance;

(v) it will not be necessary to devise new procedures and/or institutions for implementing the agreed programme for reforms beyond those already in existence. The present system of PFPs and the various policy reforms and structural adjustment measures incorporated into SPA II will thus remain essential and integral elements of the integrated strategy;

(vi) strong and effective control will be exercised over the contraction of new debts;

(vii) the system is not open-ended. Rather, it is intended to run for a limited period of time in order to ensure more effective utilization of the resources available to SPA II. The way the system would work is shown in Figure 5.1.

The scheme assumes that debt relief is provided principally through cancellation and/or conversion of loans to grants, as at present. Both measures have immediate as well as longer-term effects on the debtor's stock of external debts outstanding and the flow of debt service payments. The former is reduced by the value of the amount of relief granted. This, in turn, determines the amount by which its debt service payments are reduced in the initial and subsequent years over the life-span of the debts which have been cancelled or converted. More importantly, it provides an additional stream of foreign exchange income so that the debtor can reduce its debt burdens further and finance its reform programme. Debt relief thus performs two important functions: first, it achieves the short-term goal of dealing with the debt crisis; and secondly, it acts as a catalyst, by supplementing available

Figure 5.1 Diagrammatic representation of the integrated strategy

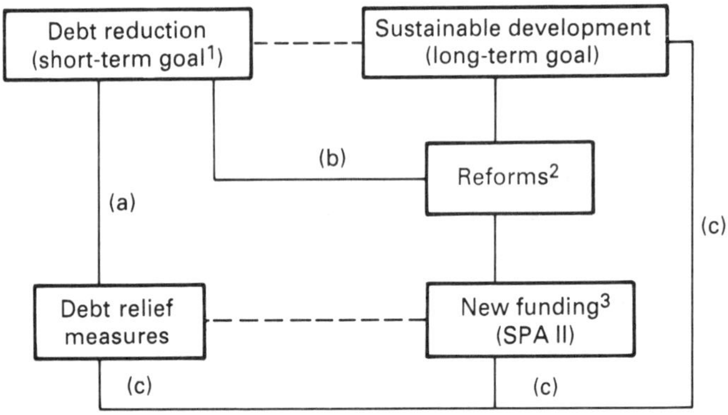

Notes

1 The goals of debt reduction are two-fold and interrelated: (i) to reduce the stock of debt and the flow of debt service payments, and (ii) to provide a flow of resources for financing reforms.
2 As outlined in each reforming country's PFP.
3 As provided under the five main sources of funding for SPA I and SPA II.
(a) System starts with initial round of debt relief.
(b) Debt service payments for financing reforms.
(c) Secondary round triggered by achievements of goals and targets as specified in [2] above.

foreign exchange for reforms and helping to dynamize the economy towards sustainable development.

However, for this to happen, two conditions are necessary. First, the amount of debt relief must be enough to make a significant impact on both fronts. So far, this has not happened. Consequently, its impact has been symbolic rather than significant. The range and scope of relief measures must, therefore, be increased and expanded beyond present modalities. Secondly, debt relief must be fully integrated into the debtor's existing reform programme and utilized specifically to relieve critical foreign exchange constraints, or tied to the implementation of high priority reforms and the achievement of precise development-related targets. The essential point of the exercise is to ensure that effective utilization, performance and results remain the driving force of the integrated strategy.

The nature and prioritization of reforms and targets are obviously a matter for each reforming country to determine for itself. However, much of the groundwork for this has already been done, and each country's formal commitment to policy reforms and structural adjustment are contained in its PFPs. All that needs to be done is for these targets and reforms to be refined, updated and consolidated into a viable debt/development strategy which is not only capable of being implemented, but can also be evaluated. *Inter alia*, this would require the participants in the scheme to devise the appropriate economic, financial and social criteria by which to evaluate the success (or otherwise) of the new integrated strategy.

Such criteria could take any number of forms and requirements as well as be based on the achievement of specific and/or quantifiable targets. To give a few examples:

(i) a reduction in either the stock of debts outstanding or debt service payments (or both) by a given percentage for each year of the scheme's operation;

(ii) an increase in the rate of growth of output by a given percentage over and above that contained in the PFP. More specifically, improvements in the agricultural sector could be targeted, and success measured in terms of the achievement of specific sectoral targets, such as annual increases in the rate of growth of food production or individual crops (whether for home consumption or export), progress towards food security and/or improved self-sufficiency ratios, the provision of research and extension services, more efficient marketing and distribution systems, and so on;

(iii) examples of fiscal and financial criteria to include such targets as increasing government tax revenues by a given proportion over a specified period of time; improving the efficiency and administration of domestic fiscal systems on the basis of predetermined requirements and criteria; cutting back military expenditure to an agreed proportion of GDP; reducing budgetary deficits to bring them into line with the average for developing countries as a whole; and improved systems of government with greater local participation and accountability;

(iv) social progress and achievement could be measured by such criteria as the number of new schools built, and/or new school places provided annually; the provision of hospitals, clinics and health centres; new doctors and paramedics trained and/or serving in the rural areas, and various other social indicators currently in use.

Success in achieving these targets (or an agreed menu of them) would indicate that the debtor country had not only satisfied the necessary preconditions for reform and recovery, but was on course to achieve sustainable development: the long-term goal of the integrated strategy. More importantly, it would render that country eligible for another round of debt reduction measures and additional inflows of new funding, which would start the process all over again, with two new and important features. First, the system creates its own dynamism and is essentially self-sustaining. Secondly, although additional inflows of new funding would facilitate the process, they are not essential to the success of the scheme, which is intended to operate as a closed and fully integrated system.

(b) Scope and Administration

The new scheme is intended to be integrated with and operate alongside existing debt relief and reform programmes, rather than to replace them. In this capacity, it basically performs a dual role, namely, to improve procedures and performance and to generate additional resources from within the system; and also, by utilizing these resources more effectively and efficiently, to catalyse the process of recovery and reform and accelerate progress towards sustainable development. Further, it is assumed that the scheme will be financed from funds already allocated to SPA II. No additional external funding would be needed, therefore, to activate it. In so far as these become necessary, they would enter once the system became operational and achieved its own momentum. They would also be minimal and performance related. The concept of additionality would thus be built into the scheme.

In terms of its scope of operations, the integrated scheme would cover all bilateral official and multilateral loans. As indicated in Chapter 2, the former accounts for the largest share of SSA countries' external debts. Consequently, they exercise a decisive influence on both the stock of debts outstanding and the level of debt service payments. The latter, though quantitatively smaller, is rising steadily and will in time create serious servicing problems for the majority of SSA debtor countries. The rapid build-up of arrears shows that this has already happened in many of them. Unless, therefore, action is taken on the widest possible front, SSA countries are unlikely to achieve sustainable development.

Significant progress has, in fact, been made in reducing current debt levels. These efforts[14] should be continued and expanded. The present proposal in no way attempts to supplant, or be a substitute for, those measures which are already in place. It seeks, rather, to supplement and strengthen them. Therefore, it envisages that the various bilateral initiatives by the creditor countries will continue and intensify, now that the principle of cancellation has been fully accepted and the positive contribution which debt relief makes to the development of the poorer countries recognized.

However, these initiatives by themselves are not enough to cope with the debt crisis or to promote sustainable development in SSA countries. Additional measures and procedures are required, particularly in respect of non-concessional bilateral public debt. The Toronto Summit Agreement makes a valiant effort to resolve this aspect of the crisis, but it does not go far enough. The amount of relief which it has provided is minimal, compared with the size of the problem or the rate at which it is growing. Negotiations are slow, cumbersome and expensive. Procedures need to be speeded up but, more importantly, the range and scope of its operations need to be liberalized and extended. Non-OECD creditor countries, for example, need to be brought within its ambit in order to give it wider acceptability and credibility and to make it a truly international cooperative effort.

These limitations have, in fact, been recognized and action taken to redress some of them. The so-called Trinidad Terms are a case in point. This scheme builds on that tradition. It is intended to improve existing modalities and procedures and to introduce a limited element of automaticity in relief operations based on the debtor's economic prospects and performance. It also seeks to provide a more flexible framework for facilitating and speeding up the work of the Paris Club, which is the principal international forum for debt relief negotiations.[15]

Although the Paris Club was set up as an *ad hoc* committee without any formal administrative structure and machinery, the scale and scope of its responsibilities and activities have changed in response to the frequency of its meetings and the additional workload created by the need for repeated reschedulings. It is now, to all intents and purposes, a semi-permanent body with an immense amount of administrative experience and technical expertise in dealing with the problems of debt relief operations, all of which can be put to good effect in implementing and administering the new strategy. There would be no need, therefore, to create another international institution. Most of the preparatory work has already been done, and policies, position papers and programmes defined. The amount of additional work needed to get the scheme off the ground is not only marginal, but falls within the scope and competence of the Paris Club sphere of operations.

Multilateral debts create different problems for SSA countries.[16] They are a major and growing constraint on these countries' ability to achieve sustainable development, and urgent and effective measures must be taken to reduce them. It is indefensible and illogical for the IMF and the World Bank, the principal holders of these debts, to stand on their status as preferred creditors and insist that multilateral debts cannot be rescheduled. Such a position is not only unnecessarily legalistic and negative, ultimately it seeks to shift the problem elsewhere. Having contributed to the problem, they have an obligation to help find a just and equitable solution.

It is illogical for them to provide additional concessional long-term assistance on the one hand and, on the other, to insist that SSA countries continue to service their outstanding multilateral loans on harder terms. What this amounts to, in effect, is that in so far as new funding is concerned, SSA countries are considered a special case, but when it comes to debt relief and repayment, they are treated no differently from other borrowers of these institutions' funds. Debt relief and new funding in fact constitute two of the main sources of financing recovery and reform for these countries, yet they sit separately and work in opposite directions. This glaring inconsistency urgently needs to be resolved.

On a more practical level, although multilateral debts are a major burden for SSA countries, they are, literally speaking, 'the small change' of the operations of multilateral financial institutions. They do not pose any threat to the stability of the world monetary and financial system, or compromise the integrity of either the IMF or the World Bank. Indeed, it can be argued that both institutions have already compromised their own much-vaunted neutrality in debt relief operations by actively participating in the Baker and Brady Plans and underwriting private debts with multilateral funds. No great or irreconcilable principle is thus at stake.

Further, having adopted a proactive or 'hands-on' approach to the private debts of the HICs, a 'hands-off' attitude to the multilateral debts of SSA countries is, at best, a strange inversion of priorities and, at worst, shows an amazing insensitivity to the needs and concerns of their poorer members. Such disparity in treatment is counterproductive and unhealthy for international cooperation and North–South relations. It engenders much unnecessary ill-will and suspicion of their motives and priorities. The inclusion of multilateral debts within the scope of the integrated scheme and the active involvement of both the IMF and the World Bank in its administration would multilateralize the scheme and immeasurably improve its chances of success.

Both institutions are already heavily involved in the operation and administration of SPA II; the amount of additional work and institutional support necessary to service the integrated scheme would thus be marginal. Among other things, it would require new procedures for closer and more effective coordination of disbursements from the various sources of new funding and evaluating performance under SPA II with measures to reduce outstanding arrears and mounting service payments on multilateral debts.

One possibility, for example, would be for the IMF and the World Bank to impose sanctions on performance, or more precisely, on the non-achievement of agreed targets and goals, rather than on repayment of arrears and servicing of multilateral debts, as at present. This would be a more effective way of reducing arrears. More importantly, it brings sanctions closer to the root of the problem. Better economic performance ultimately and directly increases the ability of SSA countries to repay their debts. Major benefits would thus result from the inclusion of multilateral debts in the integrated scheme.

Private debts are not a major problem for SSA countries as a whole. The vast majority of them are too poor to contract debts of this kind, the obvious exceptions being Côte d'Ivoire, Nigeria and Zaire, which ran up substantial amounts of private debts over the last two decades. Although they rank among the most highly indebted countries, they have not benefited from any of the major international schemes for debt and debt reduction. Côte d'Ivoire and Nigeria, were among the original members of HICs, for which the Baker and Brady Plans were devised. However, they have not benefited from either plan.

Also, African commercial debts were the most heavily discounted in the secondary markets, but they failed to attract many takers. Similarly, attempts to engage in debt equity swaps or to convert them to other non-debt-creating flows failed to take off, as did the Warburg Proposal which was devised specifically to facilitate African commercial debts. In brief, the private debts of SSA countries have been largely bypassed by all the important international initiatives and schemes. The commercial banks, for their part, have strengthened their balance sheets by reducing their exposure in problem debtor countries as well as provisioning against losses on these accounts. In every important respect, therefore, the debt crisis is behind them.[17]

The same cannot be said for SSA countries. Urgent action needs to be taken to redress the imbalance in the way their commercial debts have been treated as compared with those of the HICs. One way of doing this is to include them in the integrated scheme, and for both the IMF and the World Bank to provide appropriate guarantees to enable the debtor countries to service them, as they have done in respect of the Baker and Brady Plans. Another possibility is to reactivate the Warburg Proposal and/or extend its provisions to include some of the procedures and schemes for debt and debt service reduction which have been devised for the HICs. There are other possibilities. The point is that the problem is not insoluble, provided that goodwill and earnest intention exist.

(c) A Major Improvement

The integrated system has a number of advantages and improvements on existing practices and procedures. These include:

(i) By starting with debt relief, it directly and immediately reduces debt burdens, thus achieving its short-term goal. This provides a major psychological boost and creates the necessary momentum and resources to catalyse the system towards its long-term goal of sustainable development. There is thus a close and direct functional and sequential relationship between both goals.

(ii) Being performance related, its benefits and achievements can be readily identified and quantified. It also enables debtors to earn additional debt relief on the basis of results and the achievement of specific targets. The more successful a country is, the more debt relief and new funding it is eligible to receive. These additional resources would, in turn, further reduce its debt burden and provide extra resources for financing reforms and accelerating progress towards sustainable development, thereby setting off another round of relief and new funding to sustain the process.

(iii) In effect, the system gives rise to a series of interdependent virtuous circles that spiral cumulatively in opposite directions. Whereas the debt crisis gets progressively smaller as the process continues, recovery and reforms enter an expanding virtuous circle of cumulative causality which ends with the achievement of sustainable development. In other words, the system enables SSA countries to make a virtue of the interdependence of the debt crisis and their own critical economic situation. It gives them the opportunity to utilize this interdependence positively and effectively, and to become active rather than passive agents in achieving its twin goals.

(iv) The scheme not only provides an incentive for SSA countries to earn relief but to grow out of their debts at differential rates consistent with individual debtor's growth prospects and performance. It can thus be administered flexibly and on a case-by-case basis, the approach which has been consistently advocated and adopted by the creditors countries and institutions.

(v) Unlike existing debt relief operations, the new scheme looks forward, not backward. It is thus positive rather than negative and defeatist, and allows the debtors to contribute positively and constructively to its success. It also enhances and revitalizes the principle of maturation and graduation which has fallen into disuse and disrepute.

(vi) As a self-contained and fully integrated system, the new scheme relies on funds which are generated internally and recycled within the system to finance its operations. The cost to the creditor countries and international institutions would thus be minimal, and unlikely to disrupt or destabilize the international monetary and financial system. In so far as new funding comes into the system, this would have already been allocated to it from the overall new funding provisions for SPA II, the main source of funding open to it. It would, of course, be possible to increase the amount of new funding from other sources, but this would largely depend on the success of the scheme.

(vii) Further, it incorporates both expenditure-reducing and income-generating activities into a composite and fully functioning system. This is a major improvement on existing practices which concentrate on minimizing the creditors' losses. It will go some way, therefore, to helping SSA countries reduce their balance of payments and budgetary deficits.

(viii) At present, crucial decisions on debt relief, such as who gets what, how much, and when, are determined by the creditors, and reflect a complex mixture of their own economic, financial and foreign policy considerations. These would be replaced by a more open and transparent system of international cooperation in which participation, performance and outcomes can be objectively evaluated, and the rights, responsibilities, duties and obligations of all parties formalized.

(ix) Given the nature of the exercise, the integrated scheme has a determinate life-span. Also, it does not require any major injection of new funding, either to get it started or to ensure that it continues to function. These are generated internally and will diminish as the recipient country's external debts decrease and it approaches sustainable development. It provides, therefore, a fresh impetus and dynamism into the present system, which is rapidly losing momentum as creditors and debtors alike suffer from fatigue: the former from aid and debt relief fatigue, and the latter from structural adjustment fatigue.

(x) Finally, the scheme can be incorporated into and administered as part of SPA II, without detriment to that programme. In fact, it will have the opposite effect. Not only does it accept that SSA countries are a highly differentiated group of debtors, it enables individual members to earn debt relief and proceed with reforms at their own pace. It thus adds flexibility, improves efficiency and enhances the prospects of SPA II achieving its goals.

While it builds on the basic framework of SPA, the integrated scheme provides a set of general principles and operational guidelines for dynamizing the process of debt relief, without institutionalizing it. Although these principles are expressed in general terms, they can accommodate a selective approach which is consistent with and reflects the vast diversity of conditions in individual debtor countries and the highly differentiated nature of the problem. The debt crisis is, in fact, more severe in some countries than others, and it would be necessary to establish which debts and debtors should receive priority, given that the scheme is not open-ended. The operational guidelines are sufficiently flexible and comprehensive to enable this to be done.

The process of prioritization will have to be determined by SSA countries themselves. This is not going to be easy, and will require a lot of hard bargaining, much patience, diplomacy and negotiating skills, but it would be worth the effort. Among other things, it will mean that, for the first time,

SSA countries will have to consider the regional dimensions of the crisis, rather than concentrating solely on its impact on their individual economies. This, in turn, will help to encourage and promote greater regional cooperation and integration, streamline and expedite negotiations and improve the efficiency of relief operations. It will also promote greater coordination and cooperation among international aid agencies, credit countries and debt relief institutions. More directly, it will give SSA debtors a greater say in deciding their priorities and influencing the course and outcome of relief operations. It would not only involve them in all stages of the process, but change the status of their role from that of supplicants (which is what they are at present) to that of active participants. It would effectively multilateralize the system.

E. CONCLUDING REMARKS

Long-term sustainable development is the goal to which all SSA countries aspire. This aspiration is also shared by the rest of the international community of nations who have provided substantial amounts of resources to help them achieve their goal. In the 1980s opinions differed widely as to the most appropriate strategies and policies for SSA countries to pursue, with the sharpest differences being reflected in the controversy surrounding the need for reform and the costs and requirements of structural adjustment. This controversy has virtually burnt itself out and there is now a new sense of realism concerning the nature and scale of the crisis facing the region and what needs to be done, and by whom, to put things right.

This augurs well for the future. But two things are clear. First, despite the enormous effort and resources which have been poured into the region, the economic performance of SSA countries has not improved materially over the last decade. Indeed, many of them are poorer now than when the crisis began. With no real progress or prospects of growth in the immediate future, disillusionment is bound to set in and the commitment of both the international community and SSA countries themselves to long-term sustainable development falter and, ultimately, be superseded by more pressing international and national problems and priorities. SSA countries cannot continue to be the focus of international attention and assistance indefinitely, without showing results. Other poor countries are already beginning to demand similar 'special' treatment from the multilateral financial institutions and creditors. Also, the demise of communism in Eastern and Central Europe and the break-up of the Soviet Union have created a new set of problems and opportunities for the international economy. This is the international environment in which the need for long-term sustainable development in SSA countries and the level of international financial support for it must now be viewed.

Secondly, notwithstanding the amount of relief provided by the various initiatives, the debt crisis in SSA countries shows no signs of abating. Given that the relief programme for the next few years (as set out in SPA I and SPA II) has already fallen behind schedule, and that there are no additional initiatives on the agenda, it will become harder for them to cope with the debt crisis and at the same time continue their drive for sustainable development. Whereas the latter can be postponed or pushed into the future indefinitely, the former cannot, without seriously jeopardizing the limited progress which has already been achieved. It is the critical link in the relationship between the two goals. It has therefore to be tackled now. Also, no one knows what will happen after 1994 when SPA II expires. Will it be replaced by another SPA, thereby institutionalizing the programme, or will it be allowed to lapse? Either possibility opens up all sorts of problems and uncertainties for SSA countries and the multilateral financial institutions. It is imperative, therefore, that a fresh initiative be launched now in order to reduce the uncertainty and to maintain the momentum towards sustainable development. This is the role which the integrated strategy outlined in the preceding section is intended to fulfil.

NOTES

1. During the 1980s, gross domestic investment and savings rates for SSA countries consistently lagged behind those of other low-income developing countries; see *The World Bank Annual Report 1991*. Washington, D.C.: World Bank, August 1991, Tables 2.3 and 2.4.
2. Daniel P. Hewitt, 'Military Expenditure in the Developing World', *Finance and Development*, Washington, D.C.: IMF and World Bank, September 1991, pp. 22–5.
3. For details of individual country progress towards implementation of UNPAAERD, see UNCTAD, *Final Review and Appraisal of the United Nations Programme of Action for African Economic Recovery and Development, 1986–1990*. New York: United Nations, 1991 (TD/B/1280/Add.1/Rev.1), Annex Table 1, pp. 64–9.
4. Ibid., p. 56.
5. See *Financing Africa's Recovery, Report and Recommendations of the Advisory Group on Financial Flows for Africa*. New York: United Nations, February 1988.
6. See *Financing Adjustment with Growth in Sub-Saharan Africa, 1986–1990*. Washington, D.C.: World Bank, 1986, pp. 2–4.
7. *Sub-Saharan Africa: From Crisis to Sustainable Growth. A Long-Term Perspective Study*. Washington, D.C.: World Bank, 1989, p. 176.
8. *Africa's Adjustment and Growth in the 1980s*. Washington, D.C.: World Bank and UNDP, 1989, p. 3.
9. For the full text of its criticisms, see *Statistics and Policies, ECA Preliminary Observations on the World Bank Report: Africa's Adjustment and Growth in the 1980s*, Addis Ababa, Ethiopia: United Nations Economic Commission for Africa, April 1989, 24 pp. (mimeo). The World Bank's rejoinder to these criticisms is contained in *Comments on*

ECA's Response to World Bank/UNDP Report on Africa's Adjustment and Growth in the 1980s, 89–0038a: C. Humphreys, 9 May 1989, 12 pp. (mimeo).

10. See George C. Abbott, 'Two Perspectives on Adjustment in Africa', 50 pp. (mimeo); 'Africa Conference Issues Paper', Maastricht, The Netherlands, 2–4 July 1990 (mimeo); and Stanley Please, 'ECA and World Bank Strategy: Learning and Reassessment', 37 pp., 13 July 1989 (mimeo).
11. *The World Bank Annual Report 1991*. Washington, D.C.: World Bank, August 1991, p. 109.
12. See *Sub-Saharan Africa: From Crisis to Sustainable Growth* pp. 1–15, 185–94.
13. This point has been exhaustively discussed in the literature; see H.W. Singer, 'External Aid: For Plans or Projects?', *Economic Journal*, no. 299 September 1966, pp. 539–45; Alan Carlin, 'Project Versus Programme Aid: From the Donor's Viewpoint', *Economic Journal*, March 1967, pp. 48–58; Barend A. de Vries, 'External Aid: For Plan or Projects? An Alternative Approach', *Economic Journal*, September 1967, pp. 653–5; and H. W. Singer, 'Project versus Programme Aid: a Rejoinder', *Economic Journal*, December 1967, pp. 963–4.
14. These are fully discussed in Chapter 3.
15. For a discussion of the operations and activities of the Paris Club, see Henry J. Bitterman, *The Reshaping of International Debts*. Durham, N.C.: Duke University Press, 1973; Chandra S. Hardy, *Rescheduling Developing Countries' Debts, 1956–1981: Lessons and Recommendations*. Washington, D.C.: Overseas Development Council, 1982; Marko Milivojevic, *The Debt Rescheduling Process*. London: Frances Pinter, 1985, Ch. 3; and 'Debt and Managing Adjustment: Attracting Non-debt-creating Financial Flows and New Lending'. Geneva: UNCTAD Secretariat, May 1990 (DOC. TD/B/C.3/234).
16. These have already been discussed in Chapter 2.
17. See George C. Abbott, 'Loan Loss Provisioning', Intereconomics, vol. 24, September/October 1989, pp. 233–45.

Appendices

Appendix A.1 Basic indicators for Sub-Saharan African countries[a]

	Population (millions) mid-1987	Area (thousands of square kilometres)	GNP per capita[b] Dollars 1987	Average annual growth rate (%) 1965–73	1973–80	1980–87	Average annual inflation rate[c] (%) 1965–73	1973–80	1980–87	Life expectancy at birth (years) 1987
Ethiopia	44.8	1,222	130	1.1	0.0	–1.6	2.0	5.7	2.6	47
Chad	5.3	1,284	150	–1.3	–3.5	2.4	4.6	8.3	5.3	46
Zaire	32.6	2,345	150	0.3	–4.7	–2.5	19.0	42.1	53.5	52
Guinea-Bissau	0.9	36	160	..	–4.2	0.8	..	5.6	39.2	39
Malawi	7.9	118	160	4.3	1.4	0.0	3.7	8.5	12.4	46
Mozambique	14.6	802	170	..	..	–8.2	..	..	26.9	48
Tanzania	23.9	945	180	2.0	–0.9	–1.7	3.4	15.4	24.9	53
Burkina Faso	8.3	274	190	1.2	2.5	2.5	1.9	11.2	4.4	47
Madagascar	10.9	587	210	1.1	–1.5	–3.7	4.6	10.2	17.4	54
Mali	7.8	1,240	210	..	4.3	0.7	..	10.8	4.2	47
Gambia	0.8	11	220	1.7	0.2	0.8	3.0	13.5	13.8	43
Burundi	5.0	28	250	3.2	1.9	–0.2	3.0	15.4	7.5	49
Zambia	7.2	753	250	–0.5	–2.2	–5.6	5.8	8.9	28.7	53
Niger	6.8	1,267	260	–3.7	2.6	–4.9	4.1	8.5	4.1	45
Uganda	15.7	236	260	0.7	–6.2	–2.4	5.6	45.4	95.2	48
São Tomé and Príncipe	0.1	1	280	..	7.2	–6.0	..	2.1	4.9	65
Somalia	5.7	638	290	0.1	4.6	–2.5	4.5	17.6	37.8	47
Togo	3.2	57	290	2.0	1.5	–3.9	2.9	8.2	6.6	53
Rwanda	6.4	26	300	3.2	2.2	–1.0	7.2	17.1	4.5	49
Sierra Leone	3.8	72	300	2.3	–0.8	–2.0	2.1	14.5	50.0	41
Benin	4.3	113	310	0.0	–0.3	–0.6	2.9	11.6	8.2	50
Central African Republic	2.7	623	330	1.5	–0.5	–0.7	3.0	14.8	7.9	50
Kenya	22.1	583	330	4.7	1.3	–0.9	2.4	11.6	10.3	58
Sudan	23.1	2,506	330	–1.7	3.5	–4.3	7.2	15.3	31.7	50

Comoros	0.4	2	370	..	..	..	..	..	..	56
Lesotho	1.6	30	370	4.2	6.6	–0.9	4.1	11.3	12.3	56
Nigeria	106.6	924	370	5.3	1.2	–4.8	9.1	16.2	10.1	51
Ghana	13.6	239	390	1.0	–2.1	–2.0	8.1	45.4	48.3	54
Mauritania	1.9	1,031	440	1.2	–0.6	–1.6	4.1	8.5	9.8	46
Liberia	2.3	111	450	2.4	–0.7	–5.2	1.6	9.1	1.5	54
Equatorial Guinea	0.4	28	..	..	..	..	..	..	..	46
Guinea	6.5	246	..	1.2	1.3	–0.1	2.9	2.4	55.1	42
Cape Verde	0.3	4	500	..	7.3	1.2	..	9.7	13.9	65
Senegal	7.0	196	520	–0.8	–0.5	0.1	3.0	8.8	9.1	48
Zimbabwe	9.0	391	580	2.6	–2.0	–1.3	2.3	10.6	12.4	58
Swaziland	0.7	17	700	5.8	0.3	1.2	4.3	13.3	10.2	55
Côte d'Ivoire	11.1	322	740	4.5	1.2	–3.0	2.7	16.0	4.4	52
Congo, People's Republic	2.0	342	870	4.2	1.1	1.7	4.4	9.2	1.8	59
Cameroon	10.9	475	970	–0.4	5.7	4.5	7.5	10.4	8.1	56
Botswana	1.1	582	1,050	9.3	7.3	8.0	4.4	11.6	8.4	59
Mauritius	1.0	2	1,490	0.8	3.9	4.4	5.5	12.5	8.1	67
Gabon	1.1	268	2,700	4.9	–1.2	–3.5	5.8	15.8	2.6	52
Seychelles	0.1	0	3,120	2.6	4.5	1.3	7.3	18.3	3.7	70
Angola	9.2	1,247	..	1.1	–9.8	..	6.9	22.4	..	44
Djibouti	0.4	22	..	..	..	..	..	..	..	47
Total[d]	451.2	22,245	330[w]	2.9[w]	0.1[w]	–2.8[w]	7.5[w]	6.8[w]	15.2[w]	51[w]

Notes

[a] Listed in ascending order of GNP per capita except for those for which no GNP per capita can be calculated.
[b] Calculated according to World Bank Atlas method. For method of calculation, see Technical Notes of *Sub-Saharan Africa: From Crisis to Sustainable Growth*, Washington, D.C.: World Bank, 1989, pp. 283–4.
[c] See ibid., p. 284.
[d] Includes estimates for missing country data.
[w] Weighted average
.. Not available.

Source: *Sub-Saharan Africa: From Crisis to Sustainable Growth*, Statistical Appendix, Table 1, p. 221.

Appendix A.2 Terms of trade for selected SSA countries, 1970–88 (1980 = 100)

	1970	1975	1985	1986	1987	1988
Angola	43	63	102	70	67	55
Benin	166	128	103	82	94	112
Burkina Faso	127	110	102	98	102	106
Cameroon	93	74	78	86	69	69
Centr. Afr. Rep.	81	72	94	96	86	86
Chad	77	104	113	106	115	117
Congo	17	62	106	64	70	53
Côte d'Ivoire	81	75	85	87	78	75
Ethiopia	131	104	82	123	87	76
Gabon	16	61	101	60	66	56
Gambia	146	134	116	94	85	83
Ghana	88	80	59	67	64	66
Kenya	77	78	91	92	73	72
Liberia	165	125	101	107	97	102
Madagascar	96	93	102	111	82	81
Malawi	137	131	103	100	105	101
Mali	114	103	112	107	112	115
Mauritania	172	125	96	90	88	86
Mauritius	104	219	94	116	123	116
Mozambique	96	113	93	90	83	87
Niger	157	126	81	80	89	88
Nigeria	19	56	94	51	56	45
Rwanda	77	58	71	71	52	53
Senegal	89	153	102	99	96	101
Sierra Leone	129	104	96	99	88	90
Somalia	138	102	101	97	99	84
Sudan	96	115	92	81	76	94
Tanzania	96	100	89	99	70	78
Togo	66	217	87	78	63	67
Uganda	90	69	95	108	64	63
Zaire	181	97	90	85	85	100
Zambia	234	107	77	73	85	115

Source: *African Development Report 1990*, Abidjan, Côte d'Ivoire: African Development Bank, 1990, p. 174 (as amended).

Appendix A.3 Net resource flows to Sub-Saharan Africa, 1980–88

	Current $ billion									Per cent of total		
	1980	1981	1982	1983	1984	1985	1986	1987	1988	1980	1985	1987
I Official Development Finance (ODF)	10.6	10.3	10.9	10.7	12.5	12.1	15.4	18.1	20.4	65.8	81.8	82.6
1. Official Development Assistance (ODA)	8.9	9.1	9.2	9.1	10.0	11.0	13.4	15.1		55.3	74.3	68.9
of which: bilateral disbursements	6.4	6.5	6.7	6.5	7.2	7.6	9.4	10.7		39.8	51.4	48.9
multilateral disbursements	2.5	2.6	2.5	2.6	2.8	3.4	4.0	4.4		15.5	23.0	20.1
2. Other ODF	1.7	1.2	1.7	1.6	2.5	1.1	2.0	3.0		10.6	7.4	13.7
of which: bilateral disbursements	1.2	0.7	1.1	0.9	1.8	0.5	1.2	2.1		7.5	3.4	9.6
multilateral disbursements	0.5	0.5	0.6	0.7	0.7	0.6	0.8	0.9		3.1	4.1	4.1
II Total export credits	1.8	1.9	1.9	0.3	0.2	1.1	–0.1	–0.2	0.6	11.2	7.4	–0.9
1. DAC Countries	1.7	1.8	1.8	0.2	0.1	1.0	–0.2	–0.2		10.6	6.8	–0.9
of which: short-term	0.1	0.3	0.2	–0.7	0.2	0.9	0.5	1.5				
2. Other countries	0.1	0.1	0.1	0.1	0.1	0.1	0.1	x		0.6	0.7	x
III Private flows	3.7	4.4	4.9	2.1	–0.5	1.6	4.2	4.0	4.2	23.0	10.8	18.3
1. Direct investment (DAC)	1.0	1.8	2.2	0.3	–0.3	–0.2	0.6	0.9		6.2	–1.4	4.1
2. International bank lending[a]	2.0	2.0	2.0	1.1	–1.0	0.8	2.5	1.4		12.4	5.4	6.4
3. Total bond lending	x	x	x	x	x	x	x	x		x	x	x
4. Other private	x	x	x	x	x	0.1	0.1	0.7		x	0.7	3.2
5. Grants by non-governmental organizations	0.7	0.6	0.7	0.7	0.8	0.8	0.9	1.0		4.3	6.1	4.6
Total net resource flows (I + II + III)	16.1	16.6	17.7	13.1	12.2	14.8	19.5	21.9	25.2	100.0	100.0	100.0
Related data:												
Use of IMF credit, net	0.6	1.6	1.2	1.6	0.6	0.1	–0.3	–0.7	–0.4			
Net capital outflows by LDCs	x	–0.7	–0.2	–0.3	–0.5	–0.2	0.4	0.3	..			
Flight capital (estimated)	–4.0	–4.0	–3.0	–3.0	–2.0	–1.0	–1.0	–1.0	..			
Interest and dividends paid by LDCs, gross	–5.4	–5.3	–6.0	–5.1	–4.9	–5.2	–4.6	–5.0	–5.5			
	At 1987 prices and exchange rates											
Total net resource flows	21.3	22.8	24.9	18.5	17.6	21.1	22.4	21.9	23.5			
Total official development finance	14.0	14.1	15.3	15.1	18.0	17.2	17.7	18.1	19.0			
Total ODA receipts	11.8	12.5	12.9	12.8	14.4	15.7	15.4	15.5	..			

Notes

x Less than half the smallest unit shown.

[a] Includes long- and short-term transactions.

Note: See Technical Notes in Chapter VI of source.

Source: *Financing and External debt of Developing Countries, 1988 Survey*, Paris: OECD, 1989, Table III.6, p. 29.

Appendix A.4 Cancellations of SSA countries' ODA debt, by donor country, 1980–90 ($ million)

	Belgium		Canada		Denmark		Finland		France		Fed. Rep. of Germany		Italy	
Debtor country	80–7	88–9	80–7	88–9	80–7	88–9	80–7	88–9	80–7	88–9	80–7	88–9	80–7	88–9
Benin		2.9			19.6						56.3	20.4		
Burundi		12.7								92.1	30.1			
Central African Rep.										139.7	13.3	0.7		
Chad										64.1	6.1			
Comoros										29.0				
Equatorial Guinea										15.9				
Gambia										18.7	10.9			
Ghana			59.7	65.2		1.1				18.1		242.2		
Guinea						5.5				197.5	23.6	30.5		
Guinea-Bissau										0.8				
Kenya		5.7	98.0	91.6						146.7		370.0		
Liberia										5.9				
Madagascar		1.9	17.6	19.2						444.4		113.0		
Malawi					25.9					16.8	49.1			
Mali										165.1	93.3	33.7		
Mauritania			3.0		13.1					63.5		69.8		
Mozambique		0.2				10.7				139.7		79.6		
Niger		6.3			8.7					246.0	93.1			
Senegal		2.5	12.9	14.1	5.2					571.4		206.2		
Sierra Leone										4.3	53.6	7.7		
Somalia										37.0	56.8		12.1	
Sudan					7.6					45.6		1.9	7.4	
Tanzania		27.0	11.2		95.7					25.9	198.6			
Togo			12.0		11.0					150.8	101.1	4.0		
Uganda			8.8							29.7				
Zaire		124.2	1.1	26.3						142.9		270.9		
Zambia			65.0		0.6	3.2				4.0	236.9			
Total	0	184	290	217	188	23	23	0	118	2874	999	1671	20	0

Notes

Amounts in local currencies were converted into dollars at annual average exchange rates (from *International Financial Statistics*) at the time of cancellation. The amounts of the cancellations are mostly the face value of debt at the time of forgiveness. Data for some countries may include small amounts of debt not on ODA terms; for example, in the case of France, cancellations include earlier loans for adjustment on non-concessional terms, estimated to account for 15–20 per cent of total cancelled stock of debt in 1989. Some 1990 cancellations are pending government implementation.

The following countries cancelled ODA loans in 1978 and 1979: Finland ($23 million), France ($118 million), Germany ($576 million), The Netherlands ($75 million), Sweden ($56 million), Switzerland ($7 million), and the United Kingdom ($153 million). These amounts are included in the 1980–87 totals.

[a] Amounts represent the value of grants provided to finance debt service obligations falling due in the respective years.

[b] Figures include approximately $5 million, $21 million, and $18 million in debt service forgiven for 1978–9, 1980–7 and 1988–9, respectively, in addition to the value of other debt that was cancelled.

Source: Based on SPA donors' reports as of February 1990 and on *World Debt Tables 1989–90*, and published as Appendix Table B.1 in Development Committee no. 26, *Development Issues*, Presentations to the 39th Meeting of the Development Committee, 24 September 1990, Washington, D.C.: World Bank, 1991, pp. 54–5 (as amended).

Japan[a]		Netherlands[b]		Norway		Sweden		Switzerland		UK		United States		All donors	
80–7	88–9	80–7	88–9	80–7	88–9	80–7	88–9	80–7	88–9	80–7	88–9	80–7	88–9	80–7	88–9
													22.0	40.0	81.3
															104.8
														13.3	140.4
														6.1	64.1
															29.0
															15.9
										4.2	0.6			15.1	22.3
										12.3	6.4		79.7	72.0	412.7
		3.2											4.5	26.8	237.9
		8.0												8.0	0.8
3.5	0.8	20.9	16.0							63.0	6.8		101.3	185.4	738.9
															5.9
													5.9	17.6	584.5
3.1	1.1	5.8								23.2	3.3		29.0	107.1	50.2
													5.1	93.3	203.9
														16.2	133.3
	1.1	2.3	32.5							6.1	2.3			8.4	266.1
													2.9	101.9	255.3
											0.1			18.1	794.4
		3.0								11.3	0.6			67.9	12.6
														68.9	37.0
1.7		16.9				10.3				7.8	0.8			51.7	48.3
2.1	1.0	66.7		110.6						5.6	0.1			490.2	54.0
														124.1	154.8
2.2	0.6	4.5								34.6	1.1		8.8	79.9	10.5
													144.6	1.1	708.9
		6.2				8.3								80.2	244.1
13	5	144	49	111	0	79	0	7	0	339	22	0	404	2082	5412

Appendix A.5 Rescheduling agreements for SSA countries under Paris Club application of Toronto Terms, as of July 1990 ($ million)

Debtor country & date of meeting	Contract cut-off date	Treatment of previously rescheduled debt	Treatment of arrears	Consolidation of principal & interest (%)	Amount consol-idated	Consolidation period	Net cash savings during consolidation period[a]	Decrease in present value of scheduled debt service[a]	Comment
Mali 27 Oct 88	1 Jan 88	No PRD	Included	100	56	Jul 88/Oct 89 (16 months)	...	3	
Madagascar 28 Oct 88	1 Jul 83	Excludes 85, 86 PC (incl. 81, 83, 84 PC)	Included	100	265	Apr 88/Dec 89 (21 months)	4	34	
Tanzania 13 Dec 88	30 Jun 86	None excluded (incl. 86 PC)	Included	100	341	Jan 89/Jun 89 (6 months)	4	68	
Central African Rep. 14 Dec 88	1 Jan 83	Excludes 85 PC & interest on 81, 83 PC (incl. princi-pal 81, 83 PC)	Included, ex-cept interest on PRD	100	30	Jan 89/Jun 90 (18 months)	1	4	PRD ex-cludes interest
Niger 16 Dec 88	1 Jul 83	Excludes 86 & Apr 88 PC; (incl. 83, 84, 85 PC)	No arrears	100	43	Jan 89/Dec 89 (12 months)	1	11	
Senegal 24 Jan 89	1 Jan 83	None excluded (partially incl. 81, 82, 83, 85, 86, 87 PC)	No arrears	100	136	Nov 88/Dec 89 (14 months) PRD Nov 88/ Jun 89	3	27	

Uganda 26 Jan 89	1 Jul 81	None excluded (incl. 81, 82, 87 PC)	Included	100	90	Jan 89/Jun 90 (18 months)	3	16	Arrears include late interest
Guinea 12 Apr 89	1 Jan 86	None excluded (incl. 86 PC)	Included (90 per cent for 86 PC)	100	124	Jan 89/Dec 89 (12 months)	...	6	
Mauritania 19 Jun 89	31 Dec 84	Excludes 87 PC: 85 and 86 PC to be re-paid within 1.5 years	Included	100	52	Jun 89/May 90 (12 months)	1	7	
Togo 20 Jun 89	1 Jan 83	Excludes 84, 85 & 88 PC; (incl. 79 PC principal, 81 & 83 PC)	No arrears	100	76	Apr 89/Jun 90 (14.5 months)	1	15	Excl. cement plant debt
Benin 22 Jun 89	31 Mar 89	No PRD	Included	100	193	Jun 89/Jun 90 (13 months)	...	13	Arrears incl. late interest; excl. sugar and cement plant debt
Zaire 23 Jun 89	30 Jun 83	None excluded but 86 & 87 PC to be paid over 1.5 yrs (incl. 76, 77, 79, 81 83, 85 PC)	Included, ex-cept for arr-ears on 86 & 87 PC to be repaid over 1.5 yrs	100	1,530	Jun 89/Jun 90 (13 months)	26	197	Excludes late interest

Appendix A.5 – continued

Debtor country & date of meeting	Contract cut-off date	Treatment of previously rescheduled debt	Treatment of arrears	Consolidation of principal & interest (%)	Amount consol-idated	Consolidation period	Net cash savings during consolidation period[a]	Decrease in present value of scheduled debt service[a]	Comment
Chad 24 Oct 89	30 Jun 89	No PRD	Included	100	52	Oct 89/Dec 90 (15 months)	1	5	Bilateral arrange-ments out-side the Paris Club
Guinea-Bissau 26 Oct 89	31 Dec 89	None excluded (incl. 87 PC)	Included	100	21	Oct 89/Dec 90 (15 months)	...	1	Includes late interest
Mali 22 Nov 89	1 Jan 88	No PRD	Included	100	21	Nov 89/Dec 91 (26 months)	...	1	Includes short-term debt and late interest up to 30 Jun 89; PRD incl. all int. & principal between 1 Jan 90 & 30 Jun 90 under 86 & 87 PC
Senegal 12 Feb 90	1 Jan 83	Excl. 89 PC (partially incl. 81, 82, 83, 85, 86, 87 PC)	Excluded	100	158	Jan 90/Dec 90 (12 months)	2	34	

Equatorial Guinea 1 Mar 90	1 Jul 84	Only arrears rescheduled	Included	100 of arrears	6	As of Dec 88	...	1	Bilateral arrange-ments out-side the Paris Club
Tanzania 16 Mar 90	30 Jun 86	None excluded (incl. interest due to 86 PC; 20% of included due on 88 PC)	Included	100	199	Jan 90/Dec 90 (12 months)	3	42	Incl. late interest on arrears; principal on PRD not reorganized
Mozambique 14 Jun 90	1 Feb 84	None excluded (incl. 84, 87 PC)	Included	100	707	Jul 90/Dec 92 (30 months)	30	155	Incl. late interest due on arrears for original maturities
Central African Rep. 15 Jun 90	1 Jan 83	Excl. 81, 85 88 PC & Jul 84 Aug 84 bilateral (incl. only amounts due from the 83 PC)	Excl. except for arrears on 83 PC	100	4	Jan 90/Dec 90 (12 months)	...	1	Incl. only those amounts due from 83 consolida-tion; no other pay-ments are consoli-dated; late int-erest is excluded

Appendix A.5 – continued

Debtor country & date of meeting	Contract cut-off date	Treatment of previously rescheduled debt	Treatment of arrears	Consolidation of principal & interest (%)	Amount consol-idated	Consolidation period	Net cash savings during consolidation period[a]	Decrease in present value of scheduled debt service[a]	Comment
Togo 9 Jul 90	1 Jan 83	Incl. 81, 83, 84 85, PC; excl. 79,88,89 PC	Excluded	100 of P/I of 81, 83, 84 PRD; 100 of principal from 85 PRD	84	Jul 90/Jun 92 for 81, 83, 84 PRD; Jan 91/ Jun 91 for 85 PRD	3	10	Incl. only PRD; excl. cement plant debt; excl. late interest
Madagascar 10 Jul 90	1 Jul 83	Excl. 81, 85, 86, 88, PC (incl. only amounts due from 82, 84 PC)	Excluded	100	139	Jun 90/Jun 91 (12 months)	2	20	Excl. late interest
Zambia 12 Jul 90	1 Jan 83	None excluded (incl. 83, 86 PC)	Included	100	965	Jul 90/Dec 91 (18 months)	14	136	Incl. late interest on arrears
Total or average				100	5286	16 months	97	807	

Notes

... Less than $500,000

P/I Principal and interest

PC Paris Club

PRD Previously rescheduled debt

[a] In relation to standard reschedulings with a 20-year maturity and a 10-year grace period. A discount rate of 9% was used to calculate the present value of scheduled debt service payments.

Source: As Appendix A.4, Appendix Table B.2, pp. 56–9 (as amended).

Appendix A.6 Summary of proposed policy instruments and measures under AAF-SAP

Description of policy instruments and measures	Effects for adjustment with transformation
Strengthening and diversifying production capacity	
(a) Land reforms for better access and entitlement to land for productive use; enhancement of the role of women as agents of change and the modernization of the food production sector.	Increased production and opportunities for gainful employment; poverty alleviation and more equitable income distribution.
(b) Devoting at least 20–25 per cent of the total of public investment to agriculture.	Improved rural infrastructure and agricultural institutions; increased agricultural productivity; expansion or rural employment.
(c) Allocation of an increasing share of foreign exchange for imports of vital inputs for agriculture and manufacturing sectors; expansion of agricultural and industrial employment, increased domestic output of essential commodities and avoidance of import strangulation; and increased interlinkages between agriculture and industry.	Satisfaction of critical needs.
(d) Sectoral allocation of credit using guidelines that would favour the food subsector and the manufacture of essential goods.	Increased production of food and essential manufactured goods; increased gainful employment.

Appendix A.6 – continued

Description of policy instruments and measures		Effects for adjustment with transformation
(e)	Adoption of investment codes and procedures tailored to the promotion and development of small-scale industries.	Better enabling environment with greater involvement of local entrepreneurs.
(f)	Use of selective nominal interest rates in such a way that interest rates on loans for speculative activities would be greater than the rates on loans for productive activities, and resulting weighted real interest rates for savings would be positive.	Increased mobilization of domestic savings; reduction of speculative activities; shifting resources to productive activities.
(g)	Creation and strengthening of rural financial institutions.	Increased mobilization of rural savings and improved financial intermediation.
(h)	Rehabilitation and rationalization of installed productive and infrastructural capacities; and setting up of an effective national maintenance system.	Fuller capacity utilization; economic growth; savings in foreign exchange.
(i)	Utilizing the existence of *de facto* multiple exchange rate systems in a rationalized manner and/or creating and streamlining such a system for purposes of resource transfers, resource mobilization and reversal of capital flight and ensuring availability of essential imports.	Encouragement of capital inflows, especially by nationals working abroad, and discouragement of capital flight; improvement in balance of payments; satisfaction of critical needs.

Appendix A.6 – continued

Description of policy instruments and measures	Effects for adjustment with transformation
(j) Creation of a special fund for loans at subsidized interest rates to certain groups of economic operators.	Encouragement of greater productive activity.
Improving the level of income and the pattern of its distribution	
(a) Enlarging the tax base, improving efficiency and probity of the tax collection machinery.	Increased government revenue.
(b) Reduction of government expenditure on defence as much as possible, and on non-productive public sector activities.	Release of resources for investment; improvement in resource allocation; improvement in balance of payments.
(c) Removal of subventions to parastatals other than those in the social sector and nationally strategic basic industries.	Release of resources for productive investments; better fiscal balance.
(d) Use of limited, realistic and decreasing deficit financing for productive and infrastructural investments that have little import content.	Sustaining growth through support to relevant production units.
(e) Guaranteed minimum prices for food crops managed through strategic food reserves.	Food production on a sustained basis; assured income to farmers; increased access to food for majority of the population; control of inflation.
Pattern of expenditure for the satisfaction of needs	
(a) Expenditure-switching (without necessarily increasing total government spending) to raise government outlays	Satisfaction of critical social needs; investment in human capital; raising living standards of majority of the population.

Appendix A.6 – continued

Description of policy instruments and measures	Effects for adjustment with transformation
on the social sectors, particularly those aspects of education, health and the integration of women in the development process that are likely to increase productivity, such that an average of 30 per cent of total annual government outlays is devoted to the social sectors; and thereafter to maintain a growth rate in public outlays on these sectors at above the population growth rate.	
(b) Selective policies through subsidies, pricing policies, etc., to increase the supply of essential commodities required for maintaining a socially stable atmosphere for development.	Increased affordability of essential goods and services as well as critical intermediate inputs; increased production of industrial raw materials; control of inflation.
(c) Selective use of trade policy, including banning of certain specified luxuries; high tax rates on conspicuous consumption and competitive factor inputs that have domestic substitutes; and mass education towards consumption of domestic goods.	Changes in consumption patterns; enlargement of markets for domestic goods; changes in production patterns; internalization of production of factor inputs; improvements in balance of payments.
(d) Strengthening intra-African monetary and financial co-operation as well as	Increased self-reliance and capacities to finance adjustment with transformation.

Appendix A.6 – continued

Description of policy instruments and measures	Effects for adjustment with transformation
payments and clearing arrangements.	
(e) Limitation of debt service ratios to levels consistent with sustaining and accelerating growth and development.	Freeing of resources for productive activities to sustain adjustment with transformation; improvement of balance of payments position.
(f) Specific export incentives for processed exports and carefully selected primary commodities.	Increased diversification; reduced vulnerability to fluctuations in commodity prices; export growth and increased export earnings.
(g) Differential export subsidies; removal of trade barriers; and encouraging barter trade to boost intra-African trade.	Reduced external dependence and better product mixes and integration in Africa.
(h) Bilateral and multilateral agreements on primary commodities.	Improved and more stable balance of payments.
Institutional support for adjustment with transformation	
(a) Creation of adequately funded 'supervised food production credit systems' in rural areas with easy access by farmers in terms of limited collaterals, etc.	Sustained increase in food production and adoption of technologies to reduce vulnerability to weather through increased investments in areas such as small irrigation schemes.
(b) Strengthening agricultural research focused on production; creation of extension services and systems for the diffusion, application and operationalization of research.	Will accelerate process of achieving a green revolution in Africa, especially in the five food crops that are basic to food self-sufficiency in the region (maize, sorghum, millet, rice and tubers), as well as accelerate the building up of a viable industrial base.

Appendix A.6 – continued

Description of policy instruments and measures	Effects for adjustment with transformation
(c) Creation of rural institutions to suppport cottage industries and small-scale industries with emphasis on indigenous technology, domestic finance, rural infrastructure and women's participation.	Promotion of integrated rural development; enhancement of the attractiveness of rural areas, promotion of rural technological development; employment generation.
(d) Legislation of a clear framework of ownership and participation of the different socio-economic groups such as rural co-operatives, artisans, traders, etc.	Will enable popular participation in production, marketing and development in general; and the strengthening of the informal sector and its ultimate integration into the mainstream of development.
(e) Establishment of community development institutions, especially indigenous NGOs and self-help programmes.	Will enable use of direct community labour on a voluntary basis for the provision of rural infrastructure, such as feeder and access roads, health centres and dispensaries, school buildings and small irrigation schemes.
(f) Greater mass participation in decision-making and implementation of programmes.	Greater confidence of the people in their own societies and government; greater commitment to and sacrifice for development; more efficient use of highly motivated human resources.

Source: *African Alternative Framework to Structural Adjustment Programmes for Socio-economic Recovery and Transformation*, Addis Ababa, Ethiopia: United Nations, Economic Commission for Africa, July 1989, pp. 38–43 (as amended).

Appendix A.7 Summary of policy instruments and measures to be modified under AAF-SAP

Description of policy instruments and measures	Effects for adjustment with transformation
(a) Drastic budgetary reductions, especially with respect to expenditures and subsidies on social services and essential goods.	Undermines the human condition, the enabling environment and the future potential for development; necessitates massive retrenchment in the public sector.
(b) Indiscriminate promotion of traditional exports through price incentives offered only to the 'tradables'.	Undermines food production and self-sufficiency, and can lead to undesirable environmental degradation; could result in over-supply and fall in prices (fallacy of composition).
(c) Across-the-board credit squeeze.	Leads to overall contraction of the economy; declines in capacity utilization and closure of enterprises; and an accentuated shortage of critical goods and services.
(d) Generalized devaluation through open foreign exchange markets; currency auctions and large and frequent currency depreciations.	Leads to socially unsupportable increases in prices of critical goods and services; raises the domestic cost of imported inputs and undermines capacity utilization; triggers general inflation; diverts scarce foreign exchange to speculative activities and exacerbates capital flight; worsens income distribution patterns; undermines growth and can result in structural entrenchment of traditional exports through price incentives for such commodities or 'tradables'.
(e) Unsustainably high real interest rates (inflation-adjusted nominal rates of interest).	Shifts the economy towards speculative and trading activities by becoming a disincentive to productive investment; fuels inflation.

Appendix A.7 – continued

Description of policy instruments and measures	Effects for adjustment with transformation
(f) Total import liberalization.	Leads to greater and more entrenched external dependence; intensifies foreign exchange constraints; jeopardizes national priorities such as food self-sufficiency; erodes capacity of infant industries and thereby slows industrialization.
(g) Excessive dependence on market forces for getting the 'prices right' in structurally distorted and imperfect situations.	Worsens inflation through sharp rises in production costs and mark-ups; causes deviations from desirable production and consumption patterns and priorities, and may derail entire process of transformation.
(h) Doctrinaire privatization.	Undermines growth and transformation; jeopardizes social welfare and the human condition.

Source: As for Appendix A.6, pp. 37–8 (as amended).

Bibliography

Abbott, George C. (1972), 'Aid and Indebtedness – a Proposal', *National Westminster Bank Review*, May, pp. 55–67.

Abbott, George C. (1975), 'Debt Consolidation: the Case for Cancellation', *Intereconomics*, July, pp. 217–21.

Abbott, George C. (1979), *International Indebtedness and the Developing Countries*. London and New York: Croom Helm and M.E. Sharpe.

Abbott, George C. (1987), 'Retroactive Terms Adjustment', *Intereconomics*, vol. 22, July/August, pp. 182–9.

Abbott, George C. (1989), 'Another Round of Retroactive Terms Adjustment', *European Journal of Development Research*, vol. 1, no. 2, pp. 60–77.

Abbott, George C. (1991), 'The Toronto Summit and Sub-Sahara African Countries', *African Review of Money, Finance and Banking*, January, Supplementary issue on Savings and Development, pp. 64–84.

Adams, Martin E. (1989), 'Aid Co-ordination in Africa: a Review', *Development Policy Review*, vol. 7, no. 2, June.

African Development Bank (annual), *African Development Report*. Abijdan, Côte d'Ivoire: ADC.

African Development Bank (1987), 'A Proposal for Refinancing African External Debt'. London: S.G. Warburg & Co. Ltd, November.

African Development Bank (1988), 'The Challenge to Recovery and Growth: Finding Solutions to Africa's External Debt', papers presented at *Financial Times* Conference, London, 18–19 April.

Alexandratos, N. (ed.) (1988), *World Agriculture Towards 2000: An FAO Study*. London: Belhaven Press.

Berg, Elliot and Batchelor, Alan (1985), 'Structural Adjustment Lending: a Critical View'. Washington, D.C.: World Bank CPD Discussion Paper 1985–21.

Bitterman, Henry J. (1973), *The Refunding of International Debt*. Durham, N.C.: Duke University Press.

Cencini, Alvaro and Schmitt, Bernard (1991), *External Debt Servicing: A Vicious Circle*. London and New York: Frances Pinter.

Chhibber, Ajay (1991), 'Africa's Rising Inflation: Causes, Consequences and Cures', *Working Papers* WPS 577, Policy, Research and External Affairs, Washington, D.C.: World Bank, February.

Commander, Simon (ed.) (1989), *Structural Adjustment and Agriculture*. London: James Curry and ODI.

Commins, Stephen K. (ed.) (1988), *Africa's Development Challenges and the World Bank: Hard Questions, Costly Choices*. Boulder, Col.: Lynne Rienner.

Commonwealth Secretariat (1987), *Persistent Indebtedness: The Need for Further Action*. London: Commonwealth Secretariat, April.

Commonwealth Secretariat (1988), *Debt Distress: A Problem for Low-income Developing Countries*. London: Commonwealth Secretariat, April.

Corbo, Vittorio, Goldstein, Morris and Khan, Moshin (eds) (1987), *Growth-Oriented Adjustment Programs*. Washington, D.C.: IMF and World Bank.

Cornia, Giovanni, Jolly, Richard and Stewart, Frances (eds) (1987), *Adjustment with a Human Face*, vol. 1. Oxford: Clarendon Press.

De Rosa, Dean A. (1990), 'Protection and Export Performance in Sub-Saharan Africa', *IMF Working Paper* WP/90/83. Washington, D.C.: International Monetary Fund.

Finance and Development, quarterly publication, Washington, D.C.: International Monetary Fund and World Bank.

Green, Reginald H. (1988), 'Unmanageable – Towards Sub-Saharan African Debt Bargaining', in Stephany Griffith-Jones (ed.), *Managing World Debt*. New York: St Martin's Press; Hemel Hempstead: Harvester Wheatsheaf.

Green, Reginald H. (ed.) (1985), 'Sub-Saharan Africa: Towards Oblivion or Reconstruction', *Journal of Development Planning*, no 15.

Green, Reginald H. and Griffith-Jones, Stephany (1986), 'Sub-Saharan Africa's External Debt Crisis', *Third World Affairs*.

Guitian, Manuel (1987), 'Adjustment and Economic Growth: Their Fundamental Complementarity', paper presented at *Symposium on Growth-Oriented Adjustment Programs*, 25–7 February. Washington, D.C.: International Monetary Fund and World Bank.

Hardy, Chandra S. (1982), *Rescheduling Developing Country Debts, 1956–81: Lessons and Recommendations*. Washington, D.C.: Overseas Development Council.

Harvey, Charles (1988), 'Recovery from Macro-disaster in Sub-Saharan Africa'. Sussex: IDS, November (mimeo).

Hawkins, A.M. (1986), 'Can Africa Industrialize?' in Robert Berg and Jennifer Seymour Whitaker (eds), *Strategies for African Development: A Study for the Committee on African Development Strategies*. Berkeley: University of California Press.

Helleiner, Gerald K. (1986), 'Policy-based Lending: a Look at the World Bank's New Role', in *Between Two Worlds: The World Bank's Next Decade*. Washington, D.C.: Overseas Development Council.

Helleiner, Gerald K. (1988), 'Growth-oriented Adjustment Lending: a Critical Assessment of IMF/World Bank Approaches', discussion paper written for the South Commission, Geneva, May (mimeo).

Helleiner, Gerald K. (ed.) (1986), *Africa and the IMF*. Washington, D.C.: Overseas Development Council.

International Bank for Reconstruction and Development (1981), *Accelerated Development in Sub-Saharan Africa. An Agenda for Action*. Washington, D.C.: World Bank, October.

International Bank for Reconstruction and Development (1986a), *Financing Adjustment with Growth in Sub-Saharan Africa, 1986–1990*. Washington, D.C.: World Bank, April.

International Bank for Reconstruction and Development (1986b), *Recovery in the Developing World: The London Symposium on the World Bank's Role*. Washington, D.C.: World Bank.

International Bank for Reconstruction and Development (1988a), *Lending for Adjustment: An Update*, *World Bank News*, Special Report. Washington, D.C.: World Bank, April.

International Bank for Reconstruction and Development (1988b), *Adjustment Lending. An Evaluation of Ten Years Experience*, Policy and Research Series. Washington, D.C.: World Bank, December.

International Bank for Reconstruction and Development (1988c), *Report of the Task Force on Food Security in Africa*. Washington, D.C.: World Bank (processed).

International Bank for Reconstruction and Development (1989a), *Africa's Adjustment and Growth in the 1980s*. Washington, D.C.: World Bank/ UNDP, March.

International Bank for Reconstruction and Development (1989b), *Sub-Saharan Africa: From Crisis to Sustainable Growth: A Long-term Perspective Study*. Washington, D.C.: World Bank, November.

International Bank for Reconstruction and Development (1991), *Food Aid in Africa: An Agenda for the 1990s*. Washington, D.C.: World Bank and World Food Programme, August.

International Bank for Reconstruction and Development (annual a), *The World Bank Annual Report*, Washington, D.C.: World Bank.

International Bank for Reconstruction and Development (annual b), *World Debt Tables. External Debt of Developing Countries*, vol. 1. Washington, D.C.: World Bank.

International Bank for Reconstruction and Development (annual c), *World Development Report*. Oxford: Oxford University Press, for World Bank.

International Bank for Reconstruction and Development: Development Committee no. 13 (1987), *Protecting the Poor during Periods of Adjustment*. Washington, D.C.: World Bank, August.

International Bank for Reconstruction and Development: Development

Committee no. 16 (1988), *Proposals for Enhancing Assistance to Low-income Countries that Face Exceptional Difficulties*. Washington, D.C.: World Bank, June.

International Bank for Reconstruction and Development: Development Committee no. 21 (1990), *Progress of Initiatives to Benefit Sub-Saharan Africa*. Washington, D.C.: World Bank, January.

International Bank for Reconstruction and Development: Development Committee no. 23 (1990), *Problems and Issues in Structural Adjustment*. Washington, D.C.: World Bank, February.

International Bank for Reconstruction and Development: Development Committee no. 26 (1990), *Development Issues, Presentation to 39th Meeting of the Development Committee*. Washington, D.C.: World Bank, September, pp. 40–59.

International Bank for Reconstruction and Development: Development Committee no. 27 (1991), *Presentations to the 41st Meeting of the Development Committee*. Washington, D.C.: World Bank, April, pp. 78–88.

International Bank for Reconstruction and Development: Development Committee no. 28 (1992), *Presentations to the 42nd Meeting of the Development Committee*, Bangkok, Thailand, pp. 59–76, Washington, D.C.: World Bank, October.

International Bank for Reconstruction and Development: Economic Development Institute (1989), *Successful Development in Africa: Case Studies of Projects, Programs and Policies*. Washington, D.C.: World Bank.

International Labour Organization (1988), 'African Employment Report'. Addis Ababa: Jobs and Skills Programme for Africa, (processed).

International Monetary Fund (1987), 'Theoretical Aspects of the Design of the Fund-supported Adjustment Programs', *IMF Occasional Paper no. 55*. Washington, D.C.: IMF, September.

International Monetary Fund (annual), *International Monetary Fund Annual Report*. Washington, D.C.: IMF.

International Monetary Fund (semi-annually), *World Economic Outlook*, Washington, D.C.: IMF.

Khan, Moshin S. (1988), 'Evaluating the Effects of IMF-supported Adjustment Programs: an Empircal Survey'. Washington, D.C.: IMF (mimeo).

Khan, Moshin S. and Knight, Malcolm D. (1985), *Fund-supported Adjustment Programs and Economic Growth*, IMF Occasional Paper no. 41. Washington, D.C.: IMF, November.

Killick, Tony (1987), 'Unsettled Questions about Adjustment with Growth', in *International Monetary and Financial Issues for the Developing Countries*. Geneva: UNCTAD.

Killick, Tony (1990), 'The Developmental Effectiveness of Aid to Africa'. London: Overseas Development Institute, February (mimeo).

Koester, Ulrich, Schafer, Hartwig and Valdes, Alberto (1987), 'Structural Adjustment and the Outlook for Agricultural Export Earnings in Africa'. Washington, D.C.: International Food Policy Institute, December (mimeo).

Krumm, Kathie L. (1986), 'The External Debt of Sub-Saharan Africa – Origins, Magnitude and Implications for Action', *World Bank Staff Working Paper no. 741*. Washington, D.C.: World Bank.

Lancaster, Carol and Williamson, John (eds) (1986), *African Debt and Financing*, Special Report no. 5. Washington, D.C.: Institute for International Economics, May.

Lele, Uma (1989), *Agricultural Growth, Domestic Policies, the External Environment and Assistance to Africa: Lessons of a Quarter Century*, MADIA Discussion Paper no. 1. Washington, D.C.: World Bank.

MacDonald, Scott B., Lindsay, Margie and Crum, David L. (eds) (1990), *The Global Debt Crisis*, London and New York: Frances Pinter.

McDonald, D. C. (1982), 'Debt Capacity of Developing Country Borrowing: a Survey of the Literature', *IMF Staff Papers*. Washington, D.C.: International Monetary Fund.

Mehran, H. (ed.) (1985), *External Debt Management*. Washington, D.C.: International Monetary Fund.

Mellor, John W., Delgado, Christopher L. and Blackie, Malcolm J. (eds) (1987), *Accelerating Food Production in Sub-Saharan Africa*. Baltimore, Md: Johns Hopkins University Press.

Michalopoulas, Constantine (1987), 'World Bank Programmes for Adjustment and Growth', paper presented at *Symposium on Growth-oriented Adjustment Programs*. Washington, D.C.: IMF and World Bank, February.

Milivojevic, M. (1985), *The Debt Rescheduling Process*, London and New York: Frances Pinter.

Mistry, Percy S. (1988), *African Debt: The Case for Relief for Sub-Saharan Africa*. Oxford: Oxford International Associates.

Mosley, Paul, Harrigan, Jane and Taye, John (eds) (1991), *Aid and Power. The World Bank and Policy-Based Lending*, vol. 1: *Analysis and Policy Proposals*; and vol. 2: *Case Studies*, London and New York: Routledge.

Mosley, P. and Toye, J. (1988), 'The Design of Structural Adjustment Programmes', *Development Policy Review*, vol. 6, pp. 395–413.

Onimode, B. (ed.) (1989), *The IMF, the World Bank and the African Debt*, vol. 1: *The Economic Impact;* and vol. 2: *The Social and Political Impact*. London: Zed Books.

Organization of African Unity (1980), *The Lagos Plan of Action for the Economic Development of Africa, 1980–2000*, Lagos. Nigeria: Organization of African Unity, April.

Organization for Economic Co-operation and Development (1988), *The Sahel*

Facing the Future: Increasing Dependence on Structural Transformation: Futures Study of the Sahel Countries, 1985–2010. Paris: OECD.

Organization for Economic Co-operation and Development (1989), *Financing and External Debt of Developing Countries, 1988 Survey*. Paris: OECD.

Organization for Economic Co-operation and Development (1990), *Financing and External Debt of Developing Countries, 1989 Survey*. Paris: OECD.

Organization for Economic Co-operation and Development (annual), *Development Cooporation Report of the Chairman of the Development Assistance Committee*. Paris: OECD.

Osunsade, F.L. and Gleason, Paul (1992), *IMF Assistance to Sub-Saharan Africa*. Washington, D.C.: IMF, January.

Overseas Development Institute (1990), 'Recent Initiatives on Developing Country Debt', *ODI Briefing Paper.* London: Overseas Development Institute, April.

Pickett, James and Singer, Hans (eds) (1990), *Towards Economic Recovery in Sub-Saharan Africa*. London and New York: Routledge.

Please, Stanley (1984a), *The Hobbled Giant: Essays on the World Bank.* Boulder, Col.: Westview Press.

Please, Stanley (1984b), 'The World Bank: Lending for Structural Adjustment', in *Adjustment Crisis in the Third World.* Washington, D.C.: Overseas Development Council.

Ravenshill, J. (ed.) (1986), *Africa in Economic Crisis*. London: Macmillan.

Rose, Tore (ed.) (1985), *Crisis and Recovery in Sub-Saharan Africa: Realities and Complexities*. Paris: OECD, June.

Rotberg, R.I. (ed.) (1988), *Africa in the 1990s and Beyond.* World Peace Foundation, Algonac, Michigan: Reference Publications.

Salvatore, Dominick (ed.) (1989), *African Development Prospects: A Policy Modelling Approach.* New York: Taylor & Francis.

Save-Soderbergh, S. and Taxell, Per (eds) (1988), *Recovery in Africa: A Challenge for Development Co-operation in the 1990s*. Stockholm: Swedish Ministry of Foreign Affairs.

Serageldin, I. (1989), *Poverty, Adjustment and Growth in Africa.* Washington, D.C.: World Bank, April.

Singer, Hans (1989), 'The African Food Crisis and the Role of Food Aid', *Food Policy*, vol. 4, no. 3, August.

Smith, G. and Cuddington, J. (eds) (1985), *International Debt and the Developing Countries*. Washington, D.C.: World Bank.

Streeten, Paul (1987), 'Structural Adjustment: a survey of the Issues and Options', *World Development*, vol. 15, no. 12, December.

Svedberg, Peter (1988), 'The Export Performance of Sub-Saharan Africa, 1970–1985', paper prepared for *Trade and Development in Sub-Saharan*

Africa, financed by Rockefeller Foundation. London: Commonwealth Secretariat and Centre for Economic Policy Research, April.

Taylor, Alwyn B. (1987), 'The Debt Problem of Sub-Saharan Africa', paper presented at 5th General Conference of the European Association of Development Institutes (EADI), Amsterdam (mimeo).

United Nations (1986), *Africa. United Nations Programme of Action for African Economic Recovery and Development, 1986–1990 (UNPAAERD)*. New York: United Nations.

United Nations (1988), *Financing Africa's Recovery. Report and Recommendations of the Advisory Group on Financial Flows for Africa*. New York: United Nations, February.

United Nations (1989a), *African Recovery Programme Briefing Paper*, 'African Debt: the Search for Solutions', by Tony Killick and Matthew Martin. New York: United Nations Africa Recovery Programme Information Unit, June.

United Nations (1989b), 'African Debt: the Search for Solutions', *UN Africa Recovery Programme Briefing Paper No 1*. New York: United Nations, June.

United Nations (1990), *Africa's Commodity Problems: Towards a Solution. A Report by the United Nations Secretary-General's Expert Group on Africa's Commodity Problems*. Geneva: UNCTAD/EDM/ATF/I.

United Nations (1991), Final Review and Appraisal of the United Nations Programme of Action for African Economic Recovery and Development 1986–1990, TD/B/1280/Add.1/Rev.1. Geneva: UNCTAD, October.

United Nations, *African Recovery*, quarterly publication, New York: United Nations, Department of Public Information of the Commission and Project Management Division.

United Nations Conference on Trade and Development (1988a), *Review of the Implementation of the Guidelines Contained in Board Resolution 222 (XXI)*, Report by the UNCTAD Secretariat. TD/B/1167, Geneva: UNCTAD, February.

United Nations Conference on Trade and Development (1988b), 'Paris Club Rescheduling Practices: A Close Scrutiny', *UNCTAD Bulletin*, no. 242, April.

United Nations Conference on Trade and Development (1990), 'Debt and Managing Adjustment: Attracting Non-debt-creating Financial Flows and New Lending', Report by the UNCTAD Secretariat, TD/B/C.3/234. Geneva: UNCTAD, February.

United Nations Conference on Trade and Development (annual a), *The Least Developed Countries*. Geneva: UNCTAD.

United Nations Conference on Trade and Development (annual b), *Trade and Development Report*. Geneva: UNCTAD.

United Nations Development Programme and the World Bank (1989), *African Economic and Financial Data*. Washington, D.C.: World Bank.

United Nations Conference on Trade and Development, *UNCTAD Bulletin*. Geneva: UNCTAD.

United Nations Economic Commission for Africa (1983), 'ECA and Africa's Development, 1983–2008: a Preliminary Perspective Study'. Addis Ababa, Ethiopia: ECA (processed).

United Nations Economic Commission for Africa (1985), 'Trade Promotion Within the Context of the African Crisis: Adjustment Policies and the Lagos Plan of Action – A Policy Paper', Addis Ababa, Ethiopia: ECA, August.

United Nations Economic Commission for Africa (1988a), 'Beyond Recovery: ECA-revised Perspectives of Africa's Development, 1988–2008'. Addis Ababa, Ethiopia: ECA (processed).

United Nations Economic Commission for Africa (1988b), 'The Khartoum Declaration: Towards a Human-focussed Approach to Socio-economic Recovery and Development in Africa', in *ECA's Annual Report* 1988. New York: United Nations.

United Nations Economic Commission for Africa (1989), *African Alternative Framework to Structural Adjustment Programmes for Socio-economic Recovery and Transformation (AAF-SAP)*. Addis Ababa, Ethiopia: Economic Commission for Africa, June.

United Nations Economic Commission for Africa (annual a), *Annual Reports*, New York: United Nations.

United Nations Economic Commission for Africa (annual b), *Economic Surveys*. Addis Ababa, Ethiopia: ECA.

United Nations Food and Agricultural Organization (1986), *African Agriculture: The Next 25 Years*. Rome: FAO.

United Nations General Assembly (1988), *Critical Economic Situation in Africa: United Nations Programme of Action for African Economic Recovery and Development, 1986–1990*, Mid-term Review of the Implementation of the United Nations Programme of Action for African Economic Recovery and Development, 1986–1990. Report of the Secretary-General, Doc. A/43/500. New York: United Nations, August.

Whitaker, Jennifer Seymour (1988), *How Can Africa Survive?*. New York: Harper & Row

Yagci, Fahrettin et al. (1985), *Structural Adjustment Lending: An Evaluation of Program Design*, Staff Working Paper no. 735. Washington, D.C.: World Bank.

Index